THE CURIOUS BARTENDER'S VODKA CHRONICLES

THE CURIOUS BARTENDER'S VODKA CHRONICLES

DISCOVERING & CELEBRATING THE HISTORY OF THE WORLD'S MOST VERSATILE DRINK

TRISTAN STEPHENSON

rps

RYLAND PETERS & SMALL

CONTENTS

KONIK'S TAIL
VODKA
SPELT GRAIN
VELA

INTRODUCTION

The Vodka History Museum occupies a single floor inside the Izmailovo Kremlin, a gaudy, fairytale-coloured complex in northeast Moscow that was built in 2007 to evoke traditional Russian architecture.

Inside, there are more than 700 bottles of vodka alongside recipes from the eighteenth century, advertising posters, labels and other assorted paraphernalia. A reproduction of an early piece of distillation apparatus sits at one end of the room, staffed by a mannequin monk – a nod to the monastic origins of spirits in Russia.

In truth, the word 'museum' flatters what is essentially a well-curated collection of bottles. A single room could never adequately tell the story of a drink that has intertwined itself so completely with a nation. This raises the question of whether the modesty of the space is accidental. There are some stories that the Kremlin would prefer were not told.

And yet, in one corner, there is an information plaque bearing a single, devastating line: 'There is hardly a person in the multilingual world that surrounds us who, if Russia is mentioned to him, will not think of vodka.'

As Russian statements go, even George Orwell couldn't have argued with that one.

Victor Erofeyev, writing in his 2002 essay 'The Russian God', captured vodka's grip on Russian life with a visceral directness that could only come from someone raised inside it: 'More than by any political system, we are all held hostage by vodka. It menaces and it chastises, it demands sacrifices.'

It is, in part, Russia's complete cultural submersion in vodka, that supports their claim of historic ownership of the spirit (a better museum might aid in upholding that claim). But the roots of vodka run deeper and wider than any one country's border. The word itself first appears in a Polish court ledger in 1405, where an unknown clerk casually wrote it down while going about their daily administrative duties. The word *wódka* came from *woda*, meaning water, with the kind of diminutive suffix (-ka) that makes something sound considerably less threatening than it in fact turned out to be. Not long after Polish clerks were writing about it, monks in Moscow were almost certainly distilling an ancestral version of vodka that would later be called *khlebnoe vino*, and later still the spirit known as *polugar*. In Vilnius (in modern-day Lithuania), court records from 1501 reference a producer of *degtinė*, meaning 'burnt water'.

Three countries, various names, all converging towards one spirit.

The vodka origin debate will never be settled, which tells us something important, if a little unsatisfactory: vodka did not emerge from a single national cradle. It spread across a shared cultural zone shaped by grain, cold winters and the needs of people who had a great deal of both of those things, but very little in the way of hope or optimism. The Polish nobility turned it into an aristocratic signalling, while Russian tsars turned it into a state monopoly.

Vodka was also shaped by the availability of technology. Distillation, first in a pot and later in a column still, came about through advances in industrial engineering, which iteratively reinvented the spirit, stripping it of almost all of its odour, flavour and history. Filtration took away what little remained, producing something approaching the modern idea of vodka: clear, rectified and almost perfectly neutral.

At the close of the nineteenth century, Russian and European immigrants packed vodka in their luggage and carried it to American ports, where it was received with a mixture of curiosity and theatrical suspicion. 'Vodka is generally supposed to be a very deadly drink', wrote *The New York Herald* in 1883, with the caveat that the 'Russian drink is not half bad, taken in the right way'. That way, it turns out is to begin with caviar.

Over the 60 years that followed, America mixed just about anything they could with vodka, and by the middle of the twentieth century it had reinvented itself once again. Along came the Bloody Mary, Moscow Mule and Vodka Martini. A Smirnoff bottle found its way behind the bar at the New York's fanciest bars: the Stork Club, Rainbow Room and Waldorf-Astoria Hotel. The Hollywood set turned to it when discretion called behind the scenes, as James Bond showed us the dangerous and exotic allure of vodka on-screen. By the time Absolut arrived from Sweden in a clear bottle with a radical new approach to brand identity, vodka had already won. For the best part of 50 years it was the biggest-selling spirit in the world's most valuable drinks market. In 2021 alone, Americans consumed over 80 million nine-litre cases.

This book is vodka's biography, capturing the history, chemistry, business, mythology and cocktails that have shaped vodka, and that have been shaped by vodka. We will meet the people who built the distilleries, crafted the cocktails, designed the adverts and did the shots. This is a historical journey that will take us from ancient China, to medieval Poland, to modern Las Vegas, from the grandest imperial distilleries to craft start-ups, from the kabak to the cocktail bar. Somewhere in that span of time, vodka became the most consumed spirit on earth.

This is the story of how.

THE VODKA HEARTLAND

BASE MATERIALS

Vodka can be made from practically anything that contains starches or sugar, but in the historic 'Vodka Belt' of Central Europe, four base materials came to the fore: rye, wheat, potatoes and barley.

RYE

Rye is the traditional grain of the Polish heartland and central Russia. It gives a spirit with body, a peppery spice and a faintly oily texture that survives heavy rectification. Rye is harder to handle than wheat and yields less alcohol per kilo, which is why brands like Wyborowa, Belvedere and Chopin still pay for the privilege.

WHEAT

Wheat is the most common vodka base in the world. It produces a soft, clean spirit with a faint sweetness, which is why the majority of large commercial brands rely on it. Absolut, Grey Goose, Ketel One and almost every Russian label are wheat vodkas. It is cheap, grown right across the heartland and easy to process.

POTATOES

Potatoes took hold in Polish and German distilling through the 1800s, prized for thriving in poor soils where grain struggled. Potatoes cost several times more to handle than grain, but the payoff is a creamy spirit with mild vanilla or marshmallow notes, often detectable in blind tasting.

BARLEY

A Nordic signature crop and dominant in Finland, barley is used by both Koskenkorva and Finlandia to distil spirit at the Koskenkorva plant in the west of the country. It also turns up among Scandinavian and craft producers who make whisky alongside vodka. Barley lends a nutty, biscuity quality, a hint of toasted grain and a drier finish than wheat.

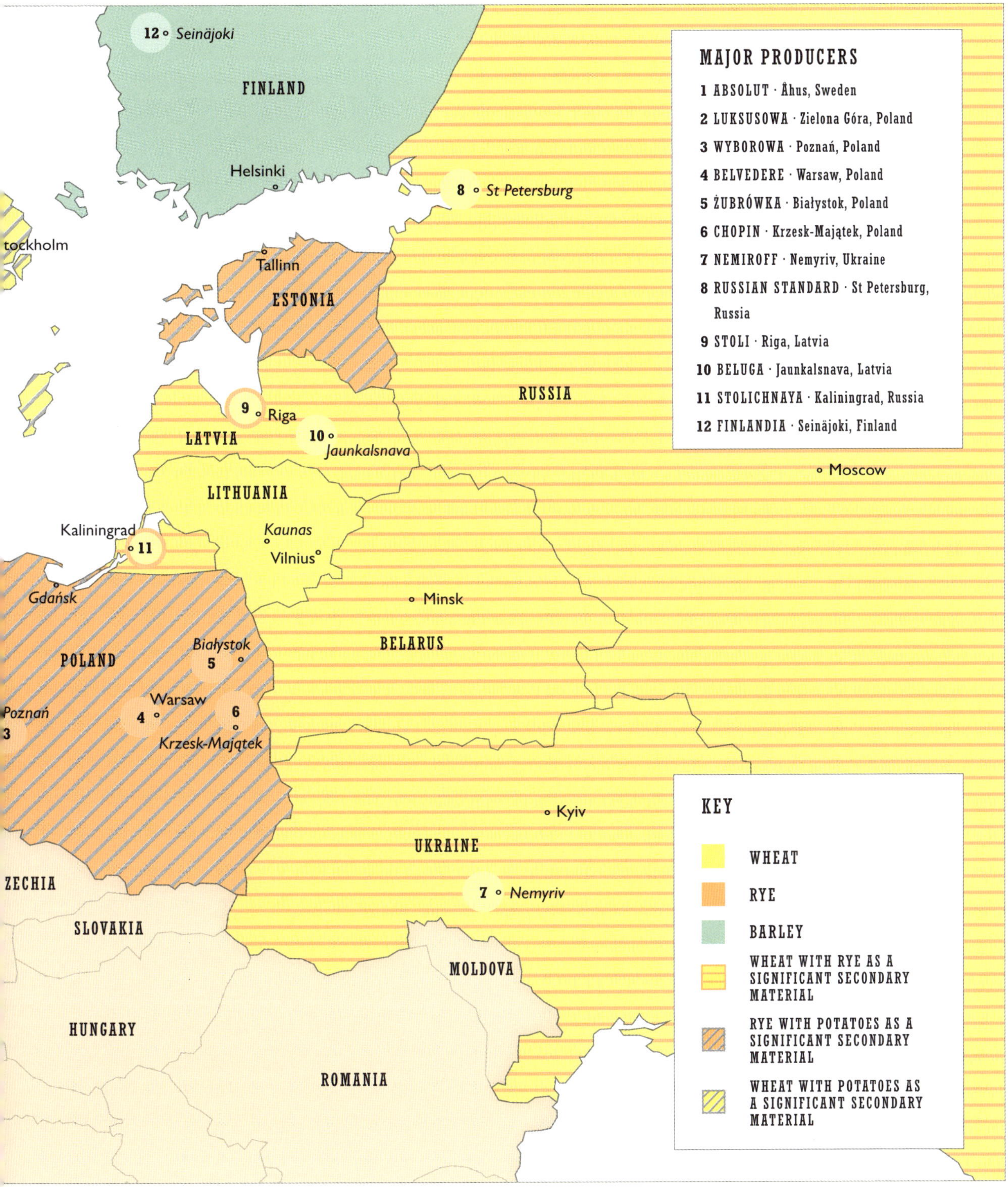
MAJOR PRODUCERS
1 ABSOLUT · Åhus, Sweden
2 LUKSUSOWA · Zielona Góra, Poland
3 WYBOROWA · Poznań, Poland
4 BELVEDERE · Warsaw, Poland
5 ŻUBRÓWKA · Białystok, Poland
6 CHOPIN · Krzesk-Majątek, Poland
7 NEMIROFF · Nemyriv, Ukraine
8 RUSSIAN STANDARD · St Petersburg, Russia
9 STOLI · Riga, Latvia
10 BELUGA · Jaunkalsnava, Latvia
11 STOLICHNAYA · Kaliningrad, Russia
12 FINLANDIA · Seinäjoki, Finland
KEY
WHEAT
RYE
BARLEY
WHEAT WITH RYE AS A SIGNIFICANT SECONDARY MATERIAL
RYE WITH POTATOES AS A SIGNIFICANT SECONDARY MATERIAL
WHEAT WITH POTATOES AS A SIGNIFICANT SECONDARY MATERIAL
12 Seinäjoki
FINLAND
Helsinki
8 St Petersburg
tockholm
Tallinn
ESTONIA
RUSSIA
9 Riga
10 Jaunkalsnava
LATVIA
Moscow
LITHUANIA
Kaliningrad
11
Kaunas
Vilnius
Gdańsk
Minsk
Białystok
5
POLAND
BELARUS
Warsaw
4
6
Poznań
3
Krzesk-Majątek
Kyiv
UKRAINE
ZECHIA
7 Nemyriv
SLOVAKIA
MOLDOVA
HUNGARY
ROMANIA

SETTING THE STAGE

Alcoholic fermentation (the conversion of sugars into ethanol) is an ancient and largely accidental pastime that gave us beer, wine and cider among other delicious and refreshing beverages. Distillation, however, is not. It requires an understanding that alcohol behaves differently from water, that vapour can be guided and captured, and that flavour and potency can be manipulated by design.

In some ways, modern vodka is the ultimate expression of a distilled spirit: pure, clean and concentrated – the end point in the evolution of a technology thousands of years in the making. But to understand it, we must first understand the origins of distillation itself: how the technology emerged, how it developed, and how it shaped the first proto-vodkas that blossomed into a global industry.

The earliest artefacts that may have been used for distillation date back to late Shang-dynasty China (1300–1046 BCE) and were all-in-one pots with a boiling vessel, domed lid and collection cup situated inside the pot. Historians theorise that, given their diminutive proportions, they were used for perfumes and medicinal extracts. There is no known record of either the knowledge or practice of distillation in China during this time, however, nor in the two millennia that followed (the first two literary references of Chinese distillation arrive in the twelfth century CE). Regardless, the practical knowledge of distillation was there, and it moved westward along the Silk Road, absorbed and refined by the great scientific cultures of the ancient world.

The Silk Road was a 2000-mile/3,200-km trail first carved out around the tenth century BCE, but it took a good 700 years to really get established. Gold, jade, silk and spices were all up for grabs, but it was as a hub of cultural networking that the Silk Road really came into its own. It was, in effect, the information superhighway of its time.

The Greek philosopher Aristotle was certainly aware of distillation in one shape or another. One section of his *Meteorologica* (circa 340 BCE) concerns experiments that he undertook to distil liquids, discovering that 'wine and all fluids that evaporate and condense into a liquid state become water.' What he was observing was not spirit as we would recognize it, but the basic principle that vapours could be captured, cooled and returned to liquid form.

In 28 BCE, a practicing magi known as Anaxilaus of Thessaly was expelled from Rome for performing his magical arts, which included setting fire to what appeared to be water. The secrets of the trick were later translated into Greek and published in around 200 CE by Hippolytus, presbyter of Rome. It turned out that he had used distilled wine, not water. Around

OPPOSITE Pliny the Elder condensed turpentine vapour using hanging fleeces. **RIGHT** The Silk Road was the information superhighway of its day – carrying goods, ideas and distillation knowledge westwards. **BELOW RIGHT** An alembic from Hieronymus Brunschwig's distilling treatise, printed in 1500.

the same time the Roman philosopher Pliny the Elder experimented with hanging fleeces above cauldrons of bubbling resin, using the expansive surface area of the wool to catch the vapour and condense it into turpentine.

One such place where this kind of thinking flourished was the Mediterranean's most famous laboratory bench: Alexandria. In the Hellenistic period, the city's ancient and epic library functioned less like a museum of books and more like a state-funded research institute, set up under the Ptolemies with the help of Demetrius of Phaleron. Alexandria's book-hoarding ambitions were legendary, but what matters for our purposes is the kind of knowledge that could flourish when mathematicians, physicians, metallurgists and philosophers were all effectively living above the same reading room. Out of that Greco-Egyptian soup came early 'chemical' traditions, including alchemy, which later writers traced back to Alexandrian Greeks in the first centuries CE.

This Alexandrian thread is where we meet characters like Maria the Jewess (also known as Mary the Prophetess), who has been credited with describing, and perhaps inventing, kit that reads like an early still-maker's catalogue: the *tribikos* (a three-armed alembic for collecting multiple distillates) and the gentle, temperature-controlled bain-marie that still bears her name. Around the same time, Zosimos of Panopolis, the world's first self-proclaimed alchemist, described apparatus and procedures that hinge on fundamentals any distiller would recognize: sealing vessels, managing vapours and capturing condensate.

Zosimos of Panopolis was also thought to be somewhat of a wizard. He provided one of the earliest definitions of alchemy as the study of 'the composition of waters, movement, growth, embodying and disembodying, drawing the spirits from bodies and bonding the spirits within bodies.' It was Zosimos' belief that distillation in some way liberated the essence of a body or object that has led to our definition of alcoholic beverages as 'spirits' today. Even the vocabulary gives the game away.

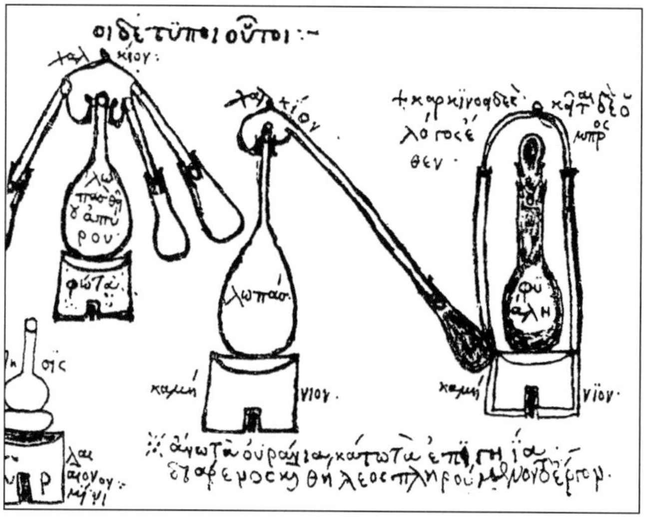

'Alembic' ultimately comes to us via the Arabic *al-anbīq*, but that Arabic term itself is built on the Greek *ambix*, meaning a cup or beaker.

The scrolls and ledgers that documented all these works were largely preserved in the great libraries of the time, such as the legendary library of Alexandria, which was thought to contain over 500,000 scrolls. That was until successive religious and political power struggles during the first half of the first millennium CE caused them to be either sold, stolen or, as was the case with Cleopatra and Julius Caesar, simply given away only to be burned. In the year 642 CE Alexandria was captured by a Muslim army and the last remaining remnants of the library were destroyed, and along with it the collective knowledge of much of the ancient world.

Or so we thought…

It would seem that some scraps of information and hastily copied texts still remained, written in ancient languages by long-dead men. The secrets to the mysteries of ardent waters and humid vapours did still exist, secreted away in monasteries and temples of learning dotted around Europe and the Middle East.

By the time we reach the Islamic Golden Age (roughly the eighth to tenth centuries), distillation found its first true institutional home. Scholars working across Persia, Mesopotamia and the Abbasid Caliphate translated inherited know-how into repeatable science, building on Greek and late- antique material that arrived through the broader translation movement (often via Syriac intermediaries) and the scholarly networks we shorthand as the House of Wisdom.

This is where Jabir ibn Hayyan (also known as Geber) looms large. He, and his eponymous school, helped to standardise apparatus and process: alembics, controlled condensation and the basic logic of separating a mixed vapour into something more useful and more concentrated.

RIGHT The Library of Alexandria, was the largest and most significant library of the ancient world.
OPPOSITE Distillation equipment described by Zosimos of Panopolis, who treated distillation as the liberation of essences.

Some time around the close of the eighth century CE, Geber invented the first true alembic still, which remains today the basic form for all pot stills. The major breakthrough was that rather than using bits of sheep hair or an old rag to collect the spirit vapours, Geber's al-ambiq incorporated a condensing retort connected by a pipe. With the alembic, Geber came tantalisingly close to realising the full potential of distillation, in what has to be one of the greatest understatements of all time: 'And fire which burns on the mouths of bottles due to boiled wine and salt, and similar things with nice characteristics which are thought to be of little use, but are of great significance in these sciences.'

Geber wasn't alone. The polymath Al-Kindi treated distillation as a tool of perfumery and formulation, concerned less with intoxication and more with capturing aroma and virtue from plants. Al-Razi (Rhazes), a physician and practical chemist, refined laboratory methods and is frequently credited in the medical-historical literature with identifying and preparing ethanol, and with the clinical use of alcohol as an antiseptic.

Alcohol occupied an ambiguous position in Islamic society: prohibited for consumption, yet invaluable in medicine, alchemy and perfumery. Distilled spirits, often starting life as wine, were used as solvents, antiseptics, and carriers for botanical compounds, their potency framed as therapeutic rather than indulgent. And the word that would eventually name the thing tells its own story. *Al-kuhl* originally referred to *kohl*, a finely powdered cosmetic,

LEFT Jabir ibn Hayyan, the eighth-century polymath known in the West as Geber, who is considered the father of distillation. **OPPOSITE** Arnaldus de Villa Nova, the Montpellier professor who popularised the term *aqua vitae* around the year 1300.

before the term migrated through medieval scientific Latin into 'alcohol' and attached itself to the volatile essence that distillers were learning to isolate.

Possibly the earliest example we have of distilled spirits being consumed for enjoyment, rather than medicinally, comes from a poem written in Arabic by Abū Nuwās, who died in 814. In one poem he describes ordering three types of wine, each of which becomes stronger as the poem continues. For the final drink he asks for a wine that 'has the colour of rain-water but is as hot inside the ribs as a burning firebrand'.

Europe entered this story late. Following the collapse of the Western Roman Empire, much technical knowledge was lost or neglected, while the Islamic world continued to translate, preserve and expand upon Greek and Hellenistic science. The turning point came through discovery rather than invention. From the ninth century onward, Islamic rule during the Moorish occupation in parts of Iberia and Sicily brought European scholars into direct contact with advanced libraries and laboratories. Translation centres, most notably at Salerno and later Toledo, transcribed Arabic medical and alchemical texts into the preferred language of the literary elites at that time: Latin.

The Englishman Robert of Chester can be thanked for completing the first Latin translation of the works of al-Kindi, al-Razi and Geber, in his book *Liber de Compositione Alchimae* (*Book on the Composition of Alchemy*) published in 1144.

European alchemists such as the Franciscan monk Roger Bacon and German Dominican Friar Albertus Magnus began experimenting with stills and, by the twelfth and thirteenth centuries, distilled wine spirits had firmly established themselves in European medical practice. Known as *aqua vitae* (water of life), they were believed to preserve youth, strengthen the heart and balance the humours. These early spirits were often steeped with botanicals: juniper for digestion, wormwood for fevers, chamomile for calm. In this regard, aqua vitae was just another tool in the medieval pharmacopoeia.

Around a hundred years later Arnaldus de Villa Nova, a professor from the University of Montpellier, successfully translated Arabic texts that revealed further secrets of distillation. He went on to write one of the first complete sets of instructions on the distillation of wine, and it's this man that we have to thank for the term *aqua vitae,* a name which stuck in the Scandinavian *akvavit*, French *eaux de vie*, and Scottish *uisge beatha*, which was later corrupted to whisky. Around 1300 he wrote, 'We call it aqua vitae, and this name is remarkably suitable, since it really is the water of immortality. It prolongs life, clears away ill-humors, strengthens the heart, and maintains youth.'

While this may seem like a sales pitch with more than a bit of hyperbole, Villa Nova's observations pervaded for the next century or more. But how?

Strong liquor was able to retain a place in the physician's toolkit because it appeared to do a little bit of everything, and often did something when nothing else did. It disinfected wounds that would otherwise fester, dulled pain that had no other remedy, steadied nerves, warmed cold bodies, preserved herbs, extracted their virtues, and, crucially, could be trusted not to spoil. In a world where medicine was guided as much by observation and tradition as by theory, distilled spirits earned their place through sheer reliability. If a treatment failed, it could at least fail cleanly, and if it succeeded, the results were visible and immediate. For a very long time, strong liquor belonged to the sickroom and the apothecary's shelf, not the bar, and its authority came not from taste but from the simple fact that it seemed to work.

With that in mind, practically all distilled spirits of the time were enhanced with herbs and spices that were deemed to have medicinal benefits (most notably juniper, angelica, fennel seed and wormwood) and therefore could be most closely compared to gin.

Production remained small-scale and almost entirely monastic or academic, carried out in infirmaries and laboratories rather than commercial distilleries. And with scant understanding of the underlying chemistry, the spirits were harsh and unstable. But the symbolic power of a liquid that could burn with a flame stayed with people, because it suggested something more than a medicine. It suggested a hidden essence you could coax out of grapes, bottle, and carry with you. And yet, while wine remained the raw material of choice in the vineyards and monasteries of southern Europe, further north and east the logic of distillation was already beginning to shift. Grapes were scarce, winters were long, and the crops that sustained everyday life were cereals rather than fruit. If distilled spirit truly was a way of concentrating the essence of a thing, then it followed that barley, rye, wheat and oats had essences worth coaxing out too. In these colder regions distillation would gradually be pulled out of the infirmary and into the household, away from the Latin of learned physicians and into the hands of farmers, traders and soldiers. What emerged there would be less concerned with immortality or the balancing of humours, and far more interested in warmth, preservation, taxation and trade… and eventually, taste. The stage was quietly being set for a very different kind of spirit.

VODKA BEFORE VODKA

The City of Genoa in the late Middle Ages was a state that thought in sea lanes not acreage. Perched on the Ligurian coast, it grew into a merchant republic whose power stemmed from a fleet of ships that could turn up and build relationships wherever profit was waiting. By the fourteenth century, Genoa was competing with Venice for influence across the Mediterranean and crucially, for our story, pushing through the Bosphorus into the Black Sea. Trading privileges, secured in the wake of Byzantine politics, opened the door and Genoa walked straight through it, planting a forest of outposts and establishing fortified 'factories' that linked Italian money to eastern goods.

The jewel in the crown was Caffa (modern Feodosiya) in Crimea, effectively the administrative heart of the Genoese colonial possessions that became known as Gazaria. Other stations along the rim of the Black Sea fed the network and kept the lanes open. But commerce did not stop at the shoreline. Goods and people flowed inland via river routes and overland tracks that tied Crimea and the Sea of Azov to the principalities of the Rus people, including the fast-rising Principality of Muscovy.

It is this piece of Genoese trading history that provides the scaffold for the oft-repeated tale first recounted in *The History of Taverns in Russia* by Ivan Gavrilovich Pryzhov in 1868, where Genoese ambassadors arrive in Moscow in 1386 with a gift of aqua vitae for Grand Duke Dmitry Donskoy. This act that allegedly kickstarted the story of vodka in the region. And the story has a certain logic. Diplomats followed trade, and diplomatic gifts were often expensive, portable signals of sophistication. We can be confident that Genoese envoys did indeed reach Moscow in the fourteenth century, and it is also

LEFT Genoese merchants treated the medieval Mediterranean as one large market place, sailing wherever profit looked likely and turning up uninvited everywhere else.

plausible that such envoys were granted an audience with the Grand Duke. However, Pryzhov supplies this story without citation of any surviving document that explicitly records the event, and so it should be approached with a fair degree of scepticism.

Had Genoese ambassadors presented aqua vitae to the Duke, he would likely have regarded it as an exotic Western curiosity – something to be examined, perhaps cautiously sampled, then set aside among the many strange novelties that arrived from abroad, such as pepper, saffron, resins and balms. Aqua vitae would have fitted neatly into the same category. Potent, unfamiliar, expensive, and not yet embraced as a drink of pleasure. If Dmitry did taste it, it was almost certainly in drops rather than gulps, and probably with more suspicion than enjoyment.

Old Russia was no stranger to alcohol, of course. Records describe how ingredients, strength and social application were delineated by name. There was *pivo*, a broad term covering beers and ales. *Med* referred to mead (fermented honey), which carried deep ritual and seasonal importance. *Kvas* sat at the everyday end of the scale. A lightly fermented drink made from bread or grain, it was nourishing, sour, and rarely very alcoholic. Wine appears too, usually as *vino*, but this was imported, expensive, and of marginal interest in a grain-growing society.

Alongside these sat *syta*, a simple mixture of honey and water. On paper it looks non-alcoholic, but left to its own devices, it would ferment easily and drift imbibers into weak intoxication. That ambiguity mattered because medieval Russians did not draw a sharp line between alcoholic and non-alcoholic drinks. Fermentation was understood as a spectrum, and many liquids lived somewhere in the middle. Even water mixed with honey could, given time, warmth, and neglect, become something stronger.

RIGHT Zurab Tsereteli's bust of Dmitry Donskoy on Moscow's Rulers' Alley, alleged recipient of the Genoese aqua vitae gift in 1386.

The same linguistic looseness applies to *berezovitsa* (birch sap wine). Fresh birch sap is sweet and refreshing but leave it for a short while and it ferments on its own. Drink it fresh and it is closer to juice. Drink it later and it begins to behave like alcohol. People drank what the season provided, and fermentation was as much a matter of chance as intention.

Mead was the most widely consumed alcohol in medieval Rus' (the federation of principalities inhabited by the Rus people) because it matched the landscape. In the forested zones of Eastern Europe, honey was abundant and wild beekeeping was well established, making mead the most practical fermented drink available. By the eleventh century, it had become common across territories such as Polotsk, Lithuania and parts of present-day Belarus, with long-aged meads becoming prized and reserved for princes and major feasts.

But the real shift came in the thirteenth to fifteenth centuries. Mongol-Tatar invasions and the weakening of Byzantine trade disrupted supplies of imported grape wine from Greece. As wine became scarce, local drinks moved to the centre of daily life. Mead brewing expanded not because it was new, but because it filled a growing gap.

LEFT Medieval distillation as illustrated in early scientific texts, is really not all that different from the production of whisky or brandy today.

At the same time, political power drifted northeast from Kiev to Moscow. Moscow sat far from vineyards but close to forests and grain, so honey and cereals became the dominant fermentable materials. As such, drinking habits increasingly reflected what could be produced locally. Some meads were matured in barrel for years but typically reserved only for the posher end of society. If you didn't have much money, you got a cheaper, stronger version. The trend for strength had been established, and while mead did not lead directly to vodka, it did set the conditions that made vodka inevitable.

Another Russian legend tied to the origins of vodka concerns a Greek monk named Isidore, who is alleged to have learned the art of distillation and produced the first distilled spirits in Russia at the Chudov Monastery in Moscow in or around 1430. The story of Isidore is another slice of history blended with legend, recounted centuries after the fact. No evidence exists of specific techniques or observations, or that Isidore was even a real person.

Nevertheless, we can be confident that a monk, or monks, somewhere in Russia, at some point in the late fourteenth or early fifteenth century, distilled spirits for the first time.

Poland, by contrast, provides something quite rare in the annals of spirits history: a dated, unambiguous written reference.

In 1405 the word *wódka* pops up out of nowhere. It appears, regrettably, neither on a tavern menu nor in a medical text – and certainly not in a cocktail book. Instead, it shows up in the court registers of Sandomierz, then an administrative province of the Kingdom of Poland, preserved in what later scholars group under the Akta Grodzkie tradition of municipal and land court books. In other words, it is a court ledger. Not the last time vodka would find itself in court I should say, and also a wonderfully unromantic debut for the spirit.

And that is precisely why it matters.

Courts recorded the everyday traffic of goods, debts, quarrels and property with a diligence that taverns rarely matched. So when wódka appears here, it is less an announcement of a new national drink than evidence that the term had become common enough to be understood by clerks and anyone else drawn into the machinery of local administration.

Etymologically, wódka was born out of the Polish word *woda*, meaning water, along with a diminutive suffix. The logic works much like English endings such as '-let' and '-ette', used to describe a smaller version of a noun. In that sense, vodka means 'little water', probably named for the distillation process that reduced a larger amount of fermented material into a smaller amount of clear 'water'. Because vodka is a diminutive it means that etymological dictionaries in both Russian and Polish convert themselves with the root form of the word (*voda* – water) and don't describe vodka until it becomes a unique, recognizable category of spirit around the middle of the nineteenth century.

As benign and unglamorous as wódka's first outing may have been, its presence in Polish records this far back is a thorny fact for anyone determined to argue that vodka is exclusively Russian.

And let's be clear: 1405 is a long time ago. It predates the first known references to gin, whisky, rum or tequila, and is therefore guarded closely by the Poles and often cited as evidence that Poland is the birthplace of vodka. The word itself is undeniable, but I would argue that it is more a linguistic landmark than a cultural one. It does not tell us that people were already drinking vodka in the way we imagine it now. In the early fifteenth century, wódka is better understood as a catch-all term for distilled or alcohol-based preparations used for washing, healing, or cosmetic purposes.

Over in what were then known as the Russian territories, we have to wait until the sixteenth century for the first secure occurrence of the word vodka. In his short paper 'From the History of the Word vodka' (1972), the linguist Kazimierz Polański notes that vodka does not appear in Old Russian sources at all, and that its first secure appearance in Russian-language material occurs in 1533, where it clearly refers to a medicinal preparation rather than a beverage. This places the Russian usage firmly in the same conceptual lane as the Polish 1405 reference, where alcohol is a tool, rather than a pleasure.

The citation comes from a chronicle account of the final illness of Grand Prince Vasily III, who died

BELOW Vasily III, whose 1533 deathbed treatment is the earliest secure Russian-language reference to vodka.

in 1533. As the story goes, Vasily suffered from a severe, festering wound, and his doctors and advisers debated treatments. One recommendation was to 'prepare vodka and apply it to the wound', language that makes sense only if vodka is understood as an alcohol-based tincture or wash. Later lexicographers, including compilers of Russian etymological dictionaries, repeatedly return to this passage as the anchor point for the word's Russian appearance, noting its medical context. The important takeaway is not national priority but continuity. Across Eastern Europe, vodka enters the written record first as something applied, infused or prescribed.

So yes, 1405 matters. It is a dated, unambiguous appearance of the word wódka in Poland, and that is chalk on the board for anyone keeping national score. But it is a not a cultural moment. The document does not show us a society drinking vodka in the modern sense, dancing on tables with espresso martinis and cursing the name vodka the next day. The continuity that matters is simpler. In both Poland and Russia, the earliest secure appearances of 'vodka' point to medicine and household use, not a national drinking habit. The drink, as a widespread and recognizable category, takes shape later.

So how and when did distillation arrive in Poland?

Unlike Russian legend, it seems likely that strong spirits flowed into Poland via academics rather than clerics. By the thirteenth century, Polish physicians were travelling abroad to study at Europe's leading medical schools, particularly Montpellier and Salerno, where distillation was part of the curriculum. When they returned home, they brought those techniques with them. One of the most fascinating figures from this period is Mikołaj z Polski (Nicholas of Poland), a Montpellier-trained doctor who, in the 1270s, served as personal physician to Prince Leszek II the Black. Mikołaj was a contrarian of the like you might find on TikTok or instagram today: he railed against what he saw as the creeping dominance of laboratory-made drugs, arguing they were a dangerous departure from the folk remedies trusted by Polish peasants for generations. In his flamboyant Latin poem *Antipocras*, he attacked the assumption that highly purified substances were automatically beneficial, and championed humble, natural ingredients. Yet for all his scepticism, he was no luddite. His medical notebook, *Experimenta*, reveals that he happily employed the very techniques he had learned abroad, including distillation in an alembic, when creating his own compound, the so-called Philosopher's Oil.

The institutional spread of these ideas followed soon after. With the founding of the Jagiellonian University in 1364 in Kraków, advanced medical training became a formal part of Polish intellectual life. One of the few surviving books from the university's fourteenth-century library, a manuscript collection titled *Opera Medica*, gives us a rare window into what students were actually learning. The first half of the volume, dated 1368, appears to have been copied by a student for practical reference, essentially a medieval study guide. Among its texts is a short Latin treatise on producing *aqua ardente*, burning water', from wine, adapted from the Salernitan tradition. In other words, distillation was not only known but part of the syllabus.

When vodka does emerge, it does so across a shared zone of grain farming, trade routes and overlapping cultures, where borders shifted more often than distilling habits did. Then add to all of this the fact that fifteenth-century wódka would have tasted nothing like the vodkas we consume today. Distillation technology was simpler, and neutral spirits were out of reach. Only later do the language and liquids begin to channel themselves into clearer lanes.

For that to happen, the spirit itself needs to offer more than just function, but also taste, provenance and perhaps a little culture too. By the late fifteenth

ABOVE Collegium Maius at Kraków's Jagiellonian University, where distillation featured in the medieval medical syllabus.

century, spirits were no longer confined to the learned world of apothecaries and monastery infirmaries. They had become familiar enough to be handled at home and talked about plainly. In Poland, imported Latin medical works on distillation remained popular at the Jagiellonian University throughout the fifteenth century, but by the sixteenth, something important happens. Local authors begin writing about these techniques in Polish. Distillation was becoming domestic knowledge, and the intellectual groundwork for vodka culture was being shaped.

I think that shift matters more than any first mention in a ledger. Once a household knows what a spirit is for, and once it can get hold of it reliably (or manufacture it themselves) it stops being a novelty and starts becoming a staple.

This wasn't a sudden explosion of knowledge however, but rather a quiet dissemination in the way most useful crafts do – rarely with names attached, rarely with fanfare. A still is simple in concept, but fiddly in practice. You need someone who can bend and hammer copper, the ability to control heat, and the patience to learn where the good run ends and the nasty run begins. Those lessons moved with clerics, merchants, travelling craftsmen and estate stewards. Sometimes they moved with books. More often, they moved with people who had watched it done once and then tried their luck at home. Once small stills began appearing in town workshops and manor outbuildings, spirits stopped being an occasional imported marvel and became something you could make from what you had. With a growing population and the demand for honey to make mead outstripping supply, distillers turned to the last remaining abundant carbohydrate: grain.

THE EXTENDED FAMILY

The Russia versus Poland rivalry lives on to this day. But the fog of this particular war also obscures an awkward geographical truth: Poland and Russia were not close neighbours when distilled spirits first began to materialize in the region. Between them lay the largest and arguably most influential political entity in Europe at the time, the Grand Duchy of Lithuania – a sprawling, multilingual state that stretched from the Baltic deep into the lands of the Rus', occupying much of present-day Ukraine and most of Belarus. Lithuania acted as a cultural, commercial and political mediator between east and west, the connective tissue of the region. Trade routes, scholars, clerics and techniques of distillation passed through its territories as readily as grain and honey. That raises an uncomfortable but intriguing question. Might Lithuania itself have been producing an early form of vodka?

The historical record is quieter in Lithuania, offering fewer named spirits and fewer patriotic champions. However, receipt books from 1501 from the court of Alexander Jagiellon, the Grand Duke of Lithuania, refer to a producer of *degtinė*.

Degtinė sits linguistically alongside the Polish word *gorzałka* ('to burn') and other Slavic terms meaning 'burnt' or 'fiery', which points to the physicality of the spirit itself rather than water or medicine. This is intriguing because it hints at a parallel vocabulary developing across the region, which is grounded in process and sensation rather than Latin medical theory.

As with the Polish 1405 reference, the Lithuanian court receipt appears as part of the court economy rather than a recipe for a drink. The record does not tell us exactly what this degtinė tasted like, how strong it was (though we can assume strong enough to burn) or how it was consumed. But it does tell us that Lithuania belongs squarely inside the early vodka story, not as a blank space between Poland and Russia. That is why I think it is important to emphasize that vodka did not spring fully formed from a single national cradle, but rather emerged across a shared cultural zone shaped in part by Lithuanian mediation. The great Polish and Russian rivalry may tell us less about where vodka was born and more about how later borders, languages and identities retroactively claimed a spirit that first belonged to a blurrier map.

Indeed, practically all of Europe was producing a clear distillate, usually young and unaged, rougher than you'd prefer it to be and shaped above all by whatever the local countryside could ferment and potentially flavour. Wine where there were vineyards. Grain where there were fields of rye, barley and wheat. Honey where beekeeping was a staple. These spirits, which we will briefly explore now, evolved

into the modern spirit categories of armagnac, whisky, brandy, aquavit and more, but they share a common ancestor with vodka. And since vodka is produced in practically every country in Europe today, it's worth inspecting their similarities for a moment to see how the history of distilled spirits has diverged and converged geographically and culturally over time.

Southwest France gives an early, unusually vivid snapshot of this shared ancestor. In 1310, the Gascon cleric Vital Dufour wrote about *aygue ardente*, 'burning water', in a health treatise. In a famous (and familiar-sounding) line he claims it 'renders men joyous' and 'preserves youth'. In a wine region, that distilled 'water' was naturally wine-based and would have been closer to an assertive young brandy than to anything neutral. Pot distillation, unintentional maturation, and a willingness to bottle what came off the still meant flavour travelled with the alcohol. Grapey notes, leesy funk (lees being the

TOP The region around Kernavė, an early capital of the Grand Duchy of Lithuania, has played host to ten millennia of settlements and is a UNESCO World Heritage Site.
ABOVE Trakai Castle, the island fortress of the Grand Duchy, that linked east and west commercially.
OPPOSITE LEFT A half-grosz of the Grand Duchy, whose 1501 court receipts mention a degtinė producer.

rich, creamy nuttiness arising from yeast cells), a little smoke from the fire and the sharp edge that comes from imperfect separation.

Move north and the spirit changes base material to something more vodka-like. Scotland's earliest hard documentary claim for distilled spirit sits in the Exchequer Rolls of 1494. The entry is crisp and almost comic in its understatement: 'To Friar John Cor, 8 bolls of malt, wherewith to make aqua vitae for the King.' This is the origin story of Scotch whisky, and it matters here because it shows the same shared European language and the same shared outcome, only now built from malted barley rather than grapes. Friar John's spirit is unlikely to have resembled modern whisky very much, however, because modern whisky relies on the civilizing effects of wood and time, as well as an understanding of the underlying principles of distillation and how to manipulate them. What the king received was a young cereal spirit, likely strong, hot and… expressive. Think warm bread crust, green fruit and a raw edge that announces itself sharply in the nose. This spirit would have sat firmly in the same family as the eastern 'bread wine' spirits that we are about to encounter and that later get absorbed into the vodka story – even if Scotland took the lineage toward cask-aged identity rather than filtration and neutrality.

In the Low Countries and Germany, the shared ancestor develops a regional quirk that becomes destiny: juniper. There are earlier medieval references to juniper being used with distilled spirits, but the key point for this period is that by the mid-sixteenth century a written recipe tradition emerges for juniper 'waters' that sits on the road to genever and gin. A Belgian distiller's history notes the Antwerp physician Phillipus Hermanni and his distilling book, published in 1552, describing a mixture of crushed juniper berries with wine to be distilled. The dedication to this particular botanical suggests an unwillingness to leave behind potential medicinal benefits in hard liquor. Besides that, of course it tasted good, which was a rarity at the time. Early 'vodka-like' spirits were not born neutral. Flavour, whether from raw material or additives, was often part of how people made these drinks palatable and meaningful. In fact, the one thing you could guarantee is that they had flavour (and not all of it great).

Scandinavia offers another close cousin. A letter dated 13 April 1531 from Danish diplomat and statesman Eske Bille to the Norwegian archbishop Olav Engelbrektsson is widely cited as the earliest known written reference to aquavit. One line in the letter offers 'some water which is called Aqua Vite'. In practice, the Scandinavian family of spirits leans into botanical signatures. Aquavit is built around caraway and related aromatics. In Sweden, *brännvin* ('burnt wine') becomes the broad category term for distilled liquor, often plain, often spiced, and later

closely bound to state control and household production. Swedish institutional histories place brännvin's arrival in the 1400s and tie its early presence to both remedies and practical industrial uses. One Swedish source even cites a Stockholm account book from 1467 to 1470 paying for '*brand wyn til krudt*', 'burnt wine for gunpowder'.

In the German lands, the same endpoint appears with the bureaucratic fingerprints you might expect. An EU technical file for Korn (not the metal band) and Kornbrand notes spirit tax records from as early as 1507 reporting ‹production of spirit› in Nordhausen. Korn is vodka-adjacent in the most straightforward way, given that it is a clear, grain-spirit, often unaged, and often intended to keep some cereal character rather than erase it.

That difference is worth some reflection. The modern idea of vodka as 'neutral' is very far from the medieval reality. Neutrality is a much later preference made possible by better rectification, more consistent fermentation and, eventually, filtration and industrial scale. In the fifteenth and sixteenth centuries, many spirits that look vodka-like on paper would have tasted like their base material.

By 1700, Europe had not produced one vodka. Instead, it has produced many local answers to the same question. What can we do with surplus fermentables, and what can we carry, store, tax and trade? Wine distillates in Gascony. Malt spirit in Scotland. Juniper water in the Low Countries. Aqua vitae in Scandinavia, shading into aquavit and brännvin. Grain spirits moving through Lithuania and the Baltic. Korn developing within German-speaking regions. All of them regional interpretations of the ferment and distil problem – and all of them closely related to proto-vodkas of Poland and Russia.

OPPOSITE Grapes and malted barley, two of the earliest fermentable bases that fed Europe's distilling tradition.
ABOVE Juniper berries and caraway seeds, botanicals that give regional distillates medicinal qualities and flavourful punch.

It is also worth mentioning, briefly, where this leaves us today. Vodka is now made in all of these countries, and from a wider range of base materials than any medieval distiller would recognize. Modern European rules still treat potatoes and cereals as the traditional raw materials, but they explicitly anticipate and allow vodka to be made from 'other agricultural raw materials' as long as the raw material is clearly stated on the label. The regulation even gives examples such as sugar beet molasses, grapes, fruit mixtures, soya, whey and grape marc.

This modern diversity does not make the word meaningless. It underlines the deeper truth. Vodka belongs to a much larger family of distilled 'waters' that took shape across Europe long before anyone argued about national ownership.

THE BOYAR'S TABLE

While vodka/wódka was occasionally used to describe distilled spirits in both Poland and Russia from the late medieval period, early spirits in the region were more commonly called other things. In Poland, *gorzałka* (derived from 'to burn') sometimes appears. In Russia you will see *zhiznennaya voda* which is a direct translation of aqua vitae 'water of life', as well as *varenoe vino* (distilled wine), *korchma* (pot wine), *goriachee vino* (burned wine), *gor'koe vino* (bitter wine), and *khlebnoe vino* (bread wine). It should be noted that the use of the word *vino* should not be taken as indication that these were spirits were made from grapes; vino was commonly used as a catch-all term for any alcoholic solution of wine-strength or higher.

In Orthodox tradition these spirits might be used as an antiseptic or added to holy water for ceremonial purposes, especially in rural communities where doctors were scarce and God was the primary physician. But the enthusiasm for these early spirits among men of the cloth didn't extend throughout the Orthodox faith, however.

Iosif of Volotsk (Iosif Volotsky) was a powerful monastic reformer who died in 1515 and whose views on distilled spirits survive in unusually clear documentary form.

His surviving writings, particularly *The Enlightener*, were polemical works aimed at enforcing doctrinal purity and moral discipline within both the Church and wider society. They are not concerned with spirits as a product in the modern sense but instead give us an early and clear indication that distilled alcohol, and the knowledge of how to make it, was already present and troublesome enough to require regulation.

'Drunkenness is the servant of sin, the door to every evil.' Iosif writes, 'From it arise fornication, anger, violence, and madness. The monk who gives himself to strong drink is no monk, but a slave to the belly and to the devil.'

Another passage, aimed specifically at monastic discipline, states:

'It is not fitting for those who have renounced the world to keep wine in excess, nor to seek drinks that inflame the flesh and darken the mind. Such things drive away prayer and invite demons.'

In later monastic rules attributed to the Josephite tradition, drawing directly on Iosif's authority, the language becomes more pointed:

'Let no brother make or keep drinks that are boiled and strengthened by fire, for such practices belong to worldly men and lead to ruin of the soul.'

Iosif of Volotsk repeatedly condemned what he called drinks 'strengthened by fire', forbidding monks from making or keeping them and treating their consumption as incompatible with monastic life. While he does not describe techniques or name a specific spirit, the language clearly distinguishes distilled drink from ordinary beer or wine and shows that such spirits were already familiar enough in Muscovy to require prohibition rather than explanation.

RIGHT Uspensky Cathedral in the Moscow Kremlin, the heart of an Orthodox Church that condemned drunkenness while granting medicinal spirits a kind of legitimacy.

Nevertheless, the church's involvement granted zhiznennaya voda a curious kind of legitimacy. It was a sacrament and a salve, something to be respected rather than simply knocked back. It is also easy to see how a therapeutic spirit, already known to warm the chest and loosen the tongue, would drift from the monastery infirmary to the feasting table.

Of the vodka precursors, the most significant was probably *khlebnoe vino* (bread wine), because it was one of the first to crop up outside of strictly medical and monastic contexts. In other words, it became a social drink, consumed for pleasure and, increasingly, in pursuit of inebriation. It also sat on the direct line that leads to what we now call vodka, even if the liquid itself would seem nothing like a modern vodka.

This 'bread wine' was distilled in pots from a mash of malted rye, barley or wheat, much the way whisky is made. And like an unaged whisky, it retained plenty of character from the fermented beer from which it was born. Often it was distilled only once, leaving it somewhere in the 30 per cent range. It tasted malty and bready, sometimes fruity, often rough. If you have ever nosed fresh new-make spirit at a distillery, you have a fair sense of the direction of travel.

From the late fifteenth century onward, distilled grain spirit slowly found a second home among the noble classes of Russia, particularly the boyars, the aristocratic elite who served as advisers, landowners and power brokers under the Grand Dukes and early Tsars. Here, it was no longer merely a tincture or remedy. It was a display of wealth, hospitality and command. As with so many fashionable intoxicants across history, part of its appeal lay in its origin story. A substance that arrived wearing the respectable clothes of medicine could be consumed with less moral fuss, at least in public, even when everyone in the room understood its real value was social rather than therapeutic. Sometimes the opposite of therapeutic was closer to the truth.

To be invited to a boyar's table was to enter a world of ceremony and opulence. Meals stretched across hours and could run to dozens of courses, with khlebnoe vino marking the transitions between them. It was served to cleanse the palate, warm the stomach and impress the guests, rather like an intermezzo. The quality of the spirit was still crude by modern standards, yet its presence was deeply symbolic. A host who could produce large volumes of clear, potent bread wine demonstrated agricultural abundance and the means to employ technically competent people. It showed they had grain to spare, equipment to distil, and the household discipline to keep it coming.

In these homes, the spirit was often infused with local herbs, spices, berries or honey, producing the sorts of flavoured infusions later grouped under names like *nastoyka*. Some recipes were handed down like family heirlooms. Others were commissioned by the head of the household from estate stewards or distillation masters.

Some instructions on how to distil spirits at that time are preserved in *The Domostroi*, a sixteenth-century Muscovite household manual that reads like a mash-up of sermon, spreadsheet, and threat. Between the fixations on obedience, discipline, and 'proper' behaviour, including how to raise a dowry for your daughter, sits a practical assumption: a good household makes things. It also bring in supplies, brews beer and kvass, manages barrels and, importantly for our story, treats distillation as a normal skill rather than a mystery. In its sections on drink, *The Domostroi* includes instructions connected to making and distilling mead and beer.

Less a technical treatise and more a record of practical observation, its brewing advice tells the master, or steward, to issue malt, flour, and hops in measured amounts and record everything. He is to supervise mashing, fermenting, and racking so nothing is stolen or 'laughed over and drunk'. It's also rather pointed about the distilling itself: 'The master should distil the spirit himself and remain there constantly. If he trusts someone else, he should give strict orders and still keep watch.' It even instructs him to note how much 'araka' comes off the boiler on the first, second and final run, and to track total yield across the whole process.

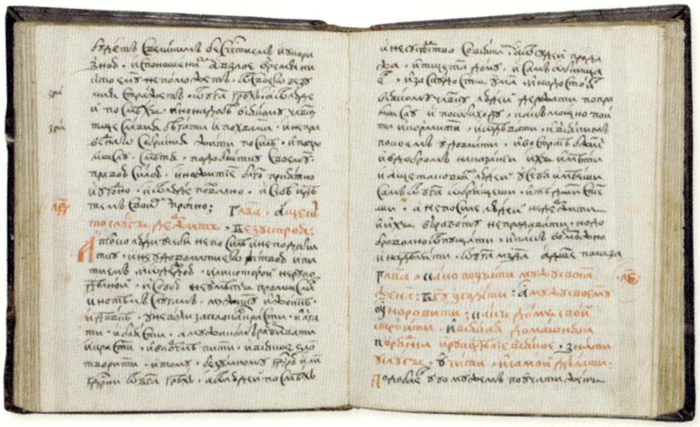

TOP A page of *The Domostroi* at Moscow's State History Museum, showing distillation treated as a household craft. **ABOVE** A banknote featuring Ivan III, who imposed an early state monopoly on the sale of khlebnoe vino in 1474. **OPPOSITE** Konstantin Makovsky's 'A Boyar Wedding Feast' captures the elaborate ceremony of elite Russian drinking, where bread wine marked transitions between courses.

A complete recipe would be lovely, but the more revealing takeaway is that *The Domostroi* assumes distillation is already a known craft, and it worries less about flavour and more about security and obedience.

That further supports our observation that this was spirit as status – a private language of taste and privilege, and a slightly dangerous thrill precisely because it was not meant for ordinary hands.

It was also spirit as control. Within boyar culture, excess projected wealth and power. To drink deeply and remain standing was a mark of endurance. To abstain risked seeming rude or weak. Guests were expected to match the rhythm of the host's toasts, and more than one courtier was undone by a drinking ritual that functioned like social combat. Toasts – ritualized, performative and always escalating – became an essential element of diplomacy and intrigue in a world of veiled threats and shifting alliances. In that sense, bread wine resembled many high-status intoxicants that came later. The liquid mattered, but the real point is what it signalled, and who was allowed to take the risk.

Perhaps because the 'haves' possessed exactly what the 'have-nots' wanted, the equipment and practical know-how for making grain spirits began to seep down through the ranks. That trickle-down came with a tightening grip from above. As distillation spread beyond noble kitchens and estate outbuildings, it stopped looking like a private indulgence and started looking like a serious economic lever.

And it was here that the idea of spirit monopolies began to emerge. Powerful noble families petitioned for, and in many cases received, exclusive rights to distil and sell within their domains. These early licenses were effectively proto-state endorsements, a rehearsal for the formal monopoly later consolidated under Ivan the Terrible in the sixteenth century.

Soon, the princes of Muscovy would be monitoring and manipulating the consumption of khlebnoe vino in the lands around present-day Moscow. Grain-based distillation was on the rise and with it came opportunity. Sensing both the cultural and fiscal potential of alcohol, Ivan III (Grand Prince of Moscow and all Russia from 1462–1505) is said to have enacted an early state monopoly on the production and sale of khlebnoe vino in 1474. It was the spark that would ignite a five-hundred-year tug-of-war between two persistent forces: the state's thirst for revenue, and the population's growing reliance on drink.

Horseradish Nastoyka

This is one of the classic Russian infusions, appearing in household manuals and folk medicine long before vodka became recreational. It was taken for colds, chest infections, fatigue and 'clearing the blood'. You can make it using your favourite vodka brand, or for a more authentic take use polugar (see pp49–51), un-aged whisky or an un-aged genever.

You can use it as the base of a Bloody Mary or in a martini if you like, but remember it was originally meant only for medicinal uses.

40–50 G/1½–1¾ OZ FRESH HORSERADISH ROOT
3–5 BLACK PEPPERCORNS (OPTIONAL)
500 ML/17 FL OZ BASE SPIRIT (SEE ABOVE)
1 TSP HONEY (ONLY IF YOU WANT TO SOFTEN THE BURN)

Peel the horseradish and cut it into thin matchsticks (don't grate it, as you want controlled extraction rather than eye-watering fumes), then place it in a clean jar, add a few peppercorns, if using, and pour over your chosen spirit. Seal and leave to infuse at room temperature for 3–5 days, tasting daily as it extracts quickly.

Once the desired intensity is reached, strain through muslin/cheesecloth or a coffee filter (absolute clarity isn't necessary – a slight haze is historically accurate). If you wish to soften the heat, dissolve a teaspoon of honey in a small measure of the infusion and stir it back in, then bottle and allow it to rest for a further 2–3 days before drinking.

FLOWING THROUGH SOCIETY

Russia's early vodka story is, in many ways, a story of the state. In Poland, drinking sat inside a looser political system and a tighter local one. Power lived with landowners, parish authorities, and Poland's landed gentry: the *szlachta*. Control was established through estates and leases rather than a single treasury in Moscow. The difference is significant, because it shaped how a medicinal 'little water' became a social drink, and how the szlachta turned it into both a badge of class and a source of income.

As we have already established, Polish records in the fifteenth century had already shown the word wódka being used as the sort of term clerks can use without explanation.

By the sixteenth century, figures like Stefan Falimirz in Kraków show how these distilled 'waters' sat at the crossroads of pharmacy, household practice and an emerging drink culture. In 1534 he published *O ziolach y o mocy ich*, which was more a practical manual of medicine and household management than a treatise on drinking, and yet a large portion of his work is dedicated to the preparation of *wódki*, 'little waters', by distillation.

Falimirz does not define what vodka is, which in itself suggests assumed familiarity. He uses the term to describe medicinal distillates, including distilled alcohol and steam-distilled essential oils. 'Wódka is good against cold of the body, it warms the stomach and chest, strengthens digestion, and drives away harmful humours.' He even repeats the old claim, inherited from earlier European medical writing, that 'Wódka, when taken in small measure, preserves youth'.

More practically, Falimirz recognizes vodka's value as a solvent and a carrier and for its ability to draw out and preserve the 'powers' of herbs more effectively than water or wine. He repeatedly recommends soaking roots, seeds, and leaves 'in good vodka' to produce medicinal waters for internal weakness, stomach complaints, paralysis, toothache and fever. In one passage he notes that vodka 'draws the strength from herbs and keeps it from corruption'.

Much of this technique was familiar in Western and Southern Europe. The leap Falimirz makes, or at least the world he reveals, is domestic because his instructions assume household handling. Vodka is used to clean wounds, rinse the mouth, warm the body in cold weather, and preserve plant matter for later use. These are not elite curiosities locked behind an apothecary's counter but everyday practices. Vodka, by the early sixteenth century, had moved out of the learned margins and into kitchens, storerooms and farmsteads.

Falimirz also offers a warning, noting that vodka 'used without measure harms rather than heals'. A late-sixteenth-century Polish medical compendium echoes the same line of thought, insisting that

OPPOSITE Infusing vodka with herbs and spices was as central to the sixteenth-century Polish stillroom as it was to the late-twentieth-century cocktail bar.

LEFT A lively medieval drinking scene. By the seventeenth century, gorzałka and wódka were used interchangeably in Polish records.

distilled and clarified wódka 'is not for gluttony but for the curing of ailments, and must be administered with care.' That concern reads like a pharmaceutical company defending its own invention as it starts slipping into the wrong hands.

In early Polish print, the vocabulary itself maps the shift. *Gorzałka* appears as a term for distilled beverages by the 1520s (after the first Lithuanian mention) and it sits alongside wódka for decades without the two meaning quite the same thing. For a time, they occupy different rooms of the same house, with wódka as the 'little water' of stillroom practice and household remedy, and gorzałka as the spirit with a wider social career ahead of it.

By the mid-sixteenth century, the political map of eastern Europe had shifted again. In 1569, the Polish–Lithuanian Commonwealth was formally created by the Union of Lublin, binding the Kingdom of Poland and the Grand Duchy of Lithuania into a single, sprawling state that ran from the Baltic deep into the lands between Poland and Muscovy. It was vast, decentralized and unusually tolerant by the standards of the time, governed less by royal command than by negotiated privilege among the nobility. For our purposes, what matters is not constitutional theory but movement. The Commonwealth functioned as a corridor rather than a barrier. Grain, people, ideas and practical skills moved across it with relative ease. In that environment, distillation did not belong to one court or one culture. It spread quietly through estates, towns and households, carried along the same routes that fed the region's economy.

The szlachta enjoyed privileges rarely seen elsewhere in Europe. Among them was the practical ability to distil and profit from alcohol on their land, whether by direct production, leasing or licensing. In practice, the still became part of estate life. Some manors featured dedicated distilling rooms. Larger estates treated it as routine infrastructure, as normal as granaries and brew kettles.

This does two things to the story of vodka.

First, it pulls spirit production into the orbit of status. A noble household that could produce clear, potent distillate was showing more than taste. It was showing command. Grain to spare. Labour to spare. Equipment and copperwork. Storage. Record keeping. The kind of competence that looks boring on paper and impressive at a gate.

RIGHT The Romanesque tower at Lublin Castle, where the Union of 1569 formally created the Polish–Lithuanian Commonwealth.

Second, it turns vodka into a language of hospitality. Szlachta culture loved ceremony, and drink made an excellent punctuation mark. Guests could be greeted with a small glass on arrival. Feasts ran long, and toasts arrived in formalized sequences. *Na zdrowie* was not just a cheerful wish. It was a social obligation. To refuse could read as an insult to the host, and in the more theatrical corners of noble culture, as an insult to the idea of Polishness itself.

There is also a useful tension here. The szlachta were tastemakers, yet they were also a target. Renaissance writers sometimes cast the gorzałka drinker as a dissolute minor aristocrat, lurching between stupor and hangover. Early commentary on distilled spirit ranges from neutral to disgusted, with some writers keen to blame outsiders for the habit. That tells you something important. Spirit has become visible enough to attract moral judgement. It is no longer just a remedy.

Once alcohol sits in the household, it starts doing what alcohol always does best. It preserves, extracts and concentrates. Before refrigeration, steeping fruit, herbs, and spices in alcohol was one of the surest ways to capture the flavours of a fleeting season. Sour cherries, blackcurrants, raspberries and quince could be locked into spirit at their peak and pulled back out months later, brightening a winter table. Alcohol preserved colour and aroma. It drew out oils and essences that deepened in the cellar. A well-made *nalewka* (a traditional fruit-, herb- or spice-infused liqueur) was practical and indulgent at the same time.

This is where the szlachta become especially relevant, because estate kitchens and stillrooms had access to both local produce and imported luxuries. Honey from the hives. Orchard fruits, forest berries, roots and barks. Also spices carried up trade routes: cinnamon, cloves, pepper, citrus peel, and the precious odds and ends that make a drink feel expensive.

Many of the classic Polish families of flavoured spirits live comfortably in this world. *Wiśniówka* from sour cherries. *Pigwówka* from quince. *Orzechówka* from green walnuts. In winter, kitchens warmed with the scent of *krupnik*, spirit married to honey and spice. In some houses, a barrel of *starka*, rye spirit mellowed with leaves and time, might be laid down for a life event and opened years later, which is less a reliable practice than a very good story. Either way, it captures the point. Spirit becomes part of lineage and memory.

On the Polish–Lithuanian Commonwealth's eastern and northern edges, similar habits appear under different names, often shaped by the same estate logic. Caraway and cumin spirits appeared around the Baltic trade world. Fruit ratafias emerged in warmer climes, steeped in sunlight then hidden in cool cellars. The details vary. The underlying mechanism stays constant. Once a household treats distillation and infusion as normal, flavour becomes local identity in a bottle.

Early Polish medical distillates that actually describe their methods of production often start from wine, which makes sense within the inherited European medical tradition of aqua vitae. Grain spirits become clearer in the record later, and they do not replace fruit and wine distillates overnight. For a long time, these drinks share space.

Szlachta drinking culture could be lavish, but the deeper story is not only taste. It is power. Alcohol sales were one of the most reliable ways for landowners to extract income from an estate economy. If you control the tavern, you control the village's social centre. If you control the still, you control the supply. If you lease the right to sell alcohol, you create a steady stream of rent and a system of dependence that sits beside labour obligations. This is where later Polish drinking problems begin to take shape, because the structure encourages volume. A tavern can form the glue of the community, but if that glue is sticky enough, the tavern becomes a trap.

Over time, this system becomes formalized in the language of *propinacja*, the feudal right to profit from alcohol production and sale. In practice, it often meant peasants had limited choice about where they drank and who earned from it. This is the Commonwealth's version of control. While it is less centralized than the kabaks of Muscovy that we will encounter in the next chapter, but it is still control nonetheless.

To understand why grain-based vodka becomes so important, we need to step back from the still and look at trade.

For much of the early seventeenth century, the Commonwealth sits inside a powerful export economy. Grain flows down the Vistula to Gdańsk and out into wider European markets. That trade enriches magnates and encourages tighter control over rural labour. Then, from the mid-seventeenth century onward, the structure buckles. War devastates the countryside. The uprising and conflicts that begin in 1648 tear at the Commonwealth's eastern territories. The Swedish invasion of 1655 delivers another deep blow. The grain export world collapses.

When export markets weaken and disruption spreads, surplus grain needs other fates. Distillation is already known and estates already have infrastructure, so turning grain into spirit becomes an attractive domestic solution – and a profitable one. So it is that from the second half of the seventeenth century onward, grain becomes increasingly central to Polish vodka's story.

This is also the moment when outside observers start commenting on the prominence of spirit drinking among the upper layers of society. A German traveller writing in the 1670s describes gorzałka as a favourite drink, consumed in striking quantities, and suggests that aristocratic Poles carried it and drank it frequently. Travel writing always deserves a pinch of salt, especially when it leans into national stereotypes, but the social temperature is clear enough: by the later seventeenth century, distilled spirit has moved well beyond remedy.

Around this time, commentators begin treating wódka and gorzałka as interchangeable labels for recreational distilled drink. The language catches up with the reality. It is tempting to assume that once

RIGHT Gdańsk in the seventeenth century. Polish grain flowed down the Vistula to its ports for export.

distillation becomes familiar, spirit rapidly becomes the everyday drink. But in late-sixteenth-century Kraków, beer still dwarfed distilled spirit in fiscal importance. Distilled drink was present and socially visible, but it has not yet elbowed beer aside as the default. To fulfil its destiny, wódka_would rise up in rural areas not towns. It would do this by moving out of the manor houses and taking up root in village life.

By the seventeenth century, distilled spirit ceased to be an elite curiosity and became part of rural routine, used for celebration, medicine and as currency. Its practical uses however remained stubbornly medieval. It was rubbed on chests for colds, poured over wounds, used to clean tools, and sipped as a cure for everything from melancholy to indigestion. In that sense, vodka kept its aura as a cure-all long after it had become a source of trouble.

It also oiled the machinery of rural ritual, at weddings, baptisms, funerals, harvest feasts and saints' days. Drink marked the calendar as surely as church bells did. If the szlachta codified vodka into ceremony, village life made it communal and raw.

Payment in drink appears in many agrarian cultures, and Polish lands were no exception. A ration to keep morale up during long hours, or a bottle used as informal currency, blurs the line between incentive and sabotage depending on the pour. Engagement rituals, too, often used alcohol as a sign. A matchmaker arriving with a bottle is a neat symbol of what vodka had become. It sealed agreements as efficiently as it loosened tongues.

Yet as vodka embeds itself in village rhythms, it also tightens its grip. Tavern systems leased out by nobles could function as debt machines, drawing future labour into present drinking. The spirit becomes a commodity with a social cost, and that cost falls unevenly. This is where the Commonwealth's decentralized model shows its darker side. Control does not always wear a crown (sometimes it wears an apron behind a bar and keeps a ledger).

By the end of the seventeenth century, Polish vodka has completed its most important transition. It still carries the smell of the pharmacy and the stillroom, but is also, unmistakably, a recreational drink. The szlachta have helped drag it into the spotlight, turning it into ritual, status and profit. The village has absorbed it into the cycle of work and worship, making it remedy, currency and escape. Between the two, a spirit that began as 'little water' becomes something with a much larger appetite.

Krupnik

Krupnik (or *krupnikas* in Lithuania) is perhaps the most delicious traditional medicinal vodka variant: think honey for preservation and softness, warming spices for digestion and spirit as both solvent and safeguard. This recipe makes approx. 1 litre/1¾ pints.

250 ML/9 FL OZ WATER (FILTERED)

1 LARGE CINNAMON STICK

4–6 CLOVES

4 ALLSPICE BERRIES

½ TSP CORIANDER SEED, LIGHTLY CRUSHED

ZEST OF 1 LEMON (NO PITH)

50 G/2½ TBSP RAW HONEY (BUCKWHEAT HONEY IS THE MOST HISTORICALLY ACCURATE BUT WILDFLOWER WORKS IF YOU WANT SOMETHING LIGHTER)

750 ML/1¼ PINTS NEUTRAL GRAIN SPIRIT, 50–60% ABV (FOR HISTORICAL ACCURACY GET HOLD OF A POLUGAR OR NEW-MAKE WHISKY, OTHERWISE GO WITH HIGH STRENGTH VODKA FOR A CLEANER TASTE)

Combine the water, spices and citrus zest in a saucepan. Bring gently to a simmer, then reduce heat and cover. Let it simmer softly for 15–20 minutes.

Remove from heat and allow the liquid to cool slightly (to around 60–65°C/140–150°F). Stir in the honey until fully dissolved. Once the honey-spice mixture has cooled to warm (not hot), add the spirit. Stir thoroughly.

Transfer to a glass jar, seal and store in a cool, dark place for 7–14 days. Taste every few days. When the spice balance feels warming but not aggressive, proceed.

Strain through fine mesh, then through coffee filters or a fine cloth. Bottle and rest for at least another 2 weeks before drinking.

Optional step: Chill the strained krupnik overnight and re-filter to remove waxes and fine honey solids for extra clarity.

THE RISE OF THE KABAK

Back in Muscovy, the story takes a slightly different direction. Whereas the Polish–Lithuanian Commonwealth's drinking economy grew outward through estates, leases and local privilege, Moscow's rulers started pulling the trade inward. They began treating distilled grain spirit as something too valuable to leave to habit and happenstance. It was a product that could be counted, licensed and taxed, then used to reward loyalty and fund expansion. Long before purpose-built drinking houses enter the picture, you can already see the logic forming. Control the still, and you control a dependable stream of money, and a dependable way to keep subjects dependent.

If only it were that simple.

The successors of Ivan III (Grand Prince of Moscow and all Russia from 1462–1505) would repeatedly rescind and reinstate the vodka monopoly, lurching between moral panic and fiscal desperation. Monopoly in principle, exemptions in practice, then crackdowns when revenue dipped. Each ruler inherited the same poisoned chalice. Close the taverns and the treasury ran dry. Leave them open and villages collapsed into debt and disorder. Vodka was both plague and lifeline.

Ivan IV, better known as Ivan the Terrible (reigning 1533 to 1584, crowned the first Tsar in 1547), was arguably vodka's first true evangelist and the architect of the first chain of vodka bars. During his siege of the Tatar Khanate of Kazan in 1552, he encountered state-run taverns known as *kabaks* and promptly imported the model to Muscovy. Loyal administrators were rewarded with exclusive rights to operate them in exchange for fixed payments to the crown.

Step inside one of these early kabaks and the first thing that hits you is the air, sour with spilled kvass, wet wool, sweat and woodsmoke. The floor is packed earth, churned into mud by boots. A tallow candle flickers on the counter, smoke curling into blackened rafters. Somewhere a musician plucks a crooked tune on his horizontal, harp-like *gusli* while men shout over each other, knuckles white around chipped wooden cups. Outside, sleigh bells jangle. Inside, time and personal constitution dissolve.

Before vodka conquered the nation, peasants drank much as their Western neighbours did. We're talking ales and beers, honeyed meads, sharp kvass brewed from rye bread, and the occasional splash of imported wine for those who could afford it. In a society rigidly divided by class, the kabak became one of the few spaces where peasants, merchants and minor officials might sit elbow to elbow. In that sense it resembled the British pub, a social equalizer, a communal hearth. From the tsarist perspective, though, this mixing disrupted the natural order even as it filled the coffers.

The first legal attempt to control the system came in 1601 under Boris Godunov, who banned private spirit sales and reserved the trade for the state. Decades later, Tsar Alexei Mikhailovich doubled down. In the Statute of 1649, he declared a full monopoly on alcohol, spirits, beer and hydromel (mead), and mandated that drinking take place only in designated kabaks, deliberately placed away from homes and workplaces. Enforcement was another matter, uneven, bribable, and elastic at the edges. What was intended to curb alcoholism ended up concentrating it.

By the mid-seventeenth century, vodka revenues funded a large portion of state expenditure. Foreign observers noted that alcohol had become one of the crown's most reliable crops, immune to drought, harvest failure or foreign blockade. In lean years, when grain yields faltered, vodka kept the army paid and the bureaucracy ticking. Poison and medicine, in equal measure. The German scholar Adam Olearius called the sums 'extraordinary.' Giles Fletcher, Elizabeth I's envoy, wrote in 1591: 'The common people are forced to spend the most part of their living in the emperor's taverns, where the keepers are bound by oath to draw from them what they can.'

Kabaks were more than cash machines. They were listening posts. Administrators drank alongside villagers, learning who grumbled about taxes, who

OPPOSITE Statue of Ivan IV, who imported the kabak system to Muscovy after 1552. **RIGHT** 'Before a Tavern' by Konstantin Trutovsky, which hangs in the State Russian Museum, St Petersburg. The kabak became the ultimate apparatus of control in Russian society.

cursed the tsar, who owed whom money. A loose tongue over vodka travelled quickly to a magistrate's ear. It was a surveillance system the KGB would have been proud of.

Presiding over it all was the tavern keeper: the *tselovalnik*, literally 'the kisser', so called because he swore loyalty to the tsar by kissing the Orthodox cross. He was also, in practice, a state-bound operator, accountable upward and incentivized accordingly. Imagine him as a rough type: fur hat pulled low, fingers stained with tar and tobacco, a little abacus behind the counter to count your misery. He knows your name, your debts, the weight of your coat. He smiles when you stagger in, because he knows what comes next.

Bound by oath never to turn away a customer, his loyalty lay firmly with the tsar's purse. Shots ran short, change ran light, and while you argued about it, a nimble accomplice might be easing your belt pouch from behind.

Drinking followed the seasons. After harvest, pockets briefly full, kabaks overflowed. By winter, the same men returned barefoot, credit exhausted, promising next year's grain to pay for last year's hangover.

But what was the booze like? Kabaks poured raw bread wine and rye or wheat spirit, which was crudely pot-distilled, often only once, and full of fusel oils and harsh congeners. It might have smelled of damp grain and varnish, burned like solvent, and punished you the next day. There was no charcoal filtration, and certainly no careful cuts between heads and tails. Tavern keepers routinely watered it down, selling weak swill as ‹vodka› at full price, colouring it with burnt sugar or masking faults with herbs and ash. It was stored in wooden barrels, ladled out into clay cups, with no measures and little accountability. Kvass, beer and honey mead still existed, but vodka took over because it worked faster.

The tavern worked fast too, extracting everything. Boots. Coats. Wagon wheels. Livestock. Grain meant to feed children. Wives sold embroidery to buy back pawned shoes. Children learned early that winter coats could disappear overnight.

Such was the degree of destitution that in Russia a drunkard was not a lovable rogue but a moral failure. Words like *pyanitsa* (drunkard) and *propoytsa*, literally 'one who drinks himself away', carried real social weight. To say a man had *propil rubakhu*, 'drunk away his shirt', meant total ruin rather than a hard night. There was even a specific term, *zapoi*, for multi-day benders where men vanished from normal life altogether, disappearing into alcohol until work, family and responsibility dissolved. Tavern regulars were called *kabatsky chert,* 'tavern devils', men half-claimed by the kabak, hovering between life and oblivion.

When Adam Olearius toured Russia in the 1640s, he marvelled at the 'extraordinary amount of money' the kabak system generated, 'since the Russians know no restraint in drinking vodka'. He described men drinking away their clothes, emerging barefoot, bareheaded, or in nightshirts, only to go back inside and sell those too. One man he witnessed pawned his cloak, then his shirt, then his underdrawers, finally leaving the tavern naked, clutching weeds to cover himself, singing as he went.

The parallels with Britain's eighteenth-century gin craze are striking. In London, cheap gin flooded working-class districts, earning nicknames like 'Mother's Ruin'. William Hogarth's Gin Lane shows skeletal mothers dropping babies, men collapsing in the street and families disintegrating – a visual echo of Olearius's naked drunks in Novgorod. The British state publicly condemned gin while quietly profiting from it through taxation, much as the Russian crown did with vodka. Moral panic followed when productivity dropped and public order frayed. In both cases, alcohol became a pressure valve for poverty and social unrest, a cheap anaesthetic for lives lived on the edge.

By 1648, writer Claire Suddath estimates, a third of Russian men were in debt to kabaks. Taverns had become incubators of addiction and machines of extraction, lubricated with rough ethanol.

A drunk population is easier to govern than a sober one. They're slower to organize, quicker to quarrel among themselves and trapped in debt. The kabak system helped neutralize dissent. Men who might otherwise grumble about taxes, conscription or land rights spent their evenings numbing themselves instead. Credit tied them to the state and drunken confessions fed local administrators. Hangovers dulled resistance. This was part design, part opportunity. The tsars preached morality, and they understood power. Distilled spirits softened hardship just enough to stop anger crystallizing into revolt and when uprisings did break out, kabaks were often among the first buildings torched.

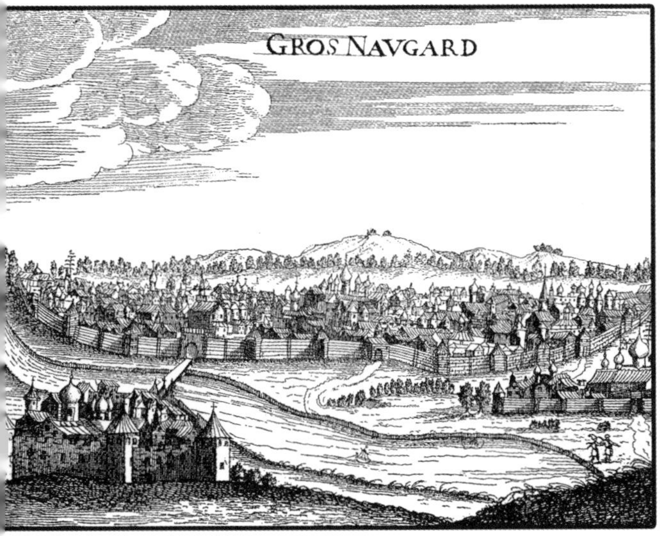

This uneasy relationship with alcohol intensified. Under Peter the Great (Tsar of all Russia from 1682 and the first Emperor of Russia from 1721– 1725), drinking would become ritualized and compulsory, with enforced toasts and hangovers as policy. The groundwork was laid here, in the kabaks. Vodka, not merely as a drink, but as an instrument of rule.

Even today, Russia's ambivalence toward alcohol echoes this legacy. It is a state that condemns drunkenness while depending on it, culturally and historically. The kabak never really closed. It just changed shape.

LEFT Novgorod the Great seen along the Volkhov River in the seventeenth century. Once one of Europe's largest cities, it housed a flourishing kabak culture.
ABOVE A reproduction of William Hogarth's 'Gin Lane' (1751). The print campaigned for the Gin Act and offered a visual echo of Russia's own kabak destitution.

Kabak Rossol Cup
(HANGOVER CURE)

Given the prevalence of hangovers during the kabak era, some kind of remedy was often needed the night after. This usually came in the form of something pickled plus some fatty meat and pepper spice. I've modified some of the traditional options into a straight brine drink that would have been the simplest 'morning after' fix in Muscovy. It is salty, sour and sharp enough to make your face remember it has bones.

60 ML/2 FL OZ CUCUMBER BRINE
(FROM SALTED CUCUMBERS OR DILL PICKLES)

120–180 ML/4–6 FL OZ COLD WATER OR COLD KVASS (IF YOU HAVE IT)

1 TSP VINEGAR (OPTIONAL, FOR EXTRA BITE)

A PINCH OF BLACK PEPPER (OPTIONAL)

A THIN SLICE OF ONION OR A SMALL SCRAPE OF HORSERADISH
(OPTIONAL, IF YOU WANT IT BRUTAL)

Pour the brine into a mug. Add water or kvass and stir.
Start with 1:3 brine to liquid if you are fragile. Go 1:2 if you are confident or foolish.
Add vinegar, pepper and a slice of onion – or horseradish if you're feeling brave.
Drink it cold, in small pulls rather than one heroic go.

PETER & POLUGAR

The coin leaves your hand at the kabak counter, caked in dirt and carrying the faint smell of kvass. You slide it across the wood and the tselovalnik pours you another *charka*, a ladle of around 150 ml (5 fl oz) of bread wine. It costs you one *kopek*, roughly half a morning's work. Cheap enough that it won't be your last, and expensive enough to keep you poor. The tselovalnik takes the coin without ceremony. You drink the spirit. Across the Empire, millions more do the same. You stay put in the kabak but the coin moves on. By the end of the day it has been counted and recorded. By the next, it is bundled with others and carried away. Clerks log it. Runners move it. Officials skim their share. With every step away from the tavern the rooms grow cleaner. As the money flows towards Moscow it dissolves into the state's accounts. It becomes wages, timber, iron, uniforms. It becomes ships and gunpowder and salaries paid on time.

By the early eighteenth century, roughly a quarter of state revenue came from the sale of spirits. One ship in four. Every fourth rifle. The dessert course at a banquet table. All paid for in khlebnoe vino. It kept courts lit and armies fed. Every rouble traceable back to a hundred measures poured somewhere like the kabak you're sat in.

Under Peter the Great, bread wine ceased to be just something people drank. It became a mechanism for extracting value from hunger, habit, and cold, and pushing it uphill into power. From barrel to ledger to palace table, the path was direct, even if the drinker never saw where it led.

Peter Alekseyevich Romanov reigned from 1682 to 1725 and is often treated as the founding figure of modern Russia. He forced the country into a new posture, militarily and culturally, driven by an obsession with efficiency and a pace that left little room for nostalgia. After the Great Northern War (1700–1721) saw Russia emerge as the dominant power in the Baltic, Peter took the title of Emperor, and in 1721 Russia was proclaimed an empire. It was a new political identity, and Peter expected Europe to recognize it.

When Peter came to power, bread wine was being distilled in three places: by the state, which needed it for revenue and sold it through the kabaks; by boyars, who treated it as both profit and privilege on their estates; and by the people themselves, who distilled illegally because the alternative was debt. Peter wanted control, and control required clarity. That meant pushing towards monopoly.

One of his most consequential moves was the destruction of the old nobility, which meant the boyars among others. Peter dismantled a system in which power flowed through lineage, household autonomy, and private economic worlds, and in its place he built a service state, where rank, land, and privilege were now earned through military or administrative service, codified most clearly in the Table of Ranks of 1722. This new nobility, the dvoryanstvo, did not derive authority from ancestry or tradition. It derived it from the state. A culture of inherited independence gave way to one of bureaucratic obedience. The old boyar household, which brewed, distilled, feasted, and drank on its own terms, was no longer the model – the empire was.

Bread wine had long been produced privately on noble estates and sold locally through taverns, with the state skimming revenue where it could and tolerating wide variation so long as the money kept flowing, but Peter pushed this loose arrangement towards something far more legible and enforceable, applying to spirits the same principles he was imposing on rank, service and administration. In practice, this meant treating alcohol production not as a household custom or inherited right, but as an activity that could be measured, judged and corrected. He didn't build distilleries but rather monopolized the output of the existing ones. As nobles were reshaped into servants of the state, vodka was reshaped into a state-facing commodity. Less an expression of lineage, hospitality or estate autonomy, and more a fiscal instrument designed to move predictably from grain to still to treasury.

The connection was structural rather than symbolic and Peter was like a new CEO looking to tighten up operations and improve efficiency. A service nobility was easier to discipline, disciplined estates were easier to tax, and grain grown on noble land increasingly flowed into stills that answered to state expectations rather than private habit.

So it was then, that khlebnoe vino and nastoyka drifted away from the world of family prestige and ceremonial generosity and towards one of counting, testing and revenue extraction. Peter did not create modern vodka, but he created the conditions that made it inevitable. By breaking the old nobility and binding the new one to service, he ensured that vodka, like rank itself, would ultimately belong not to families, but to the empire.

ABOVE The Bronze Horseman statue of Peter the Great in Senate Square, St Petersburg, the new capital he founded.

Vodka lore gravitates towards Peter because he contains Russia's long argument with drink in a single figure. He understood spirits as a powerful social solvent, something that loosened tongues, cemented friendships, tested loyalty and exposed weakness, but he also understood their cost. Families were ruined, labour was lost, violence followed. He saw this clearly, yet he also knew the treasury depended on alcohol, and he had wars to fund, cities to build, and ships to launch. Faced with a problem he could neither abolish nor ignore, he did what autocrats often do. He turned it into policy.

At court, Peter transformed drinking into performance and made himself vodka's first true

ambassador, using beer and spirits as instruments of punishment that were often comic in form and brutal in effect, the sort of spectacle that filled rooms with nervous laughter as everyone remembered they might be next. One of the most notorious artefacts of his reign was the punitive goblet known as the Big Eagle, which anyone arriving late to a feast or breaching etiquette could be ordered to drain. The cup is consistently described as holding around 1.5 litres/2½ pints, roughly the equivalent of two modern bottles of spirit, and its purpose was humiliation as much as intoxication. In 'Scenes from the Court of Peter the Great', drawn from the diary of Johann Georg Korb, we are told that there were drinking banquets lasting for three whole days, and Korb adds, without embellishment, that guests sometimes died.

At the same time, and with a hypocrisy that is entirely consistent rather than accidental, Peter publicly attacked drunken disorder. He needed

ABOVE The Winter Palace, now the State Hermitage, in central St Petersburg. Peter's new capital announced Russia's imperial ambition to Europe.

soldiers who could fight and labourers who could build, and his punishments were designed to be seen. The most infamous was the so-called Medal for Drunkenness, a cast-iron weight hung around the neck of offenders for days at a time. Accounts vary and some surviving examples are later replicas, but the core details remain consistent. It weighed close to 7 kg/15 lb 7 oz and was fixed so the wearer could not remove it themselves. It was punishment as theatre, drunkenness rendered ridiculous and physically miserable, while the machinery of alcohol revenue continued to turn.

If you're going to act as the sole supplier of alcohol to a population, you need to have some idea around how a product should taste and what strength it should be supplied at. In the early 1710s, several fiscal and administrative orders directed at taverns, distillers and tax farmers specify that khlebnoe vino supplied to the state must be 'good' and 'proper', and that it must pass the burn test, meaning it should ignite cleanly and burn away by roughly half its volume. This method of testing strength before the invention of alcohol meters is somewhat analogous to the British Royal Navy's 'proof' test where rum was burnt with gunpowder to 'prove' its veracity. In the case of khlebnoe vino, the spirit was ignited and judged by the volume of spirit left when the flame eventually went out. If the volume dropped by half or (one would assume) more then you are good to go. When later measured, the traditional strength associated with this practice came out at 38.5% ABV. In knowing both the total volume and (approximate) volume of alcohol in a barrel you could then begin assigning a value to it.

Most historians point to the year 1714 as the time this becomes clear policy rather than recommendation, and from then onwards decrees tied to tavern supply and state purchasing require inspectors to reject watered down or under-strength bread wine and to fine or punish those selling spirit that failed the burn test.

Over time this semi-standardized spirit evolved from being called khlebnoe vino and instead became known as *polugar* ('half burned') – vodka's forgotten parent. Polugar became the spirit that would shape Russian life for the next two centuries. It warmed, fed and entertained, easing hunger and cold while marking feasts, friendships, and everyday ritual. At the same time it trapped people in debt, pulled wages back across the tavern counter, and quietly deepened poverty. It satisfied and ensnared in equal measure.

A great deal of what we now know about polugar comes by way of the Russian historian and archivist Boris Rodionov. His research in the 1990s centred on imperial excise records, technical instructions, and

ABOVE Peter the Great, the reformer who reshaped Russia and turned vodka into a state-facing commodity. **LEFT** The cast-iron Medal for Drunkenness, hung around offenders' necks by order of Peter the Great. The inscription reads: 'For Drunkenness'.

legal definitions of bread wine, particularly the boring yet functional texts written for tax inspectors and distillery supervisors rather than for producers. The sources he cites repeatedly, in interviews and Russian-language publications, come from eighteenth-century administrative and technical writing, which exist for one clear reason. The state needed to know precisely what it was taxing, and that necessity forced a degree of clarity about how bread wine was made and what counted as acceptable quality.

Rodionov's key source is generally identified as an eighteenth-century instruction describing 'bread wine of proper quality'. Although it doesn't survive as a tidy standalone recipe, a core passage appears consistently across scholarly summaries and reconstructions. Translated, it runs along the lines of: 'Bread wine is to be made from grain malt, brewed into beer, and distilled twice in copper vessels, until it burns evenly and, when ignited, is consumed by half.' From this, a coherent production method emerges: the raw material is entirely grain, most often rye in central Russia, with wheat or barley used elsewhere. The grain is malted, mashed and fermented into a low beer, with no sugar addition, no neutral base spirit, and no rectification. Distillation takes place in copper pot stills, producing a spirit that can be diluted with water but not so far that it fails the burn test.

Polugar is a time capsule of what early Russian 'vodka' was supposed to be: grain-forward and aromatic, made in copper pot stills and expected to taste of its raw material. Rye tasted of rye. Wheat tasted of wheat. Barley tasted of barley. Whereas modern vodka culture tends to treat character as a flaw, polugar treats character as the point.

In recent years, polugar has been deliberately revived as a historical style by Boris Rodionov and his sons. Their range is essentially a menu of what bread wine can taste like when you stop trying to polish the character out of Russian spirits. Classic rye, single malt rye, wheat, barley, buckwheat, and a run of numbered bottlings built around old-fashioned flavourings: juniper, honey, pepper, caraway, horseradish and various rye and wheat

combinations. All typically sit at the historical 38.5% ABV.

Ironically (and for reasons we shall get into in later chapters) polugar production is banned in Russia, so Rodionov & Sons operate out of a distillery in Poland. On one of my first visits to Russia in 2012, I was fortunate enough to go to a bar in Moscow that stocked the entire range of Polugar brand products, and had a very enjoyable evening with the proud owner of the bar tasting our way through them and imagining ourselves in an eighteenth-century kabak.

Polugar is not a museum piece, though it trades heavily on memory. It is a useful tasting tool. It lets the modern drinker get closer to the world that khlebnoe vino occupied, where grain mattered, where distillation left fingerprints, and where 'vodka' had not yet been trained into anonymity. Once vodka later becomes defined as a rectified, neutral spirit, both terms fall away. Khlebnoe vino fades as language, and polugar survives mainly as a historical reference to the last moment when Russian grain spirit still had an officially recognized taste.

TOP LEFT Rye, the dominant base material for early Russian and Polish grain spirits.
ABOVE CENTRE Kvass, the lightly fermented Russian drink made from rye bread or grain.
ABOVE RIGHT Copper pot stills, vessels in which polugar and bread wine took shape.
ABOVE & LEFT Two of the polugar offerings from Rodionov & Sons, which supply abundant flavour and provide a remarkable time capsule.

THE EMPRESS OF VODKA

By the time vodka began to matter seriously to the Russian state, most of the people drinking it were no longer free to walk away from the system that sold it to them. Serfdom (Russia's version of indentured servitude) did not arrive overnight but hardened gradually, in parallel with the state's drive for order and dependable revenue. It began with The Sudebnik of 1497 – the legal code introduced by Ivan III – which restricted peasant movement to a single week a year around St George's Day. Further decrees tightened that window through the sixteenth century, and the Law Code of 1649 abolished legal movement altogether, binding peasants permanently to their estates. By the mid-eighteenth century, the scale of this arrangement was vast. Of a total population of roughly 23–25 million in Russia, around 10–11 million people were serfs owned by private landlords, with a further 8–9 million classed as state peasants, who were technically free but still heavily constrained by obligation and economic slavery. In other words, well over three quarters of the rural population lived under some form of coercive attachment to land.

Serfdom was not evenly distributed. In the fertile central and southern agricultural zones (which supplied grain to Moscow and later St Petersburg) privately owned serfs often made up 60 to 70 per cent of the population. In the north and northeast, where soil was poorer and grain yields lower, free peasants were more common and estate distilling less dominant.

A serf's home (called an *izba*) was typically a low, single-roomed log hut, built from rough pine trunks hauled in from nearby forests. The roof sloped to shed snow and rain, and the walls pressed inwards, darkened by smoke and years of use. Windows were few and small, little more than narrow openings, sometimes covered with stretched animal bladder that admitted a dull, milky light while doing little to keep out the cold. Space was tight, and families, often three generations at once, ate, slept, worked,

OPPOSITE Empress Elizabeth, daughter of Peter the Great, whose 1751 decree formalized 'vodka' in Russian law for the first time. **RIGHT** Most Russian peasants in the eighteenth century were bound to noble estates by serfdom.

and gave birth within the same few hundred square feet. Privacy barely existed. Warmth, when it came, arrived via the stove at the centre of the room or, of course, from khlebnoe vino.

Under Empress Elizabeth, Peter's daughter, the word 'vodka' entered official documentation in a decree dated 8 June 1751 that regulated ownership of vodka distilleries. We've established that the word appears much earlier, usually referring to flavoured or medicinal distillates, but what makes this moment significant is that vodka was being named so it could be governed. Once vodka was written into law, it became separable from other spirits. Rules could be attached to it: who could distil and sell it, where it could be served, and what counted as vodka. The more clearly vodka was defined, the more effectively it functioned as an instrument of policy – and the more intensely the state became marinated in it.

At the same time, vodka in this period remained a spectrum rather than a singular product. Production continued in noble houses but it was now monitored and part of a wider state-shape system. Foreign observers had long described spirits being offered as markers of rank and hospitality. Adam Olearius recorded vodka being presented by the mistress of the house 'from her own hand', a gesture heavy with status and etiquette. Ottoman clergyman and chronicler Paul of Aleppo described similar scenes of ritual hospitality among the elite. Then there was the serf spirit, sold by the state or its agents to the kabaks, designed for volume and revenue. Threaded through all of it was bread wine at polugar strength, familiar to ordinary drinkers and varying by place.

This was the world Catherine the Great inherited when she came to power in 1762. She ruled until

1796 and cultivated the image of an enlightened monarch. She read widely, corresponded with philosophers, and styled herself as a modern ruler (she also liked a drop of London stout, and is responsible for promoting the strong Russian Imperial Stout which was consumed in court). Catherine was also a pragmatist. Empires cost money, and Russia already had a dependable way to raise it.

Under Catherine, liquor revenue rose from roughly 11 per cent of total net revenue in the 1720s to around 43 per cent by 1780, before easing back toward 30 per cent by the end of the century. These figures explain why moral objections to drink repeatedly lost to fiscal rationality. When alcohol accounted for nearly half of state revenue, vodka was no longer a social problem at the edge of politics but rather one that was central to it.

Catherine's reign is often described as a high point of noble privilege, and in vodka's story that is true. She relaxed some of Peter's reforms and from 1767 estates increasingly became distilling centres again. Practically speaking, this meant that wealthy *otkupshchiki* (tax-farmers) were allowed to purchase concessions that gave them a monopoly on vodka sales in a specified region. Otkupshchiki paid the state a fixed amount based on their expected sales. This meant the local tavern, the local still and the local landowner could merge into a single economic circuit, and within that circuit, vodka became both commodity and control. Wages could be paid in drink and addiction managed by drink. This new vodka aristocracy became very well established and increasingly powerful, to the point where the tsars of the early nineteenth century would fail at their attempts to restore a state monopoly (more on that later).

It was also during Catherine's reign that science began to creep into the production and regulation of vodka. Hydrometers, alcoholometers and related floating devices, calibrated to show the density of a liquid relative to water, offered a new way to express alcoholic strength numerically rather than theatrically with a flame. A spirit could now be tested without fire and recorded without argument. The result was better accuracy, but also a new administrative mindset. Strength became a number that corresponded to yield and value and became something that could be calculated in advance. This also meant that fraud became something that could be demonstrated rather than merely suspected. Scientific advances no doubt improved quality and consistency, but more than anything they tightened control.

The adoption of these tools was neither smooth nor universal. Hydrometers arrived unevenly, were often mistrusted, and required a degree of mathematical literacy that many local officials did not yet possess. Different regions used different scales, different reference temperatures, and different units of measure, which meant that 'proof' was still a moving target. Even so, the direction of travel was unmistakable. Once alcohol content could be expressed in degrees, percentages or standardized strengths tied to excise tables, it could be slotted neatly into the growing bureaucratic apparatus of the modern state.

ABOVE Catherine II of Russia, who drank strong, dark beer while her subjects made and consumed vodka. **OPPOSITE** Tsarskoe Selo, the Catherine Palace, the eighteenth-century summer residence of the tsars near St Petersburg.

Russia did not adopt this language overnight, but the influence is visible long before full industrialization arrived. Vodka began to be discussed less in terms of custom and more in terms of grades, taxation brackets and excise logic. Officials concerned themselves with output per unit of grain, loss during distillation, and the gap between theoretical and actual yield. This is a quiet prelude to industrial modernity rather than its full expression. The still remained a pot still and the spirit still tasted of grain but the mindset has shifted.

As vodka spread more systematically across the countryside under these increasingly rationalized systems, the urge to make it at home intensified rather than faded. This is where samogon comes

TOP LEFT Bread wine started life as flour, ground for the mash in a rotary mill stone (like the one pictured) and then fermented. **LEFT** Portable distillation equipment, the sort that allowed peasants to produce samogon away from official eyes. **ABOVE** An old moonshine flask alongside potatoes, one of the cheapest and most fermentable bases for samogon.

fully into view – vodka's moonshine. The word means 'self-distilled', and it sat as the shadow twin of the state's drink, a parallel economy running alongside licences, monopolies and tax farms. Samogon was not an act of ignorance or obstinacy so much as a practical response to a drink that had become paperwork.

And because it was illegal and unregulated, the production of samogon could be fermented from grain, potatoes, beets, honey, fruit, bread or sugar, depending on what was available and what could be hidden. It could be distilled in copper if the distiller had access to it, or in improvised equipment assembled from scrap. Sometimes it was made with care and was probably quite tasty but most of the time it would have been fairly nasty. However, the popular image of samogon as dangerous is probably not true. Most illicit distillers had the same aim as legitimate distillers, which was to produce something saleable and repeatable. The real risks lie in inconsistency, contamination, poor separation, and the absence of any corrective feedback when mistakes are made.

Samogan was a thorn in the side of the state. Empress Elizabeth's 1751 decree that first regulated vodka, complained of peasants 'making wine for themselves' rather than purchasing it from licensed taverns. Later edicts repeat the same grievance with

RIGHT A Russian izba interior. Multiple generations would eat, sleep and work in this single room, warmed by the central stove.

increasing frustration, and an internal finance report from the 1780s complains that 'peasants, instead of attending the kabaks, distil spirits themselves, depriving the treasury of its lawful income'.

For the peasants, samogon represented more than just a cheap alternative but also an emblem of cultural identity and even craft – the countryside's answer to a spirit that has been reduced to categories, units and ledgers. It was also a useful way of concealing value. Grain was bulky, perishable and easy for landlords or officials to seize. Spirit was compact, divisible and concealable. This was how samogon became an informal currency for weddings, wakes, bribes, favours and everyday exchange, allowing the rural economy to make itself legible on its own terms even as the state tried to impose a different accounting system.

Crackdowns followed of course, and they failed in predictable ways that have played out across the world whenever a state over-legislates alcohol production and citizens innovate around it. Each tightening of control raised the value of illicit spirit and deepened the incentive to produce it. Enforcement pushed distillation further into private space, into sheds, bathhouses, barns and forest edges where heat and secrecy can coexist. Informants appeared because poverty produces them. Stills were seized and rebuilt. The more the state depended on alcohol revenue, the harder it fought the shadow market, and the harder it fought, the more profitable that market became.

Through all of this, the spirit itself changed in meaning as much as in taste. In the kabak it was revenue and oblivion. At court it was endurance and status. On the estate, it was profit and leverage. In the shed, it was independence and risk. When later generations speak of vodka as Russia's national drink, they usually mean a clear, measured liquid. In the Russia of Peter, Elizabeth and Catherine, vodka was already national, but it is not yet tidy.

Imperial Boilermaker

Strong British stout beer was all the rage in Catherine's court and Imperial Russian Stout remains to this day an extra-strong style of the stouts and porters we are familiar with. Stout actually takes its name from being more 'stout' of character, which is to say, strong. In the past, stout porters would have been sold at around seven or eight per cent, but over time the potency dropped to the Guinness-like strength you see today (between four and five per cent). The birth of the craft beer industry gave rise to the exploration and marketing of some historical styles however, so it's not too difficult to come by the type of beer that Catherine and her courtiers would have been sloshing back. Needless to say, there would have been *vedros* of vodka to accompany it, too.

330-ML/11-FL-OZ BOTTLE IMPERIAL RUSSIAN STOUT
(CHECK THORNBRIDGE'S SAINT PETERSBURG
OR STONE BREWING'S BOTTLING)

35 ML/1 FL OZ VODKA

Pour into separate glasses and enjoy sipping from one to the other.

INGREDIENTS FOR AN INDUSTRY

The eighteenth century opens with the Polish–Lithuanian Commonwealth still intact but economically strained. Grain exports, which were once the engine of noble wealth, were faltering. Distillation, already established on estates, became less a secondary use of surplus and more a deliberate strategy for concentrating value with excess grain. Turning bulky, price-sensitive grain into compact, durable alcohol offers a practical advantage, particularly in a world where markets are unstable and borders porous. Vodka did not replace grain as an economic foundation, but it increasingly shadowed it.

Raw material choices during this period remained conservative. Grain dominated, especially rye, which sits at the centre of Polish agriculture, bread culture, and earlier distilling practice. Scott Simpson from the Institute of European Studies at Jagiellonian University in Kraków notes that 'grain vodka, particularly rye, had been produced from at least the seventeenth century and remained the dominant raw material well into the nineteenth'.

The potato entered this world gradually… and then decisively. Introduced earlier as a food crop (King Jan Sobieski III is traditionally held to have brought the first potatoes to Poland from Vienna in 1683, though the first noted sale of potatoes as a food item in a Krakow market was in 1739), it gained momentum in distilling towards the end of the eighteenth century and spread rapidly through the nineteenth. The reason was agricultural – potatoes thrived in poorer soils, delivered high yields, and produced a fermentable mass that suited volume production.

There was one technical problem that needed overcoming, though.

Unlike grain, which carries its own enzymes capable of converting starch into fermentable sugars (diastase produced during the malting process), potatoes need a little help. They require an additional step to unlock usable sugars before yeast can do its work. That hurdle probably delayed their adoption as a distillable raw material, even as they spread rapidly as a food crop.

The breakthrough was enzymatic conversion. Early potato distillers learned to introduce enzymes from malted grain into cooked potato mash, using crushed or mashed malted barley or rye as a saccharifying agent. The potatoes were first cooked to gelatinize the starch, then mixed with malt so that

ABOVE King Jan Sobieski III, traditionally said to have brought the first potatoes back from Vienna in 1683.
OPPOSITE Potato fields in West Pomerania. Potatoes need an enzyme source (like malted barley) to convert their starch before fermentation can begin.

the enzymes could break those starches down into sugars. Only then could fermentation proceed. Later refinements improved temperature control, mash consistency and enzyme efficiency, but the principle remained the same.

This technique appeared first in the German-speaking world. David Mollinger's distillery at Monsheim in the Palatinate (a historical region in southwestern Germany), is credited as the site where potato spirit was first distilled commercially, around 1750. By the 1790s, improvements in technique had followed, and knowledge of potato fermentation was circulating widely across Europe through technical manuals and agricultural publications.

There is no firm record of when potato vodka first appeared in Polish territories. Writing before 1786, Jan Krzysztof Kluk described potatoes as already popular in Europe but still relatively recent in Poland and not yet fully exploited. Even so, he noted that '...in some places distilleries are already making vodka from them'.

The Polish–Lithuanian Commonwealth began to unravel in the latter part of the eighteenth century, however, with the First Partition in 1772,

LEFT Monument to Jan Kiliński in Lviv, the Galician city where Baczewski began distilling in 1782. **OPPOSITE** The Łącko region of southern Poland, home of the fierce 70% ABV plum spirit Śliwowica Łącka.

when Russia, Prussia and Austria each annexed large territories from a weakened state. Reform efforts, including the Constitution of 3 May 1791, failed to halt the process, and the Second Partition in 1793 further reduced Poland's land and autonomy. After the defeat of the Kościuszko Uprising in 1794, the Third Partition in 1795 erased Poland entirely, dividing its remaining territory between the three powers and leaving the country without sovereignty for the next 123 years. By the time the third and final partition erased Poland from the map in 1795, potato vodka, later so closely associated with Polish identity, was already taking hold.

Piątkowski's 1809 distilling manual *Gorzelnik i piwowar doskonały* discusses potato vodka as a familiar practice, though he judged it 'the worst of all kinds of vodka'. His preferences are revealing. He considered spirits made from beetroot, chestnuts and acorns superior, alongside fruit distillates from apples, pears and grapes. Grains occupied a middle ground in his estimation, yet the extended attention he gives them suggests they remained the most commonly used bases in practice.

Even here, innovation still flowed west to east. Piątkowski looked explicitly to German sources for the most up-to-date methods of producing potato vodka, underlining how closely distilling developments in Eastern Europe were tied into wider European technical exchange.

Speaking of fruit spirits, in Jewish communities, *śliwowica* occupied a distinctive and practical place in the landscape of spirits. Made from plums rather than grain or potato, śliwowica was not *chamec* (from the Hebrew *chametz*), meaning it could be owned and consumed during Passover when fermented grain products were forbidden. Grape spirits were subject to stricter religious rules, which helps explain why Jewish grape brandies remained relatively uncommon, while fruit distillates flourished.

With Jews accounting for roughly one tenth of the Commonwealth's population for much of its history, this was not a small market. Śliwowica circulated widely, both as a domestic spirit and as a commercial product, and its status persisted into the modern regulatory era. Polish law repeatedly treated so-called Passover vodkas (*pejsachówka*), largely fruit-based spirits such as śliwowica, as a special category. Even the 1927 regulation of the spirits industry granted them a degree of freedom from the state monopoly that grain vodkas did not enjoy.

That survival instinct is still visible today. *Śliwowica Łącka*, the fiercely strong (typically 70% ABV) plum spirit associated with a small mountain town, remains technically illegal, yet appears on the Polish Ministry of Agriculture's list of Regional and

Traditional Products. Locals sell it openly to visitors, complete with homemade labels and tongue-in-cheek excise stamps, while enforcement remains sporadic at best. In recent legislation, Polish law has shifted śliwowica out of the vodka category altogether, placing it under *okowita*, a revived Polish term derived from aqua vitae. In many respects, fruit distillates such as śliwowica represent a parallel strand of Polish vodka history that may predate the grain spirits we now think of as canonical. They also proved more resilient than rye vodka when potato spirit swept through the industry at the end of the eighteenth century, altering the economics of distillation almost overnight.

In addition to the wide range of ingredients used to make vodka, the dissolution and partitioning of Poland resulted in different administrative bodies overseeing vodka production. Distillers in Poznań adapted to Prussian excise discipline and agricultural rationalization. In Galicia, under Austrian rule, producers operated within a bureaucratic but commercially minded imperial framework that encouraged export and branding. Meanwhile, in the semi-autonomous Kingdom of Poland, under Russian control, vodka was pulled into a centralized fiscal logic that echoes the industry in Moscow.

The effect was a fragmented but technically literate vodka landscape. Polish producers learned to operate under multiple systems at once, often supplying different markets with the same spirit finished to different specifications. This reorganization also underpinned export as Polish spirits moved beyond local and imperial markets into Western Europe, not in vast anonymous volumes but as identifiable products.

The history of the world's oldest vodka brand, Baczewski, illustrates this trajectory most clearly.

Founded in 1782 by Leopold Maksymilian Baczewski in Wybranówka, near Lviv, in what was then Austrian Galicia, the company emerged at the intersection of estate distilling, imperial bureaucracy and a rapidly professionalising spirits' trade. From the outset, Baczewski was less interested in novelty than in refinement. The firm invested early in improved distillation and rectification techniques (more on this in the next chapter) aiming for consistency and clarity at a time when much vodka production was still irregular and locally variable.

The company's trajectory was shaped by the decentralized multinational Habsburg system, which favoured documentation, standards, and export readiness, and Baczewski adapted quickly. By the early nineteenth century, the firm was producing a wide range of spirits, including vodkas, fruit brandies and liqueurs, with vodka at the commercial core. What set Baczewski apart was their technical competence but also their branding and presentation. The company pioneered the use of distinctive bottles and cohesive visual identity, moving away from generic glass long before this became common practice. This helped shift vodka from a bulk commodity towards a recognizable product.

Baczewski's portfolio initially relied on descriptive naming rather than invented brands. Products such as Starka, Pomarańczowa and Wiśniowa were clearly labelled according to style or flavour, reflecting an older logic where trust was grounded in transparency rather than storytelling. Over time, however, the firm became adept at aligning quality with prestige. In the nineteenth century, Baczewski secured the title of official purveyor to the Austro-Hungarian imperial court, a designation that worked as both endorsement and export passport. By the late nineteenth and early twentieth centuries, Baczewski spirits were being shipped widely across Europe and beyond, including to Britain, France, and the United States.

Within Polish vodka history, Baczewski represents an alternative path to modernity from the Russian model. Where Russian vodka increasingly became defined through state monopoly and enforced uniformity, Baczewski shows how Polish vodka could modernize through branding, export and selective adoption of industrial methods. Rectification was embraced, but flavour traditions were not erased.

LEFT The double-headed eagle, used as a symbol of the Austrian Empire in the late nineteenth century.

RIGHT J.A. Baczewski's company entrance in 1930s Lviv. The original Galician operations were destroyed in the Second World War.

Grain-based spirits, fruit distillates, and aged styles coexisted under one name, reflecting the plural nature of Polish drinking culture.

The company's original Galician operations were destroyed during the Second World War, bringing an abrupt end to continuous production. For decades, Baczewski survived largely as memory and trademark rather than as a functioning distillery. Its revival in the late twentieth century, based in Vienna, trades explicitly on that heritage. Today's J. A. Baczewski produces vodka and other spirits (whisky, gin) styled after historical recipes, positioned as premium products that emphasize the brand's history.

Seen in the long view, Baczewski is less important as a single brand than as a lens. It shows how Polish vodka learned to speak the languages of empire, industry and export while retaining an attachment to identity. In a region repeatedly reshaped by borders and regimes, that ability to remain recognizable proved as valuable as any technical innovation.

The nineteenth century saw a range of other Polish producers begin to bottle proprietary brand names that reached beyond raw material, flavour or place. The Kasprowicz distillery's Żupan took its name from a traditional noble garment, a subtle nod to the Commonwealth's vanished world. Other brands reached for historical resonance more directly by adopting figures of international stature, such as Copernicus. Others drew on local heroes, including Bartoszówka, named for Bartosz Głowacki, the peasant who briefly rose to fame and freedom during the Kościuszko Uprising of 1794 before dying soon after. In a partitioned country, vodka labels became one of the few places where history could still speak.

Trade figures are uneven across regions and years, but local studies give a sense of scale. In the town of Cieszyn in Silesia, production in the early 1850s reached roughly 2.6 million litres of spirit, much of it destined for export to Galicia, Vienna, Trieste and Upper Hungary. While we don't have hard figures for the era, total annual production would have been in the order of 25 million litres a year across the Polish territories, which may sound like a lot but represents only 5 per cent of today's output. Nevertheless, vodka and rectified spirits had become part of the cultural identity, from the countryside to the city.

INDUSTRIAL STRENGTH

Nineteenth-century Poland takes us up to the moment where vodka finally becomes recognizable as the spirit we know today – pure, neutral, odourless. Everything that came before then, whether it was called vodka or not, was something else entirely. This is because the technology required to rectify a spirit as neutral (like most modern vodkas) was not invented until the 1820s. This change came about not through better grains, more skilled distillers, or nifty filtration techniques, however. It came from plumbing.

For centuries, the spirits of Poland, Lithuania, Germany and Russia were made in fits and starts, as every pot still forces you to be: you charge the still with beer or wine, you heat it, you draw off something stronger than what you started with, you empty it, and you do it again. If you want something cleaner, you distil again, and again, and then you start sorting fractions by taste, smell, and experience. But after two or three distillations you would be hard pushed to produce anything above 80 per cent alcohol. And even a fourth or fifth distillation wouldn't change that much, because water wants to evaporate even at ethanol's lower boiling point of 78.3°C/173°F.

This is bad news for purity but good news for flavour: polugar was a spirit with texture, the taste of bread crust with a touch of oil. It reminded you where it came from.

But making it was a labour-intensive process and the process produced enormous variation, because every step was performed manually and every still had its own idiosyncrasies.

Continuous distillation was the industrial answer to that inconsistency. The principle was simple, even if the engineering took decades to tame. Instead of boiling a pot, stopping, and starting again, you keep feeding fermented wash in at one end and keep drawing spirit off at the other. The still becomes a machine for separating alcohol from water and congeners through repeated cycles of vapour rising and liquid falling, controlled by plates, reflux and temperature.

If that sounds like something you might use to refine crude oil into kerosene, gasoline, diesel, etc., based on their boiling points then you're not far off. And it might not be a coincidence that one of the world's first industrial oil refineries was built by Ignacy Łukasiewicz in Jasło, Poland, in 1856.

In the early nineteenth century, Europe was getting good at stacking inventions on inventions. There wasn't just one inventor of the continuous still but rather a series of engineers including the French chemists Edouard Adam (studying at that great institute of distilling technology, the University of Montpellier), Charles Derosne and Jean-Baptiste Cellier-Blumenthal, and the Scotsman Robert Stein, who improved the idea in the 1820s. In 1830, Aeneas Coffey patented the design that became the archetype, the 'patent still' or Coffey still, which is the basic still design still used in every vodka distillery today (albeit with some modifications).

In the 1911 *Encyclopaedia Britannica*, the intention is described with brisk Victorian confidence:

LEFT & ABOVE A copper column still, where wash feeds in at one end and spirit flows out the other… continuously.

it was designed 'in one operation' to do what needed 'several operations in the pot-still,' while saving 'time, fuel, and material,' and producing a purer spirit on demand.

For vodka's heartlands, the column still arrived at the exact moment the region was being remade by railways, cities, bureaucracies and a new kind of consumer. You can see it in Poland first, because Polish vodka was already a commercial, branded product long before it was a strictly defined category. Distilleries such as Hartwig Kantorowicz's operation in Poznań were selling 'fine' vodka as early as 1823, at a time when 'fine' still meant skill and repetition, not stainless steel and metres of copper plates. In the Polish lands, vodka sat at the junction of estate distilling, Jewish merchant networks, urban taverns and, increasingly, industrial plants. That ecosystem was ready to adopt any technology that let it sell a cleaner product, more reliably, to more people.

This shift is visible in the language of quality that survives from the period. Vodka is no longer described only by place or base material but by grade. Terms such as *zwykła*, *wyborowa*, and *luksusowa* appear not as marketing inventions but as working categories tied to purity and repetition. (Perhaps you will recognize Wyborowa and Luksusowa as names of modern vodka brands which we'll cover in detail in later chapters).

Zwykła literally means 'ordinary'. In vodka terms, it referred to the most basic category, intended for everyday consumption, produced with minimal rectification and little concern for finesse beyond drinkability. It was cheaper, more variable, and often retained noticeable character from its raw material. Zwykła was not necessarily crude, but it was not expected to be elegant, and belonged firmly to taverns, village trade and working households rather than ceremonial tables.

Wyborowa translates as 'select' or 'choice'. This term signalled an intermediate level of refinement. A wyborowa vodka would typically have undergone more careful distillation or rectification, with greater attention paid to purity, clarity and consistency. It was smoother, more predictable and more suitable for urban consumers and hospitality settings where reliability mattered. Importantly, wyborowa did not imply complete neutrality. Some grain character was often expected to remain.

Luksusowa means 'luxury', and this category sat at the top of the informal hierarchy. A luksusowa vodka was defined by repeated rectification, careful dilution and visual perfection. It was intended for prestige consumption, gifting, and export, and it aligned most closely with emerging ideas of vodka as a refined, modern spirit. By the late nineteenth century, luksusowa vodkas were often the ones most likely to be bottled distinctively, branded, and associated with reputable producers rather than anonymous sources.

Most importantly, these terms allowed vodka in Poland to be categorized and priced. That change supports urban growth, export trade and administrative oversight without demanding a single national definition of what vodka must taste like.

The scale of production by the late nineteenth century confirms that distilling had moved well beyond cottage or estate margins. A Warsaw newspaper report from 1897 lists 355 *gorzelnie* (producers of raw industrial alcohol) alongside dozens of rectification plants (where the raw spirit is further purified), distilleries (which may have carried out pot distillation), breweries and mead producers operating in the Kingdom of Poland. Even allowing for imprecision in terminology, the numbers point to an industry of national economic weight.

Warsaw emerges as a particularly important node in this system. By the second half of the nineteenth

RIGHT The Copernicus Monument in Warsaw, around 1890. Under Russian rule, the city's vodka trade was a commercial powerhouse.

century, the city hosts large rectification operations designed to process spirit at scale. Later known as the Warsaw Vodka Factory, 'Koneser' began life with a rectification plant working alongside a state wine repository. The development of these specialist rectification firms in the 1880s and 1890s reflects a wider European pattern, but one shaped locally by Polish commercial practice. Rectification separates production from finishing. Agricultural distilleries supply raw spirit. Urban plants purify, dilute, bottle and store.

In Russia, the relationship with the continuous still is more overtly political, because Russia's relationship with vodka is always political. As we've already learned, the empire had long relied on alcohol revenue, and it had long struggled with the social fallout. The shift to column distillation offered something the state had wanted for generations: controllable sameness. A neutral base spirit could be made in large quantities, shipped, blended, diluted, filtered and taxed with far fewer variables than pot distillate. It also made enforcement simpler, because you could define the legal product more tightly and attack anything outside that definition as illegitimate.

The *Oxford Companion to Spirits & Cocktails* notes that with the reintroduction of a state monopoly in 1895, Russian authorities standardized what we would recognize as vodka as 'the product of industrial rectification through modern distillation columns', and that traditional polugar distillation through copper pot stills was outlawed. That is an astonishing moment when you step back. A state does not just tax a spirit. It defines what the spirit is, then bans its older form.

Even before that formal standardization, private producers were already learning what the new technology could do for branding. Pyotr Smirnov (a man who we will discuss in more detail soon) is the obvious example, because his name is still with us, and because his success was bound up with modern production methods and an almost obsessive focus on 'cleanliness' and consistency. Secondary summaries vary in the details, but they consistently tie Smirnov's rise in the second half of the nineteenth century to the marriage of filtration and more advanced distillation, producing a cleaner spirit than many competitors. Whether we treat Smirnov as the first mover or simply the best marketer, he represents the new model: vodka as a repeatable industrial product with a reputation that can travel.

This is also the point where we can start spelling out, plainly, what people were actually drinking, because the technology creates distinct rungs on the ladder.

At the bottom is the wash, the fermented beer made from grain, potatoes or whatever starches were available and economical. Above that is low wine, the first distillate from a pot still or an early apparatus. In older British technical language, 'low wines' are weak spirit, then rectification turns them into 'high wines'. East of the Vistula the terms shift, but the concept is identical. Each pass removes water and, depending on the cut points and design, either concentrates congeners or strips them away.

In the older polugar world, you might stop at a strength where flavour still rides along, then you might filter through charcoal, or rest, or redistil, but you are still dealing with a spirit that tastes like its raw material and its still. In the new rectified world, the goal is a high-strength, near-neutral spirit that can be diluted to a standard bottling strength and still taste clean. Continuous stills dominate global spirits production precisely because they can produce high-proof spirit efficiently and continuously. Once that becomes possible at scale, vodka becomes less like a rustic distillate and more like a designed commodity.

ABOVE A distillation pot (on the right), used for producing spirits of varying quality in the comfort of your backyard.

Who drank which rung, and where? The simplest answer is that the further you are from cash, regulation and distribution networks, the more likely you are to drink something that still tastes like its origin (a trend that, for many, has reversed itself in the modern world). In cities and at court, status attaches itself to consistency, refinement and the ability to buy the same thing again tomorrow. In rural areas, where people still distilled at home or bought locally, the spirit remained more variable and shall we say interesting. The rise of rectification didn't erase the older styles overnight, but it did begin to demote and ostracize them. It pushed them into the shadows as 'rough' or 'illegal', while the state and the big producers claim 'real vodka' as the clean, taxed, standardized article.

This is why the continuous still is more than just a piece of technology but rather a hinge between two ideas of vodka. Before, vodka was a family of spirits made from local starches, distilled in batches, with an accepted range of character. After, vodka was increasingly treated as a base material, purified industrially and then finished by dilution and filtration into something predictable. In Russia, that predictability becomes a tool of governance. In Poland and the former Polish–Lithuanian territories, it becomes a tool of commerce, branding, and export, with a parallel tradition that keeps arguing that vodka ought to taste of something.

That is where the idea of taste memory becomes crucial. For centuries, bread wine and polugar trained drinkers to expect flavour. Even when spirits were filtered or redistilled, they carried enough character for people to recognize origin and skill. You learned what your household made, what your estate poured, what your region preferred. Vodka had a sensory identity that encapsulated culture and agriculture.

The arrival of rectification disrupts that memory unevenly. Among elites and urban consumers, neutrality quickly becomes aspirational. A cleaner spirit signals money, modernity and access to new technology. In cities, consistency matters more than familiarity, and a vodka that tastes the same every time is easier to trust and easier to brand. For rural drinkers and estate cultures, the shift is slower and more ambivalent. Flavour does not vanish overnight but is gradually pushed aside. What had once been a sign of quality is reclassified as roughness or backwardness. Breadiness becomes an off note. Oiliness becomes impure. Neutrality, which had no cultural meaning before, acquires one.

This is where class quietly reorganizes vodka. In both Poland and Russia, different spirits begin to map onto different spaces. In Russia, the state increasingly insists that 'real' vodka is the rectified article, while everything else becomes illegal, folkloric or invisible. In Poland, the picture is more plural. Neutral vodka grows in importance, but it never fully displaces the idea that vodka can taste like something, and that taste belongs to family, season and place.

By the time modern vodka emerges as a global product, taste memory has already been thinned out socially, surviving most clearly in illicit distilling of samogan, flavoured traditions and revivalist gestures like polugar. The irony is that neutrality presents itself as timeless, when in fact it is historically very new. It is not the natural end of vodka's evolution, or even a representation of changing tastes (in the literal sense) but rather a cultural shift made possible by technology, class aspiration and the state's preference for things that are easy to measure, tax and control.

BELOW In this modern commercial distillery, a pot still (left) is connected to a continuous still (far right) to gain flavour from the former and efficiency from the latter.

Pertsovka (Pepper Vodka)

In Russia, pepper vodka appears under the name *pertsovka* in household manuals and medical writing from the eighteenth century onwards. It is domestic drink rather than a courtly one, and by the nineteenth century it is sufficiently common that it no longer needs explanation in Russian-language sources.

Black pepper is not native to Eastern Europe, but it was widely available by the early modern period through Baltic and overland trade routes. By the seventeenth century it appears routinely in urban kitchens in both Russia and Poland, if not always cheaply. Its presence in spirits is a sign of urban domestic culture rather than peasant improvisation.

Pepper served three practical purposes: it heightened the warming effect of alcohol, which mattered in cold climates that didn't have central heating; it smoothed over rough, inconsistent spirits, masking off aromas and harshness when re-distillation was impractical; and it sat squarely in the realm of folk medicine. Pepper vodka was routinely taken for colds, digestion and general weakness, with small morning drams appearing frequently in eighteenth- and nineteenth-century domestic accounts, especially in winter.

When Absolut reintroduced flavoured vodka to a western audience in the 1980s, do you know what the first flavour they launched was? Pepper (although of course they spelled it *Peppar*).

10 WHOLE BLACK PEPPERCORNS
500 ML/17 FL OZ RYE VODKA (LIKE BELVEDERE)

Lightly crack the peppercorns with the flat of a knife but avoid grinding them otherwise they are a pain to filter out. Add to a glass jar with the vodka and leave to infuse for 2–4 days. You can infuse much longer, but I think you lose some of the pepper's aromatic quality in place of astringency and heat.

Serve chilled and neat in small glasses.

THE FRAYING FABRIC OF SOCIETY

The summer of 1831 was a brittle, nervous moment in Russia. Nicholas I had been on the throne only a few years, and the memory of the Decembrist revolt, the uprising in which army officers and soldiers tried to block his accession and force constitutional reform, still hung over the empire, sharpening Russia's long-standing instinct to see conspiracy in any form of collective behaviour. At the same time, cholera was moving through the country, spreading north from the southern provinces and triggering a wave of violent unrest as rumours took hold that officials and doctors were poisoning wells. Markets closed, movement was restricted, and soldiers were deployed with growing frequency. In towns and villages already strained by poverty, poor harvests and the hardships of serfdom, authority felt suddenly more intrusive.

Against this backdrop, any deviation from established social rhythms, including how, where and whether people drank, could be read as defiance. It was into this charged atmosphere that General Yegor Petrovich Tolstoy (no relation to the writer) was dispatched to the provincial town of Spassk, where a local disturbance would reveal just how tightly vodka had become bound to obedience and the expectations of the Russian state.

Tolstoy was a high-foreheaded, moustache-forward lieutenant-general who looked like he could organize a siege, a province and your entire day with the same unshowy, stiff-backed competence. He was also not a man unfamiliar with unrest. He had fought in the Russo–Persian and Russo–Turkish wars, in campaigns that taught him to recognize the difference between genuine rebellion and what officials usually dismissed as rural disorder. When he arrived, the reports suggested nothing more than another flare-up of peasant stubbornness in the long, grinding age of serfdom.

At first glance, the scene seemed to confirm it. Villagers gathered in tense knots while officials complained of lost revenue. The familiar language of insubordination was already circulating. Yet, as Tolstoy began to probe, it became clear that this revolt carried an unexpected and deeply unsettling twist. The villagers were not making the usual demands of cheaper vodka, better access to it or relief from tavern debts – they were refusing it altogether.

A sectarian religious movement had taken hold in the area, preaching abstinence as a moral duty. Men who had once spent evenings in taverns now avoided them. Families stopped buying drink. To the peasants, this was a matter of conscience, but to the

imperial authorities, it looked like something else entirely. In a system where vodka revenue underpinned local administration and state finance, abstinence represented a refusal to participate in the economic and social machinery of the empire.

It was treason. And that's exactly how Tolstoy interpreted it.

From horseback, addressing the assembled townspeople, he declared abstinence as shameful. Drinking was a cultural responsibility and teetotalism brought dishonour on the village and defied the order that bound subjects to the state.

His punishment was swift and theatrical. Soldiers were ordered to pull suspected abstainers from the crowd and, one by one, they were beaten with batons for an hour. The message was clear: in the Russian Empire, loyalty was not measured solely by devotion to the tsar, taxes paid, or observance of religion – it was also measured by whether or not you raised a glass when the state expected you to.

Grim as it is, the episode speaks volumes about vodka's symbolic weight by the early nineteenth century. Vodka was no longer simply a drink, or even an economic lever. Vodka had become part of the apparatus of rule, and to reject it was to step outside the rituals of obedience. Drinking vodka was

OPPOSITE Nicholas I's monument in St Isaac's Square, St Petersburg. He was the tsar who considered sobriety to be treason. **ABOVE** General Yegor Petrovich Tolstoy, before 1874. No relation to the novelist, and considerably less forgiving. **RIGHT** Russian serfs in a village between Kostroma and Yaroslavl, the world a young Pyotr Smirnov was born into and escaped.

not so much a calculated indulgence as a customary act. It was the expected gesture at any meaningful moment in Russian life. This takes vodka beyond the usual social lubricant, liquid escapism or practical anaesthetic and into the realms of cultural identity – closer to the flag, the language or the national anthem.

Vodka filtered its way into almost every cultural moment in Russia, from church ceremonies and religious festivals to weddings, political gatherings, business dealings, medicine cabinets and the *pomoch*.

The word pomoch translates as 'to help' and it was basically a call for aid within the peasant class where some form of additional labour was required. R.E.F. Smith and David Christian note in *Bread and Salt: A social and economic history of food and drink in Russia*, 'A household which had to get an urgent task done, for which it did not have enough labour, would hold a work-party, inviting friends and relatives to help them with their work, in return for a meal and some vodka'.

It should come as no surprise that the Russian military also had a long and tumultuous history with vodka and its predecessors, where it functioned as a morale booster and anaesthetic for the mind and body.

Following suit with Britain, France and Spain, along with most of the rest of western Europe, Peter the Great instigated a bread wine ration to servicemen during his army reforms in the late 1690s and early 1700s, when he was reshaping Russia along western European lines. By the time of the Great Northern War (1700–1721), in which Russia and its allies took on an increasingly powerful Sweden, regular spirit rations were firmly embedded in both the army and the navy. The standard issue for infantry soldiers was typically one charka (roughly 125 ml/4 fl oz) of bread wine, which

OPPOSITE Swedish troops crossing the Düna near Riga, 1701. By now spirit rations marched with every army. **ABOVE** Russian sailors aboard a warship, 1850. At sea the daily charka was as essential as gunpowder.

was distributed on designated occasions such as religious feast days, imperial celebrations, inspections, victories or after especially hard labour.

For the Russian navy, and all navies for that matter, spirit rations were more regular and more generous. Sailors usually received one charka a day during active service, particularly in cold conditions or at sea, where vodka was believed to have warming and restorative properties. In addition to vodka, soldiers and sailors were often issued beer or kvass when available, which, given its low alcohol content, was perceived more as an everyday drink for hydration and nutrition. This practice continued with relatively little interruption through the nineteenth century, despite periodic criticism from doctors and the odd reform-minded officer. By the 1870s, when medical objections to the ration became more vocal, the vodka issue was deeply entrenched and widely defended as essential to morale, discipline and cohesion.

Vodka infiltrated the workplace too. From estate workshops in the Volga provinces, to textile mills in St. Petersburg and mining and foundry work in the Urals, vodka was consumed.

According to historian Patricia Herlihy, a newly employed worker in the late nineteenth century was expected to provide a *prival'naia* – a welcoming gift of vodka for his fellow labourers. By paying for the drinks, the newcomer secured informal training, guidance and acceptance; failure to do so risked mockery, isolation and, more practically, a refusal

LEFT A 25 rouble banknote bearing Alexander II, the tsar who abolished serfdom in Russia and freed over 20 million peasants. **BELOW LEFT** A roadside vodka shop in 1891. Humble premises for the commodity that underwrote roughly a third of the imperial budget.

to share the skills needed to perform the job. The cost of the vodka needed to ingratiate oneself was not trivial either: two or three roubles could amount to several days' wages, and some men spent far more. Even so, it was the price of belonging.

By the late 1850s, the empire got a taste of what it meant to have vodka woven into daily life and state finance at the same time, because people discovered they could protest the system simply by stepping away from the bar. In 1858–59 a wave of organized abstinence spread across large parts of European Russia, and in places it spilled into attacks on taverns and the infrastructure of the tax farm itself.

Tax farming could keep revenue flowing in normal times, but it depended on social compliance that could fracture quickly when prices rose or when communities coordinated. Once it fractured, the state had to choose between losing money and using force to defend a revenue stream. Some contemporary accounts describe protesters being flogged and, in some cases, 'flogged into drinking', which is about as clear a sign as you can get that the vodka system had become part of public order rather than a private vice.

The sums explain the panic. The historian David Christian calculates in 'Vodka and Corruption in Russia on the Eve of Emancipation' (*Slavic Review*, 1987) that liquor revenues averaged approximately 32 per cent of Russia's ordinary revenues from 1805 to 1862, and on the eve of reform the state was still taking around 121 million roubles from vodka in 1862 alone.

Tax farming appeared to be successful because it delivered large, predictable cash to the state, but it was fiscally broken because it handed day-to-day control of pricing and collection to contractors whose profits depended on squeezing the trade, cooking the books and pushing costs and risk down onto communities. The arrangement encouraged corruption and opacity, which left the government unable to properly see, audit or manage the real economics of its single most important revenue stream. Set beside emancipation in 1861, the boycott years read like an early warning flare. Alexander II was already dismantling the structures that bound labour and land in place, and the drink

ABOVE Alexander II simultaneously freed the peasantry and dismantled the corrupt tax-farming machine behind vodka, setting the stage for the vodka kings.

economy sat in the same knot of coercion, local power and accounting darkness.

The tax-farming system was abolished in 1863, making way for an excise system and new classifications for quality control. This shift had two monumental consequences: first, it standardized pricing and production oversight, helping to curb the worst excesses of the kabak era; and second, it opened the door for independent distillers to enter the market and compete on the basis of quality rather than political patronage.

The late 1800s was the dawn of brand marketing, where companies across the world started to realize that consumers preferred recognizable, consistent products. It was the era of trademarks: Ivory Soap, Campbell's Soup, Coca-Cola and Quaker Oats. And in Russia the conditions were set for the arrival of the biggest brand name in vodka history…

THE GOLDEN AGE OF VODKA KINGS

Born in 1831, the same year as the Spassk unrest (a major peasant revolt in the far east of Russia), Pyotr Arsenievich Smirnov was the son of a serf in the Yaroslavl province, approximately 170 miles/275 km from Moscow. Destined for a life of poverty and servitude, his early years were unexceptional, save for one glimmer of hope. When Pyotr was still young, his uncle Ivan managed to save enough money to buy freedom from his landlord and move to Moscow. Ivan set up a wine trading business and likely inspired young Pyotr to earn his own freedom, which he duly did and followed his uncle to Moscow at age 16, where. There he learned the mechanics of retail working under his uncle. Smirnov presented himself for the future he desired not the past he had endured. A thick-bearded, sharp-eyed, and broad-shouldered man, he had a merchant's practical neatness about him, and the faintly weary patience of someone used to winning arguments with figures rather than charm.

By the age of 30, Smirnov was a master salesman with a keen eye for products and marketing, just as the market opened up. Emancipation and deregulation opened the door of opportunity, which Smirnov walked through, establishing P. A. Smirnov in 1864, on a corner building of Pyatnitskaya Street, near the Chugunny Bridge. To begin with, Smirnov would have purchased rectified spirit from a third party and used it to make a large catalogue of flavoured nastoykas (infused liqueurs) that he would compound in-house, ranging from cherry and honey to rowan berry and pepper.

What set Smirnov apart from his competitors was not so much the quality of his spirits (though they were good) but rather how aggressively he promoted them. Yes, he invested in modern rectification apparatus and in large-scale charcoal filtration, and sourced high-quality fruits and herbs with which to flavour his range of products, but it was the marketed quality of his vodkas that elevated the Smirnov brand. To this end, he incorporated a numbering system for each expression, which were graded and presented as reliable articles rather than anonymous bulk alcohol. Also, whereas earlier producers might have sold by the barrel, Smirnov sold by the bottle, with branding that could travel.

By the 1870s and 1880s, his firm was producing millions of litres annually. Contemporary accounts suggest that he employed hundreds of workers and controlled substantial warehouse capacity. By this point, the backbone of the business was highly rectified, charcoal-filtered spirit diluted to the

OPPOSITE Pyotr Arsenievich Smirnov, the serf-born marketing genius who built the empire's most famous bottle. **RIGHT** An 1894 Smirnov advertisement depicting hard-earned medals and imperial crests.

emerging standard. He called it Table Wine No. 21, which is a number that still adorns every bottle of Smirnoff 'Red' Vodka today.

Smirnov also understood something that many technically competent distillers did not: trust could be manufactured.

He made prolific use of printed advertising at a time when Russian alcohol promotion was still rudimentary at best. Testimonials and endorsements appeared in Moscow newspapers. Bottles carried distinctive labels and seals that reassured buyers in a market long-plagued by adulteration. Cleanliness became part of the pitch and the Smirnov distillery was presented as orderly, modern and hygienic. In a country haunted by cholera and rumours of poisoning, purity was a powerful word (and one that remains front and centre of vodka advertising to this day).

Smirnov also deployed masterful advocacy campaigns, often involving psychological theatre that pre-date modern guerrilla marketing by a century. On one occasion, he recruited a small army of shills, comprising a motley crew of impoverished students and street-smart panhandlers, whom he scrubbed clean, dressed in respectable attire, and sent into Moscow's most popular taverns with a simple, scripted mission: approach the bar and demand Smirnov's vodka by name with an air of aristocratic entitlement. Upon being told it was unavailable, they were instructed to stage a scene of vocal disgust, insulting the establishment's inferior selection before storming out in a huff. After enduring a succession of these choreographed outbursts, rattled tavern keepers – convinced they were haemorrhaging the business of the city's most discerning drinkers – would rush to Smirnov's distillery the following morning to place their first orders, unwittingly surrendering their shelf space to a demand that had been entirely manufactured.

At the All-Russian Industrial and Art Exhibition of 1882 in Moscow, Smirnov pulled of one of the greatest alcohol marketing stunts of all time. His stand reportedly featured thousands of bottles stacked in a tiered formation arranged in horizontal bands of white, blue and red to represent the Russian flag. He then stationed 'trained bears dressed in

ABOVE The All-Russian Industrial and Art Exhibition, Moscow, 1882, a vast showcase of imperial industry and self-promotion.

human clothes' by their pavilion, with the bears 'pouring vodka for visitors' until, the story goes, they got drunk themselves.

These exhibitions were also where medals were awarded. Smirnov accumulated them and printed them on his labels. Each medal became a shorthand for quality. By the late 1880s, his bottles carried a constellation of awards from Russian and international exhibitions. Some of them can still be seen on modern Smirnoff bottles.

The fulfilment of a seemingly career-long obsession arrived in 1886 when Smirnov secured the coveted title of official supplier to the Imperial Court. This achievement became a powerful commercial weapon for the brand, implying scrutiny and quality at the highest level. For urban consumers aspiring to refinement, it signalled that this was not tavern rotgut but something fit for ceremonial tables.

While Smirnov is the most famous name to survive from this golden era, he was not alone in industrial ambition. Another major figure in the nineteenth-century vodka world was Alfons Koziełł-Poklewski, a Polish–Lithuanian nobleman who built an unlikely alcohol empire in the heart of Siberia. After relocating to the Urals as part of Russia's colonization of the East, Koziełł-Poklewski purchased a small distillery in the town of Talitsa in 1869. What followed was nothing short of an industrial miracle. Over the next few decades, he constructed a vast, vertically integrated spirits business that stretched across vodka distillation, glass bottle manufacturing, tavern chains and even river shipping.

At the height of his influence, Koziełł-Poklewski controlled the vodka supply for much of Western Siberia, earning him the nickname 'The Vodka King'. His products were widely recognized for their quality, affordability and branding flair, and his marketing approach echoed some of the urban polish seen in Moscow with the likes of Smirnov. But unlike Smirnov, Koziełł-Poklewski thrived on the frontier, where he fused vodka with infrastructure and logistics, building a mini-state within the empire, powered by grain and alcohol vapour.

Vodka kings were not limited to Russia either. Mirroring what had already happened in Russia and Poland, the Swedish government of the 1850s sought to pull spirits out of the farmyard and into a system that could be properly licensed and morally defended. A key turn came in the form of new legislation on *brännvin* (more on this spirit in a second), which came into force in 1855, described as a *förordning* (regulation) that tightened household distilling and changed tax policy. In short, it killed craft distilling and pushed production to a few large distilleries.

In the 1860s, Gothenburg then trialled a retail model that reads like modern Nordic socialist policy: the city granted a sole spirits licence to a trust that capped the shareholder return at five per cent and channelled surplus profits back into local civic spending. It was a smart attempt to keep drink available while stripping away the pure profit motive. Against that backdrop, Lars Olsson Smith – an immaculately presented Swede with the cool, narrowed gaze of a man who treated bureaucracy as an obstacle course – launched the first vodka brand built on purity as a sales pitch.

Smith had begun his working life on the Stockholm docks at the age of 14, and it was there, among crates and invoices and the smell of tar and wet timber, that he noticed vodka moving through the city as a commodity rather than a mere local drink. Smith started travelling to sell spirits, picking up languages as he went, and by his early twenties he had built a reputation that mixed admiration with irritation. The mythology that swelled around him would soon proclaim him a 'vodka king'.

In 1879 he introduced Absolut Rent Brännvin, meaning 'absolutely pure brännvin'. The word comes from the Old Norse *brenna*, meaning 'to burn' and *vín*, meaning 'wine' and the same root can be found in German *branntwein* and Dutch *brandewijn*. In Sweden, 'brännvin' once covered any distilled spirit made from grain or potatoes, much as vodka did in Poland and Russia before it became a tightly defined, neutral product. Early brännvin was pot-distilled and often full of character, closer to polugar than modern vodka. What Smith did was pioneer the use of the Coffey still for production of his brännvin and he traded on the cleanliness and purity of his spirit.

BELOW A 1910 label for Reymersholms 'Absolut Rent Brännvin', the spirit whose name would outlive its founder by decades.

Stockholm's drinks market was highly regulated and Smith found himself facing what he saw as a state-backed cartel that protected entrenched producers and kept inferior vodka moving through the city. In light of this, Smith stepped just outside the boundary of Stockholm's jurisdiction and opened a retail operation on the island of Reimersholme, then made access part of the pitch by offering customers a free ferry service to his vodka island. It was a neat manoeuvre, and it worked because it turned shopping into a small act of defiance. People could buy his 'pure' brännvin and feel, at least for a moment, that they were outsmarting the system with him.

The wider Swedish spirits industry was changing however, and by the end of the 1870s a large share of production was concentrated in the south, particularly around Skåne, and Smith moved aggressively into that landscape, taking over distilleries and trying to bend supply to his will. Like Smirnov, he fought on reputation, calling his competitor's vodka inferior, pushing hard at the trade's weak points, and even courting organized labour when it suited him, encouraging boycotts of outlets that would not play along. All of these tactics made him enemies. Smith attracted resentment with the ease that other men attracted friends, and he cultivated a sense of being besieged that may have been partly real and partly useful. Stories followed him of threats and attempted assassinations, and whether or not every detail survives scrutiny, the evidence suggests that there was certainly a lot to dislike about the man.

In time, Smith fell ill with appendicitis and travelled to London for surgery, believing he might not return. He put his wealth in the hands of his wife and children, and when the operation succeeded and he came home, they refused to give it back. The great salesman who had bent a national drinks market towards his will found he didn't even have the trust of his own household. He died penniless in 1913, but the legacy of his brand was revived in the form of Absolut Vodka, but more on that later.

Back in Russia, the rise of vodka kings did not go unnoticed by the state. Indeed, where money and vodka were concerned, little in Russia ever escaped official attention. Pyotr Smirnov, Alfons Koziełł-Poklewski, Nikolai Shustov, M. A. Popov, and Alexander Shriter built fortunes by doing what the old tax farms never could: turning spirit into a brand that could be sold at scale and supported by increasingly sophisticated distribution and marketing. Yet their success also sharpened an old anxiety in St Petersburg. When vodka is your most dependable source of revenue, allowing private empires to grow around it starts to look less like progress and more like a loss of control. Quality could improve and the treasury could still feel exposed, because pricing and supply were now influenced by men whose loyalties were commercial rather than imperial.

So it was that the logic that had killed tax farming returned in a new form, and by the 1890s the state's conclusion had a familiar flavour: if vodka underwrote the budget and helped keep the streets quiet, it was too important to leave to anyone else, however talented.

The brief golden age of private vodka entrepreneurship came to an abrupt end in 1895, when Sergei Witte, Russia's brilliant but austere Minister of Finance, reinstated the state vodka monopoly. Witte, a former railway director with a mind for systems and statistics, was tasked with modernizing the empire's crumbling finances. His solution? Take back control of the nation's most reliable revenue stream. He perceived vodka like many of his predecessors had done – as a fiscal instrument which, if properly managed, could fund industrial expansion and the empire's growing administrative machinery.

Under Witte's reforms, the state tightened control over production and sale, standardizing strength, price and packaging while stripping branding back to something closer to an official commodity. Private distilleries were shut down, absorbed or forced into the new arrangement, and one of vodka's strangest contradictions came into view: the more modern it became in technical terms, the less room there was for individuality in the market. Lenin would later sneer at this sort of arrangement as 'monopoly capitalism', but for the treasury, it worked.

The monopoly was a revenue engine but a cultural flattening, crushing the fledgling identities of producers like Smirnov and bringing an end to the brief era of vodka entrepreneurialism in the Empire.

By 1902 vodka was contributing 341 million roubles per year to the treasury, rising to 594 million by 1911, and on the eve of the First World War receipts still amounted to roughly a third of imperial revenues. The Moscow State Wine Warehouse No. 1, later renamed Kristall, began production in 1901 and was filling millions of dekalitres within its first year. It was soon followed by a network of similar plants across the empire, each designed to maximize taxable output and to maintain a consistent flow of human diesel.

Smirnov did not live long into this new era. He died in 1898 – an event marked by a funeral fit for a head of state. By then his sons, Pyotr Petrovich, Vladimir and Nikolai, had joined the business in varying capacities and along with his widow Maria they attempted to navigate the new landscape. They did so poorly, in part because it was so difficult to trade under the monopoly system and partly because the Smirnov sons were born into incredible privilege and lacked the drive and ambition of their father.

Pyotr Smirnov's incredible rise to prominence therefore sits in a narrow window between deregulation and re-monopolization. He embodied

ABOVE 'The Bear's Turn', 1905. A cartoon Witte dances to the tune of the vodka-soaked spirit of Russia.

the industrial, branded, aspirational vodka made possible by column distillation, filtration and legal standardization. He was not a rustic distiller refining bread wine by nose and habit but a savvy businessman who understood that modern vodka was an engineered product that needed to be reliable to be sold at scale.

At the time of Smirnov's death, Russia stood on the edge of upheaval. Industrialization was accelerating, urban populations were swelling, and vodka receipts once again represented a third of imperial revenue. The state had reasserted its grip – for now. Within two decades, war and revolution would tear apart the world in which Smirnov and his contemporaries had inhabited and Russian vodka would never be the same again.

Vodka Punch

Before the cocktail became a single-serve-shaken-to-order fixture, the punch bowl reigned supreme and was the height of nineteenth-century conviviality. In taverns, private clubs and hotel bars, a well-made punch offered economy, sociability and balance. Jerry Thomas gave generous space in his 1862 *Bartender's Guide* to punches of every stripe, built on rum, brandy, arrack or whiskey. Vodka doesn't appear in his book and would have been unusual in an American bar of that period… but not impossible. A Russian-style grain spirit, probably closer in character to polugar than to modern neutral vodka, would have brought a faint cereal sweetness and a lightly oily texture.

With that in mind, this recipe assumes a mid-nineteenth-century grain vodka, distilled in batches and carrying a touch of bread crust and pepper rather than absolute neutrality.

30 ML/1 FL OZ SUGAR SYRUP (2:1)
60 ML/2 FL OZ FRESH LEMON JUICE
120 ML/4 FL OZ VESTAL VODKA
30 ML/1 FL OZ COGNAC
240 ML/8 FL OZ COLD TEA

SERVES FOUR

Stir the sugar syrup into the lemon juice in a jug or small bowl. Add the vodka and Cognac, then the cold tea. Stir well. Add a large block of clear ice, or several solid cubes, and stir again until the mixture is well chilled. Express the oils from a few strips of lemon over the top and drop them in. You can also grate a little nutmeg across the top before serving in small punch glasses.

The proportions follow the classic punch formula of spirit, citrus, sugar and water, with the brandy lending roundness, the tea bringing tannin and the lemon supplying depth. The vodka provides structure and weight rather than overt flavour, allowing the lemon and nutmeg to sit forward while the grain character hums quietly beneath.

CLEAN SPIRIT

Before the nineteenth century was over, the Russian Empire had two more contributions to make to the modern idea of vodka. The first addressed the problem of taste and texture in distilled spirits; the second concerned alcoholic strength. Both emerged from chemistry rather than distilling tradition, and both would shape not only vodka, but spirits produced across the world.

Filtering liquids goes back way before spirits existed, and is older even than written chemistry. Long before anyone worried about neutral spirit or mouthfeel, people were trying to make water safer, clearer and more palatable. Vodka inherited that entire lineage and then pushed the boundaries even further.

Civilizations that learned to settle near rivers learned pretty quickly that river water could sustain life but also kill you. Sanskrit medical texts in India from around 2000 BC describe methods for purifying water by boiling, exposing it to sunlight, and filtering it through sand and gravel. In ancient Egypt, wall paintings show water being poured through cloth and porous vessels. Hippocrates, writing in the fifth century BC, recommended boiling and straining water through a cloth bag (the so-called 'Hippocratic sleeve') to improve its quality and taste. Filtered water usually meant softer water, and while nobody knew about microbes, everyone understood the inconvenience of vomiting and diarrhoea!

The Egyptians used charcoal as a filter medium in medical preparations, and by the time of Pliny the Elder in the first century CE, charcoal was recognized for its ability to remove odours and impurities. The underlying mechanism would not be understood for centuries, but the effect was obvious: porous carbon trapped things and liquids that passed through it became clearer, softer and more stable.

Alcohol followed water with very little delay. As soon as wine, beer and later, distilled spirits became trade goods – and especially when they became packaged and marketed – clarity and stability became important. Medieval brewers filtered beer through straw, cloth or river sand to remove solids. Winemakers racked wine repeatedly and sometimes filtered through charcoal or ash to correct faults. Early distillers experimented with filtration too, because even though distillation concentrated alcohol and left behind particulate matter, it did not guarantee cleanliness in the sensory sense. Harshness, off smells, and oils remained, especially in spirits made from grain or other starchy materials.

By the early modern period, filtration had become part of the standard toolkit of distilling, even if it was poorly theorized. In seventeenth- and eighteenth-century Europe, distillers filtered spirits through wool, felt and paper. In Britain and France, charcoal filtration was sometimes used to 'polish' brandy or grain spirit, particularly if it was destined for compounding into cordials or medicinal preparations. In Sweden and Finland, charcoal was already being used to soften grain spirits by the eighteenth century, drawing on abundant wood resources and a long tradition of charcoal production for heating furnaces. However, many of these practices were parochial and inconsistent.

Charcoal filtration was eventually brought into the scientific literature of spirits by Tobias Lowitz, a German–Russian chemist working in St Petersburg in the late eighteenth century.

In 1785, while attempting to crystallize tartaric acid, he noticed that powdered charcoal, which had accidentally entered the solution, stripped out visible impurities. His curiosity piqued, Lowitz designed a series of systematic experiments on adsorption (the

OPPOSITE Vodka poured clear. Neutrality was a long road with a thousand year lineage. **ABOVE** Charcoal has been used to remove colour, taste and aroma from spirits for 250 years or more. **BELOW** In charcoal filtration, undesirable substances attach to the surface of the charcoal.

phenomenon in which a substance adheres to a surface, but more on this later) using charcoal made from wood and bone, and even carbon derived from tartaric acid itself. He observed that charcoal was particularly effective at removing colour and odour from organic liquids. On that basis, he recommended its use as a purifying agent for vodka, sugar syrups and drinking water. He also observed charcoal's ability to absorb gases and neutralize unpleasant smells.

By the early nineteenth century, charcoal filtration was becoming formalized in Russian vodka production. Rectified spirit, produced at high strength, would be diluted with water and then passed through tall columns packed with birch charcoal. These columns could be several metres high, and the spirit might pass through them slowly over many hours or days. The goal was not just clarity, but softness. Harsh congeners, fusel oils and trace impurities were reduced, leaving a cleaner, more neutral product.

At this point, it is important to be precise about materials. Not all charcoal behaves the same way. Hardwood charcoal, especially from birch, has a porous structure that makes it particularly effective at adsorbing organic compounds. Birch was plentiful across Russia and the Baltic regions, and birch charcoal had already been used domestically for water purification.

Not wishing to let the Russians take all the credit, next came the Polish chemist Raphael Ostrejko who is responsible for the discovery of 'activated carbon'. In his 1901 patent filings, he writes: 'The object of the present invention is to produce carbon of great decolorizing powers.' Ostrejko then lays out the mechanism by which carboniferous material is subjected to dry distillation 'with concurrent action of superheated steam or carbonic acid, or both together', a process that opens up the pore structure and dramatically increases the surface available for adsorption. In a later patent he makes the intended application explicit, describing the result as 'a highly active product suitable for the decolorization and deodorization'.

Activated carbon could do more than just remove colour and odour, however – it could also strip out impurities and even poison. A decade later, at the beginning of the First World War, the same chemistry was used in the Russian-made Zelinsky-Kummant gas mask that used a canister of activated carbon made from birch or linden wood.

The first vodka brand to introduce activated carbon into their production flow is not known, but by the early 1920s the pieces were finally in place for it to happen. Activated carbon was becoming an industrial material that performed consistently, made by specialists rather than burned in a pit behind the distillery. One of the most significant of those specialists was Norit, a Dutch firm whose own corporate history places the start of activated carbon production at Zaandam in 1916.

In Russia, a name often linked to the earliest adoption of activated carbon is Shustov. Founded in Moscow in 1863 by Nikolay Shustov, the company grew from small beginnings on Maroseyka Street into a major player in the Imperial drinks trade, operating smack-bang in the competitive market of the Golden Era where cleanliness and consistency became paramount. A later technical account claims that in 1924 Shustov began using 'Norit-grade' activated carbon in place of raw charcoal to purify vodka, cutting contact time dramatically in recognition of the new carbon's higher activity. If it is true, it marks an important shift where charcoal stops being a folk remedy for rough spirit and becomes an engineered operational process that would soon become an essential component of a modern vodka factory.

At a molecular level, carbon filtration works through adsorption rather than absorption.

Absorption is when a substance dissolves into another. Adsorption is when a gas, liquid or dissolved solid adheres to a surface. Carbon, particularly activated carbon, has an extraordinary internal surface area. A single gram of 'activated' carbon can present hundreds, sometimes thousands, of square metres of microscopic pores. These pores are created when carbon-rich material is heated in low-oxygen conditions and then 'activated' with steam or chemicals, which opens up a complex lattice of channels. When a liquid passes through this structure, certain molecules are attracted to the carbon surface and held there by weak intermolecular forces.

In spirits, the compounds most readily adsorbed are larger, less volatile organic molecules. These include higher alcohols, fatty acids, esters, sulphur compounds and trace aldehydes. Ethanol and water molecules are small and relatively non-polar, so they pass through largely unaffected. This is why carbon filtration can soften a spirit without significantly reducing its alcoholic strength. The effectiveness of filtration depends on several variables: pore size distribution in the carbon, contact time, temperature, alcohol strength and flow rate. High-strength spirit generally filters more effectively because water competes with congeners for adsorption sites. This is why filtration is often done before final dilution.

It is also why carbon filtration is selective rather than absolute. It does not remove everything, and it does not do so evenly. Some flavour compounds are stripped quickly, others barely at all. Over-filtration can flatten a spirit by removing texture and trace aromatics, while under-filtration leaves harsher elements intact. In traditional birch charcoal columns, the process was slow and gravity-fed, allowing extended contact time and gentle adsorption. Modern systems can be far more aggressive, using finely graded activated carbon and controlled pressure, but the underlying science remains the same. Carbon does not 'purify' alcohol but rather alters the balance of molecules by offering them a surface on which to stick, and the spirit that emerges is defined as much by what was left behind in the carbon as by what remains in the liquid.

This practice coincided with two larger shifts. The first was the rise of rectification through column distillation (as detailed a few chapters previous), which made very high-strength spirit available in volume. The second was the increasing involvement of the state in defining what vodka was allowed to be. When Russia reintroduced its state vodka monopoly in 1894, it effectively tied legal vodka to industrial rectification and subsequent treatment, including filtration.

As with most things concerning Russian vodka, carbon filtration became part of a political as well as technical story. It is one of the tools that helped turn vodka from a broad family of grain spirits into a narrowly defined, industrial product.

By the early twentieth century, carbon filtration was firmly embedded in vodka production across eastern Europe, and no longer simply a corrective measure applied to faulty spirit but a routine stage in manufacture. Even today, producers who choose to retain flavour often define themselves in relation to filtration, either by minimizing it or by not doing it.

Filtration becomes most prominent precisely when distillation technology has already removed much of what earlier generations were trying to filter out. Column stills produce spirit at 95 to 96 per cent alcohol, with very low congener levels. Carbon filtration at that point is less about removing obvious faults and more about texture, mouthfeel and psychological assurance. It reassures producers and consumers alike that nothing unwanted remains.

Modern vodka brands continue to employ filtration in their narratives, sometimes with

ABOVE Dmitri Mendeleev, father of the periodic table. His 1865 study of alcohol and water handed the state the science of measurable strength that standardization would later require.

impressive technical detail and sometimes with ludicrous excess. I was once asked to comment on the potential launch of a Smirnoff variant that was to be filtered through gold – a medium that is chemically inert and has a very low surface area compared to its mass (but no doubt would have appealed to some consumers). That product never saw the light of day thankfully. Beyond birch charcoal, you will find vodkas filtered through quartz sand, diamond dust and silver-impregnated charcoal, which is said to improve efficiency. These claims trade on a long cultural memory that equates filtration with care and quality but increasingly rely on connotations of luxury and rarity in efforts to improve marketability. All of this attention to filtration, whether grounded in chemistry or drifting into theatre, points to a category that is not being judged solely by taste or tradition, but by processes that could be explained and, indeed, marketed.

Once producers began asking how clean a spirit was, the next question followed naturally: how strong is it exactly? That question, and the tools required to answer it, would pull vodka even further away from craft intuition and into the hands of science. This is where Dmitri Mendeleev enters the story.

The Russian chemist is remembered almost exclusively as the father of the periodic table, a visionary who organized the elements and predicted new ones before they were even discovered. That achievement alone would have secured his place in scientific history, but Mendeleev was also a practical chemist and a state servant, deeply involved in the industrial and economic problems of late-nineteenth-century Russia. And nothing impacted industry and economics more than alcohol.

By the time Mendeleev became involved, continuous distillation and industrial rectification were making high-strength, near-neutral spirit possible at scale, and charcoal filtration was being used widely. Alcoholic strength still varied between producers and measurement, while improving, remained inconsistent. What the state lacked was a clear, defensible definition of legal vodka, and Mendeleev's role was to replace rule of thumb with numbers derived from science.

In 1865, Mendeleev defended his doctoral thesis, 'On the Combination of Alcohol and Water'. He examined how ethanol and water interact at different concentrations, measuring density, contraction and the exothermic reaction of mixing them. One of his conclusions was that alcohol and water do not behave as simple additive volumes. When ethanol and water combine, the total volume actually contracts, because the molecules arrange themselves into a tighter structure. That structure changes in a consistent, predictable way as the proportion of alcohol increases or decreases, affecting density and other physical properties. This mattered enormously to anyone trying to measure, regulate or tax alcohol accurately.

Later, in his capacity as director of the Bureau of Weights and Measures, Mendeleev helped standardise instruments and methods for determining alcohol strength. Strength then became a number that could be better verified and enforced. Within this framework, a bottling strength of 40 per cent alcohol by volume emerged as a practical standard for Russian vodka. It sat comfortably below rectification strength, diluted cleanly from high-proof spirit, and behaved predictably in solution – and it was easy to measure and reproduce. This has led some people to suggest that Mendeleev personally 'invented' 40 per cent vodka, which isn't true. What he provided was the scientific groundwork that made such standardization possible and credible.

The instantiation of the measurement came about officially in 1866 when Finance Minister Michael von Reutern stated that: 'the strength of wines, vodkas and other beverages produced from wine and alcohol should not be below 40 degrees in establishments for the sale of beverages in Great Russian provinces, Stavropol province and Siberian provinces and 38 degrees in retail trade establishments…'

The slightly lower strength for retail was to account for evaporative losses while the vodka sat in barrels, reminding us that even in the late nineteenth century, vodka could harbour some flavour.

The consequence of standardizing strength extended far beyond Russia. Once alcohol strength could be measured precisely, spirits could be classified, taxed, traded and regulated across borders with far fewer disputes. The same logic that underpinned vodka standardization fed into broader

ABOVE A pressure gauge attached to a still allows distillery workers to help monitor that distillation rates are steady.

international norms for spirit strength, labelling and excise. Gin, rum, brandy and later whisky all benefited from the same shift toward measurement and repeatability.

But the standardization of strength and almost complete removal of flavour also did something else. Vodka became more broadly inoffensive, which meant fewer barriers to entry for new drinkers and fewer objections at the table. The less flavour, the less resistance. But what does that say about the role vodka played in daily life? Was it so routine that removing any character made it easier to integrate into every occasion? Neutrality, then, was perhaps a response to the necessity of vodka consumption, and an attempt to create the most frictionless form of alcohol rather than a gustatory experience.

Or was it more to do with safety? A more consistently neutral product reduced the risks associated with poorly distilled spirit, making it psychologically more desirable and physically easier to consume in quantity. So we must ask: was this neutrality truly an end goal, or was it simply a reflection of how completely vodka was woven into the fabric of life?

VODKA REVOLUTION

By the late nineteenth century, vodka had soaked its way into every corner of Russian life, from imperial banquets to peasant wakes, from courtly rituals to backroom samogon stills. But not everyone was pulling corks. A growing number of reformers, clergy, writers and civic leaders had begun to raise alarm bells, warning that the empire's beloved spirit was, in fact, its slow-moving undoing.

The Russian temperance movement didn't emerge from one single source, but from a convergence of frustrations. Orthodox clergy began to preach against the sins of drink, particularly the state's complicity in spreading it through the kabaks. The medical profession, emboldened by new ideas in psychiatry and public health, started linking alcoholism to madness, crime and premature death. And writers, who were ever the conscience of Russian society, took up the cause with biting prose.

Perhaps the most forceful literary voice belonged to the *War & Peace* author Leo Tolstoy, who by the 1880s, had shifted from novelist to moral crusader. Tolstoy saw vodka for exactly what it was: not merely as a personal vice but a deliberate weapon of the state, used to pacify the masses and raise revenue. In his pamphlets and essays, he described alcohol as 'poison', a toxin that corrupted both body and soul. His call was simple but radical: abstain completely and refuse to participate in a system that profited from your degradation.

The temperance movement found further support in the form of voluntary societies, many of them funded or supported by the Orthodox Church. One such group, the All-Russian Society for the Struggle Against Drunkenness, was founded in 1894 (the same year that Tsar Alexander III and Sergei Witte reasserted the state monopoly on vodka). These

LEFT Leo Tolstoy, who by the 1880s had traded fiction for a moral war against the bottle.

RIGHT 'An Oath of Temperance' by Akim Karneev, 1860. Pledging sobriety in a country built on alcohol proved to be an uphill battle.

societies published educational pamphlets, hosted public lectures and even staged theatrical performances to promote sobriety. Some distributed badges to those who pledged abstinence and created the altogether modern-sounding 'sober holidays' to offer alternatives to vodka-soaked village festivals.

The public reaction was mixed. In some urban circles and religious communities, the movement gained genuine traction. In rural areas, however, the call for temperance often collided with harsh realities: alcoholism was seen not as a choice, but as a symptom of poverty and despair. For many peasants, a shot of vodka was the only warm comfort on a cold morning, or a numbing reward after a brutal day in the fields. Preaching moderation was one thing but replacing the social and psychological support structure of vodka was quite another!

Indeed, church life in some communities played an especially large part in sustaining the culture of drinking in nineteenth-century Russia. In the Ufa governate, peasants claimed that Orthodox feast days accounted for more than a third of the entire year and these occasions rarely ended when the calendar said they should. Celebrations continued for days, in an extended period of drinking known as *podgvozdki*. Festivals provided another sanctioned outlet. Vodka at festivals served a psychological purpose, compensating for the general absence of organized entertainment. Feeling a bit bored? Drink some vodka. As people drank, the atmosphere inevitably became livelier, but this form of amusement came with its own problems, as the line between celebration and excess was easily crossed.

Among the least enthusiastic supporters of temperance, understandably, were vodka producers and kabak owners. Many framed the temperance movement as foreign-influenced moralizing or classist interference. Others quietly lobbied against anti-drinking campaigns and continued to grease the wheels of local government through tax payments and concessions. The state itself maintained a characteristically conflicted superposition: publicly endorsing moderate reforms while raking in vast revenues from vodka sales.

Of course, the Russian crusade against drink bore more than a passing resemblance to the temperance movements underway in the United States and Britain. In all three countries, the late nineteenth century saw alcohol framed not just as a private vice, but as a public crisis. Where the American movement leaned heavily on Protestant revivalism and the organizational muscle of the Women's Christian Temperance Union, the Russian version was more fragmented: a patchwork of priests, physicians, philosophers and reformers, often outpaced by the cultural behemoth they were trying to slow down.

Still, their efforts planted seeds. The idea that alcohol could and should be controlled by moral or medical logic would bloom again in the twentieth century.

Concerns about the role of vodka in the Russian military resurfaced in the 1870s with figures such as polymath Peter Keppen and General Konderovskii questioning the impact of the regular vodka ration issued to soldiers and sailors. Dr. P. Suvarov argued against the ration entirely, claiming that withholding it improved 'troop morale, comportment, discipline and performance' during the campaign against Khiva in 1873. Others echoed these concerns. Colonel Butovskii described a familiar pattern of smuggling and secret consumption in barracks, followed by 'drunkenness, disorder, and crimes and misdemeanors committed by drunken soldiers'. He was particularly alarmed by how quickly new recruits were absorbed into this culture. Statistics from the 1878 draft group show the shift clearly: upon entering service, 43 per cent refused the vodka ration and only ten per cent drank beyond it; by 1883, seven per cent abstained and half of all servicemen drank beyond the ration.

In the *New York Herald* in 1859, an unnamed writer travelled to Russia and noted the military's appetite for vodka: 'Though they receive rations of vodka, and extra rations on holidays, the fact of a Russian soldier or sailor ever having refused 'another glass' is unheard of,' he wrote. 'Intoxication is, of course, quite common, and no fines, arrest or castigation have any effect in suppressing it.' When the drunkenness became too much and soldiers had to choose between alcohol or punishment, 'soldiers often declare their willingness to take two or three hundred lashes more, if they can but get another bottle of liquor'.

The Commission for Combating Alcoholism, formed under the Russian Society for the Protection of Public Health, pushed the issue into military life in the 1890s. Psychiatrist M. N. Nizhegorodtsev called for the total elimination of alcohol from camps and barracks, proposing a decidedly modern-sounding alternative involving tea rations and organized exercise. His proposals were largely dismissed. Vodka was defended as both a social glue and a necessity, particularly in the navy, where it was believed to have 'energizing and warming properties'. Meanwhile, Dr. P. V. Putilov presented far more damning evidence, estimating that alcohol poisoning accounted for 75 per cent of ailments treated in military medical facilities between 1890 and 1896, and up to 44 per cent of all deaths. The official response amounted to little more than educational pamphlets warning of alcohol's dangers.

The consequences of this complacency became brutally clear during the Russo–Japanese War of 1904–5. Official supply plans for August 1904 alone allocated 300,000 *poods* of vodka for an army of 400,000 men over eight months, with a further 255,000 poods planned for the following year. This equated to roughly 4.8 million kilograms of vodka, or about 18 bottles of vodka per soldier.

In what may have been one of the most drunken wars ever fought, one account of the war that was used to promote temperance claimed that Japanese troops found Russian soldiers 'so dead drunk that they were able to bayonet them like so many pigs', while a field physician by the name of Dr. Veresaev recalled seeing 'masses of aimlessly wandering soldiers, red-eyed from alcohol, dust and exhaustion' being ladled vodka from barrels.

In the aftermath, the military replaced vodka rations with beer or light wine, effectively closing the temperance debate until the First World War. On August 22, 1914, the Imperial government enacted a complete 'ban on sales of spirits, wine and vodkas', followed by a total prohibition on distilling beer, wine or vodka by September 29, 1916.

Five months later, in February of 1917, the Russian Empire imploded under the cumulative weight of war, starvation, political repression, a crumbling monarchy and… perhaps the bleak reality that nobody could even get a drink anymore?

What began as a wave of strikes and bread riots in Petrograd (St. Petersburg's name between 1914 and 1924) quickly swelled into a full-scale revolutionary tide, sweeping away three-centuries of Romanov rule and with it the entire imperial system. The February Revolution deposed Tsar Nicholas II and installed a shaky provisional government, but it was the October Revolution, led by Lenin and the Bolsheviks, that delivered the fatal blow to Russia's old order.

The seeds of this revolution had been sown long before the first barricade went up. Russia's peasant majority had endured centuries of landlessness, taxation and vodka-fueled debt. The industrial class laboured under brutal factory conditions with no real representation. The military, bogged down in the First World War, was demoralized, poorly supplied, and increasingly sympathetic to the cause of change. The monarchy, meanwhile, remained aloof and

TOP Tsar Nicholas II banned vodka in 1914, then shortly after lost his throne (no connection, I'm sure…)
RIGHT A Russian soldier during the First World War – badly supplied and badly in need of a drink.

ignorant, clinging to divine right while the ground shifted beneath its feet.

In the mixing of this volatile cocktail, vodka played a subtle but significant role. To reformers and revolutionaries alike, the state's reliance on alcohol revenue was emblematic of a regime that extracted profit from suffering. The kabaks were seen as state-run sedation centres, numbing the masses into submission. Lenin himself famously described vodka as 'a weapon of the counter-revolution'.

And so, when the Bolsheviks seized power in October 1917, they brought with them not just a new political doctrine, but a plan to sober up the Russian soul – and they would achieve that by force, if necessary.

Tsar Nicholas II had already imposed nationwide prohibition at the outbreak of war in 1914 (he and his advisers feared that a nation of drunk soldiers and factory workers would be no match for the might of Germany) which removed the fiscal anchor on which the imperial budget depended. Many economic historians view that decision as a self-inflicted wound that compounded wartime shortages and destabilized the state at a critical juncture. It was too little too late from the perspective of the Bolsheviks, however.

ABOVE A Bolshevik poster heralds the spectre of communism. Lenin's new order had little patience or appetite for vodka.

The tsarist state, they argued, had grown fat off a monopoly that deliberately addicted the masses, keeping them pacified and pliant while the aristocracy toasted with gold-rimmed goblets. In the Bolshevik worldview, the prohibition of 1914 wasn't a moral stand but rather a belated, panicked attempt to save a collapsing empire. So, while the drink was already banned, the memory of state-sponsored intoxication gave the Bolsheviks all the ammunition they needed to frame vodka as the pouting gasoline of autocracy. Moreover, they viewed vodka not only as symbolic of tsarist decadence but as a threat to the revolution itself – drunkenness, they believed, dulled the proletarian will, sapped productivity and opened the door to counter-revolutionary sabotage.

Following the October Revolution, Lenin, a teetotaller by principle, doubled down on the prohibition laws introduced during the First World War. State distilleries remained shuttered and the production, sale and even possession of strong spirits was banned outright, backed by raids, arrests and, in some cases, execution. Private distilleries, no matter how refined or reputable, were labelled bourgeois relics of a corrupt regime. Vodka barons like the late Pyotr Smirnov, once feted at court and envied across Europe, suddenly found themselves enemies of the people. Their factories were nationalized, their brands erased, their assets seized. Trademarks were abolished, advertising outlawed, and brand identity replaced with ideological purity. Vodka, if it existed at all in those early Bolshevik years, would be anonymous, uncelebrated and entirely under state control.

For many former producers, exile was the only option. Members of the Smirnov family fled, with Smirnov's second son, Vladimir, attempting to restart the family business in Poland before settling in Paris where he changed the name to Smirnoff, with an extra 'f' for Western appeal. It was a strange twist of fate: while Bolsheviks tried to scrub vodka's capitalist past from Russian soil, Smirnoff would go on to become one of the world's best-selling spirits, an imperial ghost haunting global cocktail menus from Paris to New York (and a story we will return to later).

With the economy in tatters, civil war raging and food supplies evaporating, bootlegging surged. The ever-dependent panacea of the people, samogon, returned with a vengeance. Makeshift stills cropped up in villages, factory basements and city alleyways. Alcoholism, far from being cured by prohibition,

BELOW The Kremlin today – the seat of every regime that has treated vodka as an instrument of state.

LEFT New York, 1934. The first Soviet vodka shipment arrives after the repeal of Prohibition – two formerly dry nations back on the sauce. **RIGHT** Soviet vodka advertising from the 1930s. Stalin didn't hesitate to reinstate what Lenin had outlawed.

became more dangerous and unpredictable, as people turned to industrial solvents and denatured alcohol for intoxication.

Then came Joseph Stalin. The Bolshevik Revolution had promised collective leadership, but a scramble for control followed between Lenin's old guard: Trotsky, Zinoviev, Kamenev, Bukharin… and one quiet, calculating Party Secretary who, initially, no one took seriously. Stalin's strength was in organization, manipulation and raw administrative power. After years of revolution, civil war, famine and ideological purges, the Soviet people were exhausted. Stalin offered certainty: food, jobs and industrial growth even if it came at a terrible cost. And he knew, better than anyone, that people were easier to govern with a ration in one hand and a glass in the other.

By the time Stalin consolidated power in the 1920s, the revolutionary fervour had begun to cool, and so too did the ideological constraints that had kept vodka off the shelves. Stalin understood what Lenin refused to admit: vodka was too valuable to ban. Not just culturally, but financially.

In 1925, the state lifted prohibition, reinstating the vodka monopoly under tight bureaucratic control. 'One cannot build socialism in white gloves,' Stalin told the XIV Congress in 1925. It was either the vodka monopoly or slavery to Western European capitalists. A spokesman for the finance commissariat explained it in similarly Orwellian terms a year later: 'The Soviet government took the path of collecting revenue from the sale of vodka because it became convinced that in practice it was impossible to combat alcoholism by simple prohibition.'

By 1928, vodka resumed its rightful position in the Russian economy, generating almost 50 per cent of excise taxes and 12 per cent of total revenue. Vodka returned at a fixed strength – typically 40% ABV – and at a price point that struck the balance between accessible and profitable. The message was clear: you could drink again, but only with permission.

НАРКОМПИЩЕПРОМ
ГЛАВЛИКЕРВОДКА
СССР
ВОДОЧН. ЗАВОД
СТАРАЯ
Старка
ВОДКА
Джин
голландский
ЗАВОДОВ ГЛАВЛИКЕРВОДКИ
Зубровка
ГЛАВЛИКЕРВОДКИ
Горькие Настойки

AMERICAN SPIRIT

The period between 1850 and 1920 marked the third great migratory wave in the history of US immigration, though it might better be described as a flood. After 1880, larger steam-powered oceangoing ships replaced sailing ships, which resulted in lower fares and greater immigrant mobility. In addition, the expansion of a railroad system in Europe made it easier for people in the east to reach oceanic ports to board ships. Millions of Europeans made the long trip in the latter half of the nineteenth century, with eastern Europeans forming a significant part of the cohort. Due to shifting borders in Europe at that time, many of these immigrants were classified as 'Russian', 'German' or 'Austrian' by the U.S. Immigration and Naturalization Service but included amongst their ranks a large number of people from present-day Poland and Lithuania.

Unlike most other ethnic groups, the Polish didn't intend on sticking around and becoming Americanized. They were here to make a quick buck and then return home to their families better off than when they started. Most found unskilled labour jobs, working in heavy industries like steel mills, iron foundries, slaughterhouses and oil and sugar refineries. They socialized mostly in their own communities and always had a few bottles of vodka kicking around – a taste of home, very far from home. Many Poles had fled after national insurgencies and famine, so when coupled with their chosen vocations and relatively closed communities, Polish immigrants were not regarded as a high-status group. Neither, then, were the things they brought with them, like vodka.

For many Americans the mere existence of vodka would simply have passed them by, but if an introduction was made, it more often than not came via newspapers reporting on the cultures and habits of this new wave of immigrants. In 1907, a writer for Oregon's *The Morning Astorian* wrote a story called 'Foreign Tastes Imported'. In the article he describes the arrival of eastern European immigrants coming into the country which 'has brought with it in the way of flotsam and jetsam a host of strange liquors, with weird names and subtle effects'. He continues, 'the thousands of Russians who for the past few years have been flocking to the United States, must have their vodka [which is] a species of whisky or brandy distilled generally from rye, but sometimes made from potatoes. An experience with it furnishes a complete and sufficient explanation for the prevalence of revolution, anarchy, and terrorism in the land of the Czar'.

Russian and Baltic merchant ships regularly docked in American ports. Sailors traded, drank and boasted. Dockside papers occasionally mention 'strange spirits' brought ashore by foreign crews. American seamen, already accustomed to rum and grog, encountered vodka here as a curiosity, harsh, unfamiliar and quickly mythologized. This blue-collar exchange complicates the idea that vodka lived only in immigrant ghettos or elite exhibitions. It was also sloshing around dockyards and boarding houses, part of the informal economy of sailors.

One notable strand often missing from the early American vodka story is the role of Jewish distillers and merchants, many of whom arrived from the same eastern European regions as Polish and Lithuanian migrants. In the Old World, Jews were deeply embedded in the alcohol economy: by the mid-eighteenth century, around 85 per cent of rural Polish Jews were involved in alcohol production or sale in some capacity, often running taverns on land leased from nobles. When these communities emigrated,

OPPOSITE A transatlantic liner brought to America new tastes and culture – and more than a few bottles of vodka.
RIGHT Foreign arrivals to the US were treated with careful curiosity or outright contempt – humans and alcohol alike.

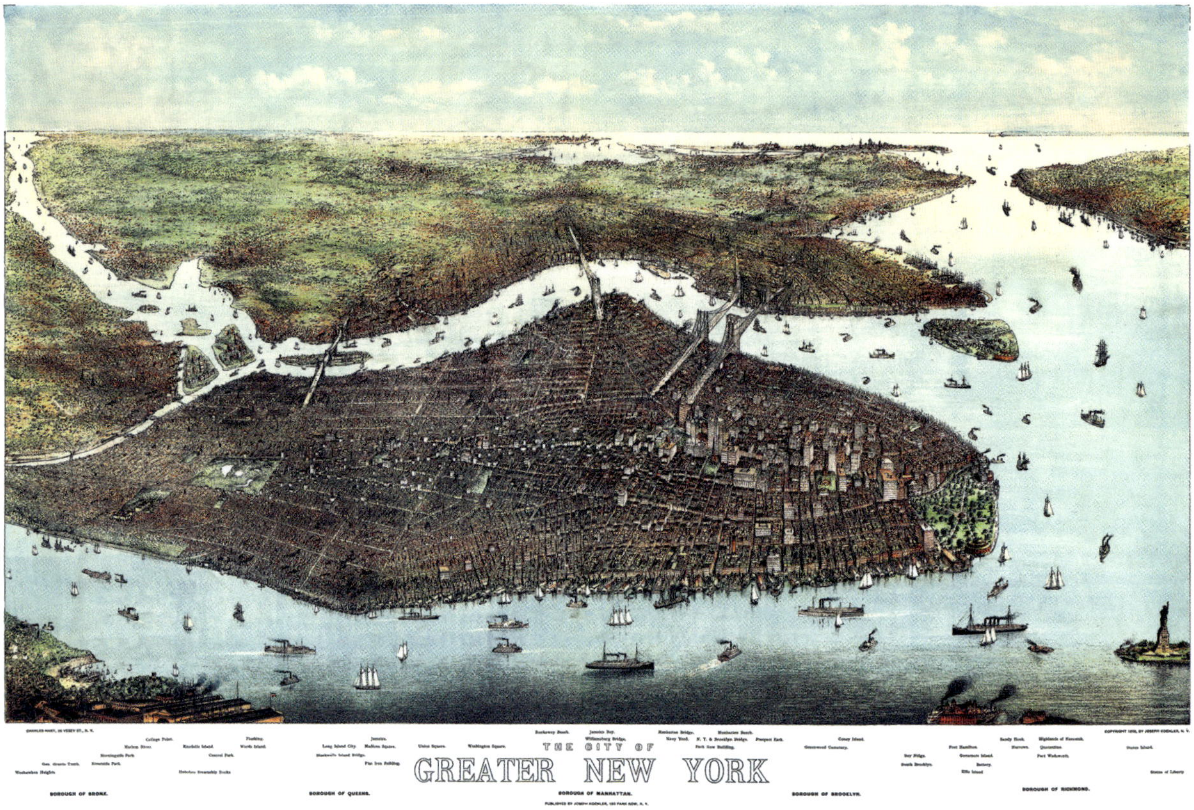

they brought that knowledge with them. In New York, Chicago and Philadelphia, Jewish wholesalers quietly imported and distributed rye spirits, while small kosher-certified operations began to appear. Vodka also solved a religious problem: unlike wine, it did not require kosher certification, making it acceptable for ritual use when wine was impractical.

The growing mythology of vodka meant that it wasn't uncommon for the spirit to be generously mixed into stories relating to the Russian Empire, which was a major economic and political power prior to the First World War. Americans were curious about Russia (some things never change) with its long history, tsars, palaces and strange customs, and journalists viewed it as fertile literary ground.

You might imagine that the tsar's close ties to the Russian vodka industry, and that royal eagle crest emblazoned upon many bottles, would have afforded Russian vodka a certain degree of prestige from the American market. All that pomp and regal flair ought to have counted for something, as it had in Russia. But the sense of drunkenness and anarchy that emanated from Russian society was deeply enough ingrained into the American narrative that no amount of royal endorsement could elevate its position.

It's possible of course that the harm that vodka was doing to Russian society was exaggerated by American commentators for artistic effect and that vodka was being unfairly scapegoated, used as a literary device to highlight the social differences between the two nations and reassure the reader how comparatively fantastic American life was. Whether or not this was the case is irrelevant however, as the damage was done and vodka had gained a reputation as a destructive force in the minds of the few Americans for whom vodka was actually on their radar.

The most positive spin you could expect to find in relation to vodka at this time was through accidental mislabelling or inaccurate description, with it being described as 'corn brandy' or 'Russian gin' on more than one occasion.

The lowly status that vodka held at this time explains its complete absence in mixed drinks through the latter part of the nineteenth century. Cocktails were fancy drinks for well-to-do types and vodka was the very antithesis of that. A bartender from 1900 wouldn't put vodka in a cocktail for the same reason that a bartender from 2000 wouldn't put moonshine in cocktail – because it has a reputation for tasting bad, because it's potentially dangerous and, most of all, because nobody would want to pay money for it. The very concept of mixing expensive drinks with cheap ingredients was as preposterous to a bartender then as it is today. Sure, if the bar at the Waldorf-Astoria was packed full of Polish steel workers pining for a vodka rickey every Friday night in 1904 perhaps a roaring trade in vodka cocktails might have been established, but this obviously wasn't the case.

Ironically though, vodka may have benefitted more than most spirits from the cocktail treatment. One of the functions of a cocktail (and the main motivations for cocktails existing) was to smooth over some of the imperfections of the ingredients you had to hand. If we're to believe that vodka really was that bad at the time, it stands to reason that it was an eligible candidate for mixing. But there was only so much a bottle of vermouth could do, and while fixing a some imported fire water from Gdansk was more than likely achievable in the hands of a skilled bartender, fixing the identity of vodka in the eyes of the average cocktail drinker was too tall an order.

For the curious kind of consumer there were occasions where it would have been possible to see and sample vodka, however. Before aeroplanes sped up intercontinental travel times, the world connected importers and exporters from every type of industry though huge fairs and expositions held in major trading cities. Besides being a chance for nations to publicize their wealth and mastery of whatever industries they excelled in, these weeks-long events were also an opportunity for normal

OPPOSITE New York has played a part in practically every stage of vodka's American domination from migrants to nightclubs. **BELOW** The 1893 Chicago World's Fair by night, where Russia displayed vodka as pure imperial spectacle.

LEFT The Russian pavilion at the 1893 Chicago World's Fair, where ornate imperial bottles spoke of tsarist grandeur to a largely baffled American public.

people to experience the cultures of countries they would never likely visit.

The Russian section of the half-mile-long Agricultura Building at the 1893 World's Columbian Exposition, also known as the Chicago World's Fair, was located in the eastern wing of the building, next to the Japanese concession. Among the exhibitors, who showcased everything from literature and household utensils to soap and tobacco, were no less than 27 vodka brands, including that of Pyotr Smirnov. With the Russian Empire encompassing much of eastern Europe and Finland at that time, these brands originated from present-day Ukraine, Belarus, Poland and Russia. Even so, one would have been hard pressed to find 27 vodka brands in the 1990s, when vodka was at the height of its powers, let alone the 1890s, when vodka was scarcely known to the average American. Most of the Russian vodka exhibitors also brought with them cordials, liqueurs and bitters, which were manufactured using vodka as a base. Indeed, many of the vodkas themselves were flavoured with herbs, fruits and spices that were available to the producer. Vodka wasn't alone in this practice, with whisky manufacturers also choosing to flavour their spirit with peaches or honey, to not only preserve the flavour of the perishable product in question, but also mask any off-notes in the spirit.

The Chicago World's Fair wasn't the first time that vodka was showcased to an American audience. The Centennial Exhibition in Philadelphia in 1876 commemorated 100 years of American independence by showing off the nation's emerging industrial prowess. Russia sent a whole contingent of exhibitors, touting agricultural machinery, candies, tobacco products and spirits. There were 36 Russian alcoholic drinks brands represented, 19 of which were vodka. 'The first thing that strikes one is the variety of wines, brandies, and liqueurs Russia must make and drink, wrote *The New York Times*,

ABOVE The 1876 Centennial Exhibition in Philadelphia, America's first world's fair. Russia sent agricultural machinery, candies and 19 vodka brands.

'here is vodki [sic] in every imaginable kind of bottle. When people travel for months in temperatures below zero such elegant bottles must be very comforting'.

But both the 1876 Philadelphia Centennial Exhibition and the 1893 Chicago World's Fair positioned vodka more as an imperial spectacle than a consumer product. Russia wasn't trying to sell bottles but rather reveal its distilling prowess. Rows of ornate bottles with imperial crests spoke of tsarist grandeur. As such, these fairs were exceptional circumstances and not a basis with which to establish any kind of rising popularity for vodka in the United States.

No, for that we would need to see evidence of the sale of vodka at scale.

The wine shop in Donaldsonville, Louisiana, probably wasn't your typical turn-of-the-century liquor store, but then Donaldsonville wasn't your typical town either. In 1904, the population sat at around 4,000 and, being home to one of the first synagogues and the first black mayor in the United States, it constituted a diverse mix of American society writ small. Perhaps this explains why a rural wine shop in the south came to stock dozens of types of vodka before most people had even heard the word vodka. With prices ranging from 25 cents to 56 cents for a bottle, you could take your pick from 'vodkas of brown and yellow, vodkas green and red, vodkas flavoured with fruit and herbs and flowers', wrote *The Donaldsonville Chief*, 'also common or garden vodka, innocent in appearance as gin, but on which the moujik can get most gloriously drunk for six cents'.

The piece finishes by telling us: 'Good vodka when mixed with soda or seltzer water makes a very enticing beverage.' That last line could have been pulled from a twenty-first-century brand marketing campaign and it is remarkable to think that a journalist from nearly 120 years ago was able to strip away all of the tropes and stigma that surrounded vodka at that time with an objective assessment of its quality and potential.

In late-nineteenth-century America, spirits carried a rigid social code, and vodka arrived wearing the wrong clothes. Bourbon was frontier grit, rye was respectable working-man's liquor, cognac signalled inherited wealth, and gin – despite its own rough past – had been domesticated into something the middle classes could tolerate. Vodka, by contrast, belonged to nobody with cultural power. It was the drink of dockworkers, slaughterhouse labourers, steelmen and seamstresses – a bottle pulled from a coat pocket in a boarding house, not ordered from a mahogany bar. Its association with eastern European immigrants cemented this divide. To drink vodka was to mark yourself as foreign, poor, transient. So while Germans slowly Americanized beer, Italians softened attitudes to wine, and Irish whiskey found its place at the bar, vodka remained stubbornly ethnic.

Things were beginning to change though, and the following year, 1905, Americans might have felt their greatest exposure to vodka yet. The Russian Empire had been at war with Japan over rival ambitions in Northeast China and Korea, and President Theodore Roosevelt called the leaders of both nations to the Portsmouth Shipyard in Maine to negotiate a peace treaty (an act that would earn him a Nobel Prize). The whole episode was reported widely in the media as far afield as Nebraska with vodka mentioned in some of the columns. *The Richmond Times Dispatch* reported that the Russian delegates were 'excellent mixers' and that 'the reference is purely social, with no allusion to the vodka cocktail etc.' *The Omaha Daily Bee* used the headline 'Vodka Suffers an Eclipse' claiming that the Russians had abandoned their vodka-drinking ways in favour of American cocktails.

LEFT Theodore Roosevelt gently nudged vodka into the public domain.

Not everyone was convinced. In 1904 the pharmaceutical journal *The Spatula* sniffed that 'the same kind of drink can be enjoyed' by drinking the deadly spirits used in alcohol lamps,' before concluding that vodka 'may suit the Muscovite for the dead of winter, but in a climate like ours it could never become popular.' The implication was clear. Vodka was not simply foreign. It was industrial, joyless and vaguely poisonous.

The comparison with lamp fuel proved stubborn. A year later, in 1905, the New York political periodical *The Tammany Times* offered what may be one of the earliest printed references to a vodka cocktail, albeit in parody. In a fictional tale, a Russian fisherman imagines himself destroying a Japanese fleet after 'soakin' in a couple train oil an' vodka cocktails to steady his nerve'. The drink was not meant to be real, just absurd. Train oil, more commonly known as whale oil, was rendered from the blubber of bowhead whales and used for lamps and soap. It was flammable, greasy and entirely unsuited to human consumption. Pairing it with vodka was deliberate exaggeration. In modern terms it was the equivalent of calling something 'rocket fuel'. The joke only works if vodka itself already occupies that space in the reader's mind, as something harsh enough to sit comfortably beside lamp oil. The humour depends on contempt.

It is tempting to overanalyze the imaginary recipe, but the detail matters less than the attitude behind it. At the turn of the twentieth century, at least among certain journalists and professionals, vodka was associated with drunken Russian sailors, industrial fuel and the bleakness of a northern winter.

The United States of America, of course, was built by immigrants and shaped by what they brought with them: Germans brought sausages that became hot dogs and hamburgers; Italians brought pizza; Chinese migrants adapted regional cooking into what became Chinese-American cuisine; Eastern Europeans brought vodka. At first it was treated as an alien curiosity. In time, it would become something else entirely.

BELOW The banana docks of New York, 1906. Vodka moved through ports like this as part of the informal cargo of sailors.

EARLY ADVENTURES IN COCKTAILS

For all of vodka's growing availability in the United States, better ways of drinking it were undoubtedly needed – preferably ones that did not involve train oil in the recipe, or any kind of oil for that matter. Fortunately, vodka did not have to wait long before bumping into the American cocktail, and when it did, the meeting happened in a place with a habit of turning ingredients into tradition: Louisiana.

More classic cocktails have emerged from the hot, humid bars of New Orleans than seem reasonable for one city. The Big Easy was an important trading hub during the colonial period and right through the nineteenth century, and for a time it was home to a remarkable concentration of wealth. New Orleans' identity formed through a steady collision of peoples, languages and tastes, and that cultural mixing did not stay out of the glass.

The wealth that passed through New Orleans can still be read in the architecture, in the luxuriant townhouses of the French Quarter and in the memory of its grand hotels. Perhaps the most legendary was the St. Charles Hotel, a building that managed to be constructed no fewer than three times and still failed to survive into the modern day. When it first opened in 1835, it was the first large building erected above Canal Street, which at the time was little more than

RIGHT New Orleans harbour, where trade brought spirits, sugar and ambitious bartenders. **OPPOSITE** Jackson Square at dusk. Beyond the cathedral spires, the French Quarter quietly rewrote cocktail history.

swamp land with half-sunken wagons and a congregation of alligators. Over the next hundred years, an enormous share of the city's business took place within its walls, and a more than fair share of the drinking too.

We do not have a surviving St. Charles cocktail menu from the early 1900s, and unlike some posh hotels of the 1920s and 1930s, the St. Charles did not publish its own cocktail book. Luckily, it didn't need to, thanks to *Beverages De Luxe* – a 1911 cocktail and spirits manual compiled by *The Wine and Spirits Bulletin*, a drinks trade magazine based in Louisville, Kentucky. The first half of the book offers descriptions of wine and spirit categories. For the second half, the editors reached out to notable clubs and hotels and asked them to supply recipes for popular drinks served in their venues. The result is a rare snapshot of what you might have been served at places like the Pendennis Club in Louisville or the Waldorf-Astoria in New York, without having to (time) travel there and pay the bill.

The maître d' of the St. Charles Hotel supplied ten cocktails to *Beverages De Luxe*, and one of them uses vodka as the base spirit. It is the first-known instance in print of a vodka cocktail actually intended for pleasure rather than punishment. The drink is called the Russian Cocktail, and the recipe is simple: 45 ml/1½ fl oz of vodka combined with a measure of Ruhinoy, a cordial made from cherry stones/pits, similar to eastern European cherry preparations that sit somewhere between syrup, liqueur and preserve. The book adds a small sales pitch of its own: 'A drink which is in the last year much appreciated in the Northern part of Europe, and is lately introduced here, where it has proven to be appreciated by connoisseurs.' It is a modest drink, and that is part of the point. Early vodka, especially when encountered out of context and out of culture, often needed taming. Fruit, herbs and sugar were the traditional tools for doing it. Whether Ruhinoy was a non-alcoholic cordial or something stronger, the logic holds either way: a sharp, perfumed modifier making a blunt spirit easier to love. Ruhinoy is obscure today, but Kirsch with a small touch of sugar gets you into the right territory, as does a restrained cherry liqueur. The aim is perfume and softening, not cherryade.

LEFT Russian support for the Union side during the American Civil War (1861–1865) meant that when visiting officers of the Imperial fleet arrived in 1863, New York society lavishly threw them a 'Great Russian Ball'.

A few years earlier, and almost a thousand miles north, vodka made a rather more theatrical entrance into American cocktails – albeit nowhere near a professional bar. *The Inter Ocean*, a Chicago daily, ran a society gossip column called 'The Whirl of Society', and on September 22, 1904, tucked between reports of upcoming weddings and garden receptions, the columnist Willie Dearborn (likely a pen name for a female society commentator) described a Monday night gathering at which an unnamed Russian Count mixed cocktails for his American guests. His recipe, retold in a phonetic impression of his Russian accent, included: 'a small measure of absinthe, a pinch of marchini, and pure vodka.' Whether 'marchini' refers to maraschino liqueur or, more intriguingly, to Martini & Rossi vermouth is left to interpretation. The former would produce a sweet, anise and cherry-forward drink. The latter, something considerably closer to an early vodka martini.

What distinguishes the Count's drink from the 1911 Russian Cocktail is that he wasn't a bartender and wasn't try to sell anything. Rather, he was deploying vodka as a cultural statement, using it to perform Russianness for a room full of fascinated Chicagoans. More than anything, it's a useful reminder that vodka's earliest appearances in American life were not behind a bar but in private rooms, and for people for whom it carried meaning.

That's one reason why vodka remains largely absent from American cocktail books and menus we can reliably point to across the first two decades of the twentieth century.

Other reasons sit well outside the bar.

Nothing stifles barroom creativity quite like a war. They interrupt production, trade, and travel, all essential ingredients in cocktail innovation. They also interrupt attention: people drink differently when the world is on fire.

Then there was prohibition, which arrived not as a single event but as a wave that swept across the vodka-producing world in quick succession. Russia banned vodka sales in August 1914, as a wartime measure, and the state monopoly that had industrialized Russian production went dark almost overnight. Finland, which had been part of the Russian Empire and shared its grain spirit traditions, had been pushing towards prohibition for years. The Finnish parliament voted for a ban unanimously as early as 1907, and though the Russian government refused to confirm it (Finland then being the Grand Duchy of Finland, and part of the Russian Empire), Finnish independence in 1917 finally cleared the path. Prohibition came into force in Finland in June 1919. Between Russia and Finland, two of the Baltic

Russian Cocktail

45 ML/1½ FL OZ VODKA

20 ML/⅔ FL OZ CHERRY-STONE OR CHERRY-LIQUEUR-STYLE MODIFIER

Stir over ice and strain into a chilled cocktail glass.

region's most developed grain spirit industries had effectively shut down within five years of each other.

Poland tells a different story. Regaining independence in 1918 after more than a century of partition, it moved quickly to rebuild, and alcohol production became one of the most developed sectors of its agricultural economy. Revenue from vodka helped finance a military that successfully held off the newly formed Red Army of the Soviet Union. But a country rebuilding from scratch, fighting a border war, and reintegrating three separately administered territories, was not in a position to be exporting to American bars.

Meanwhile, the United States was running its own argument about drink, framed as morality rather than state revenue. The temperance movement had been building for decades, with women playing a central role, because alcohol was seen as a destructive force in households and marriages. Flaunting vodka-based cocktails under the noses of placard-waving teetotallers, while Europe simultaneously burned and dried itself out, was not a convincing strategy for making alcohol look like a civilized hobby.

Even so, bartenders remain bartenders, and at least one of them saw vodka as a useful prop in the politics of the moment. Bill 'Cocktail' Boothby, one of the biggest American cocktail names of the era, used his platform to call for peace during the First World War. *The Oakland Tribune* reported the story on November 22, 1914 wherein Boothby allegedly listened to a heated argument between a German and a Frenchman, then served them a 'Peace Cocktail' built from vodka, šljivovica, schnapps, cognac and other ingredients that represented the nations embroiled in the early stages of the war. They drank, liked it and supposedly left arm in arm. It is a story made up by a famously egotistical bartender, but the point stands: vodka was present enough, at least in some bars, to be used as a recognizable national symbol.

RIGHT Four popular interwar cocktail books where vodka appears with uneven competence but persistent ambition.

Locating vodka in Europe was easier than in Prohibition America, and so too was finding Russian emigres who wanted to drink it. Hundreds of American bartenders migrated to Europe during Prohibition to work in hotels and clubs in Paris, London and Monte Carlo. Around the same time, over a million Russians fled the turmoil of revolution and civil war, and those communities brought tastes, habits and a certain nostalgia for the old world.

In theory, this should have been fertile ground for vodka cocktails. In practice, the early interwar years produced a lot of drinks that read like confusion and panic. Many vodka recipes in 1920s books feel rushed, as if bartenders were trying to prove they had heard of vodka rather than demonstrating they knew what to do with it. Vodka often appears as a supplementary spirit, sitting behind gin, brandy or a liqueur.

Take the Pépa from *Cocktails de Paris* (1929), which throws brandy, vermouth and vodka into a glass then barrels over the top with a large measure of Cointreau. Or the Yokohama in *Harry's ABC of Mixing Cocktails* (1923), which combines vodka, gin, orange juice, grenadine and absinthe. It is a dreadful drink, yet it refuses to die, haunting the pages of other books like a persistent ghost. Then there is the

Voronoff from *Recettes de Cocktails* (1928), in which vodka shares a glass with rhum agricole, Żubrówka, and Scotch whisky – less a recipe and more a dare.

One drink of marginally fairer proportions that surfaces repeatedly from the mid-1920s is the Niekla, first printed in *Drinks Long and Short* by Nina Toye and A.H. Adair in 1925. It combines vodka, orange juice and French vermouth, in something akin to the Bronx cocktail (normally made with gin), providing brightness, aromatics and a little structure. Whether or not orange juice is ever a great cocktail ingredient is another matter.

A similar instinct runs through *The Drinks of Yesteryear: A Mixology* (1930) by Jere Sullivan, which includes a vodka drink called the Czarina: vodka, orange juice, and Peychaud's bitters, noted as 'The Grande Danseuse's Demand'. Sullivan presents his book as a collection of authentic favourite formulas from Washington and New York prior to Prohibition, raising the possibility that some of these combinations existed before 1920.

What seems more likely is that this was a numbers game. Early twentieth-century cocktail books often treated quantity as proof of expertise regardless of whether or not the drinks were popular, tested or ever made outside the page. Vodka turns up in recipes as a flourish or an exotic stamp rather than a meaningful component. If you were writing a cocktail book in 1927 and wanted to look worldly (as any self-respecting bartender would) a few Russian-sounding drinks among the classics served the purpose neatly, and very few readers could check your work.

Among the chaos there were occasional flashes of genuine competence. When bartenders stopped trying to make vodka perform tricks and started using it for what it is – a canvas, a carrier, a clean platform – the results improved. One example appears in *900 Recettes de Cocktails et Boissons Américaines* (1927), a book that boasts an absurd quantity of drinks for the time – most of them not great – but proves that a stopped clock is right a couple of times a day. The Haughtinesse is a vodka martini prototype that calls for equal parts vodka and Italian vermouth (around 30 ml/1 fl oz each), brightened with a small measure of anisette and a dash of orange bitters, then served with an olive and a strip of lemon. The drink is spirit-forward, aromatic and structured, belonging to the broader family of stirred, fortified-wine cocktails that were popular long before vodka arrived in the Western mainstream. It still works today.

Devil's Torch

In London, vodka appears in UK cocktail books with increasing frequency through the same period. *The Savoy Cocktail Book* (1930) provides precisely four vodka drinks, which feels appropriate for a book so devoted to gin. Other publications do better though. The *UKBG Approved Cocktails* book (1937) includes Clubland, a simple stirred combination of equal parts vodka and white port with a dash of Angostura bitters, built over ice in a rocks glass. It is a short, honest drink that makes no pretence about what it wants to be. *The Café Royal Cocktail Book* from the same year runs to around a dozen vodka recipes, and most are best left unrepeated. One that stands out for its simplicity, balance and visual appeal (a pink drink in a martini glass) is the Devil's Torch.

30 ML/1 FL OZ VODKA
30 ML/1 FL OZ DRY VERMOUTH
5 ML/I TSP GRENADINE

Stir over ice and strain into a chilled cocktail glass.

Gypsy Queen

One venue where we can be confident that vodka cocktails were being more than just printed was The Russian Tea Room in New York. Opened in 1927 by former members of the Russian Imperial Ballet, it began as a gathering spot for Russian expatriates and soon became a magnet for the entertainment industry. After Prohibition was repealed in 1933, vodka began to appear as part of the venue's identity in a way that could be sold to Americans: Russian food, Russian atmosphere and Russian drinking, fitted neatly to Manhattan.

From 1933 the Tea Room published a souvenir booklet titled 'Russian Dishes and what they are made of...', and from 1938 onwards it included several pages of vodka cocktails, many of which sound genuinely drinkable. The Casino Russe mixes vodka with Chartreuse and lemon. The Ballet Russe swaps the Chartreuse for crème de cassis. The Sasha Special is more chaotic, combining Żubrówka vodka, Jamaican rum, port, lemon juice and sugar.

The best of the bunch is the Gypsy Queen: vodka, Benedictine and bitters. David A. Embury later included the drink in *The Fine Art of Mixing Drinks* (1948), despite his general distaste for vodka. He noted that the original recipe called for one part vodka to two parts Benedictine, but suggested that five or six parts vodka to one of Benedictine made a better drink, with a dash of orange bitters. He was right. Benedictine is sweet, herbal, and complex, flavoured with a long list of botanicals, and used sparingly it behaves less like a syrup and more like a concentrated aromatic seasoning. In a vodka drink, it supplies the impression of depth without demanding the spotlight.

45 ML/1½ FL OZ VODKA
10 ML/2 TSP BENEDICTINE D.O.M
A DASH OF ORANGE BITTERS (OR ANGOSTURA, IF YOU PREFER)

Stir over ice and strain into a chilled cocktail glass. Garnish with an orange twist.

LIQUOR
ABBATIÆ FISCANENSIS
D.O.M
BENEDICTI
Vodka

WHITE WHISKEY

LEFT Americans heartily celebrate legal beer's return in December 1933, largely oblivious to vodka's quiet arrival behind it.

While vodka's fandom in the early twentieth century may have been small, it was passionate enough that some American producers decided it was worth faking. Passing off domestic neutral spirit as Russian vodka became a minor industry in itself, aided by the fact that very few consumers had any meaningful benchmark for what real vodka tasted like. Bootlegging, mislabelling and creative storytelling were already deeply woven into American drinking culture. Vodka simply offered a new costume.

In 1912, Samuel Schochet of New York appeared in court charged with false advertising for his product, Monopol Vodka (Made and Bottled in Russia). The label claimed supervision by the Russian government, carried a St Petersburg address complete with storehouse number, and was sealed with a wax stamp bearing the imperial coat of arms. A Bureau of Chemistry investigation found that the spirit was made in the US. Schochet pleaded guilty and was fined $25. Similar cases followed, brought against companies with names like The Russian Transfer Monopole Co. and The Russian Monopole Co. of America. The thirst for vodka may have been limited, but the appetite for its mythology was already robust.

Neutral spirit itself was nothing new to America. It had been produced domestically since the mid-nineteenth century in rectification plants scattered across the country, used to make domestic gins and as the basis for liqueurs. What was new was the idea of bottling and selling it as vodka. This meant that men like Schochet could plausibly sell American spirit as Russian vodka without anyone noticing much difference. Technically, the spirit may have been almost indistinguishable.

Opening a dedicated vodka distillery in the United States would still have seemed a foolish gamble at the turn of the century. Demand was negligible, and what demand existed leaned heavily on a romanticized Russian origin story. Prohibition then flattened any remaining ambition. You would have to be utterly mad to even contemplate launching a vodka brand.

But as Aristotle said, no great genius has ever existed without some touch of madness.

Rudolph P. Kunett was born Rudolf Kunettchenskiy into a Ukrainian grain-merchant family who had established one of the biggest spirit rectification plants in the world by 1912. Prior to that, his father's firm had been one of the principal suppliers of grain to Pyotr Smirnov's distillery in Moscow, which was the most powerful vodka operation in imperial Russia. Kunett had grown up knowing exactly the weight that the Smirnov name once carried and knew exactly what had been lost when the Bolsheviks nationalized it. After the October Revolution of 1917 swept away the world his family had built, Kunett fled Russia. He arrived in the United States in 1920, rebuilt himself as a cosmetics salesman with the kind of grim determination available only to those who have watched everything they knew disappear overnight.

The Smirnov brand, meanwhile, had scattered with the family. Pyotr's second son, Vladimir, had made his way west through Constantinople and Warsaw before settling in Paris. There he had registered the family name in its French spelling, Smirnoff, with a double f, partly for Western phonetic appeal, partly to signal that this was a new chapter rather than a haunted continuation. He attempted to sell his vodka to the Parisian market with modest success. By the early 1930s, the operation had not grown into much. Vladimir was ageing, unwell and without the capital or the industrial infrastructure that had once made the original Smirnov empire so formidable. What he possessed was something rarer and, in the right hands, more valuable: his name.

Exactly when and how Kunett found Vladimir in Paris is not recorded in clinical detail, but the broad outline is well established. Sometime in the early 1930s, the two men met in the city. On one side of the table sat a destitute Russian exile with a famous surname and a small, struggling spirits operation. On the other sat a Ukrainian-American businessman who understood, perhaps better than anyone alive outside Russia, exactly what that surname had once been worth. In 1933, Vladimir Smirnoff sold Kunett the exclusive rights to produce and sell Smirnoff vodka in the United States and Canada for 54,000 francs, roughly equivalent to $50,000 today.

The timing appeared fortunate. Prohibition, which had shuttered America's legal alcohol industry for 13 years, was on the verge of repeal. The bars were coming back. The question was: what would they pour?

In 1934, Kunett opened America's first dedicated vodka distillery in Bethel, Connecticut, a quiet town of a few thousand people tucked into the Housatonic Valley in the southwestern corner of the state, roughly 60 miles/95 km from New York City. Bethel was not a place that announced itself. Its main street was lined with the modest storefronts of a small New

England manufacturing town. There was a hat factory, a few grocery merchants, a railway depot. The idea of producing tsarist Russian vodka in such a setting was strange enough to make the local papers. *The Danbury News-Times*, published in the county seat a mile or so to the west, covered the venture with a mixture of curiosity and civic pride. Here was a Russian immigrant, in a New England town, attempting to resurrect the spirit of a fallen empire.

The operation was small. Kunett had capital enough to produce and bottle but not enough to advertise properly or to weather a prolonged period of poor sales. Kunett leaned hard into the provenance the brand already carried, anglicizing the spelling and feeding American newspapers a carefully prepared history of imperial prestige, medals, and courtly favour. Bottles featured coats of arms and purveyor-to-the-court insignia. A bottle cost $1.75, less than half the price of imported vodka, and came with a booklet of cocktail recipes that included what appears to be the first written reference to a Vodka Martini and perhaps the one and only recipe for a Vodka Manhattan – Kunett was covering all the bases. Vladimir Smirnoff himself was quoted addressing bartenders directly, praising vodka's clarity and its ability to blend harmoniously with vermouths, grenadines, bitters, fruit juices, and other ingredients. It was a confident pitch for a spirit that almost nobody was asking for.

In spite of his declining health, Vladimir planned to travel to the United States to support the new venture and wrote to Kunett in the summer of 1934: 'Your business is dear to me, because I see the reconstruction of our old Smirnov company… I look at you with great hope. I'm certain of your success.'

Success would eventually come. In time Smirnoff would be the biggest spirits brand in the world. Vladimir never made the trip however, and died in Nice on 25 August 1934, just months after the distillery opened. He was 59.

Vladimir's confidence was, for the time being, misplaced however. America in 1934 was a country clawing its way out of the Great Depression. Franklin D. Roosevelt was in his first term, unemployment had reached a quarter of the workforce at its peak, and the repeal of Prohibition had sent Americans rushing back to what they already knew. Beer flowed again. Whiskey returned to the bar. Gin, which had been the illicit drink of choice through the dry years, was already domesticated enough to order without explanation. Vodka was none of these things.

In its first year, Smirnoff sold just 1,200 cases, almost entirely to Russian and Eastern European immigrants who recognized the name. Kunett later remarked that Americans were not simply uninformed about Russia, they were misinformed about vodka. The association with drunken Cossacks and revolutionary chaos, which had followed the spirit through decades of American journalism, had not faded. The bottle with the imperial crest did little to dissolve it. By 1938, the company was effectively bankrupt, but salvation came in the form of John Martin, a senior executive at G. F. Heublein and Brothers, the Hartford, Connecticut company that had been in the bottled cocktail and condiment business since the 1870s. Martin was not a vodka drinker and had no particular attachment to Russian imperial mythology. What he had was a clear eye for commercial opportunity and an unusual ability to think outside whatever category he was working in.

He bought Smirnoff, along with Kunett's equipment and the rights, for $14,000, kept Kunett on with a modest royalty arrangement, and immediately began thinking about the product differently. Where Kunett had been trying to sell vodka as vodka, Martin asked a different question: what problem does this spirit actually solve that others cannot?

The answer arrived, as good answers sometimes do, by accident. An early Smirnoff shipment had been bottled before the proper caps arrived, and the bottles were sealed with closures labelled whiskey. A South Carolina distributor, rather than treating this as a crisis, leaned into it. He ran a banner advertising Smirnoff White Whiskey: No Smell. No Taste. The campaign was technically illegal, and wildly effective. Vodka's defining characteristic – the fact that it had no characteristics – turned out to be a selling point.

This reframing coincided with a deeper structural change in American bars. Prohibition had wiped out a generation of professional bartenders. Many of the people now serving drinks had learned from pamphlets and house recipes rather than from experienced mentors. Skills were uneven and quality inconsistent. Vodka thrived in this environment because it was forgiving. It could be mixed sloppily, would not overpower a weak hand, and did not fight back if handled clumsily. This goes some way to explaining why early vodka cocktails are so often dismissed as crude or uninspired. They were not failures of imagination so much as products of their moment. A spirit that did not demand expertise was exactly what the post-Prohibition bar needed.

That practical logic found its first truly successful expression in 1940 with the Moscow Mule. The setting was the Cock 'n' Bull, a pub on Sunset Strip in Los Angeles that Jack Morgan had opened in 1937 with the ambition of giving Hollywood something that felt like an English public house. It had low ceilings, dark wood, and a back bar stocked with Morgan's own ginger beer, which he brewed himself and could not, despite considerable effort, move in sufficient quantity.

The standard version of the origin story involves three overlapping problems and a single solution. Martin needed to sell vodka. Morgan needed to shift ginger beer. A woman named Sophie Berezinski needed to find buyers for a stock of custom copper mugs she had inherited and could not get rid of. One evening at the Cock 'n' Bull, the three got talking and the drink was assembled on the spot. Vodka, ginger beer, a squeeze of lime, in a copper mug.

ABOVE The copper mug. A single solution to three separate commercial problems.

The story is almost certainly tidier in the telling than it was in the making, and the copper mug detail in particular has been disputed and embellished over the decades. Martin reportedly carried a very early version of the Polaroid camera and photographed bartenders across the country holding Moscow Mules in copper mugs, leaving one copy with the bar and keeping one for himself, building up a visual record of the drink spreading from city to city. It was an early example of both grassroots and influencer marketing, long before the advent of social media.

The drink itself worked because it did not ask vodka to emulate gin or whiskey on their own terms. Ginger beer brought spice and fizz. Lime added acid.

Vodka carried the alcohol without pulling the flavour in any particular direction. The Moscow Mule made vodka's neutrality into its best quality. It was the drink in which vodka first stopped being a liability and started being a feature.

This period also saw vodka spread through standardized service environments. Hotels, cruise ships, airlines and chain restaurants valued consistency above almost everything else. A vodka highball behaved the same in New York, Chicago or Miami. Miniatures tasted identical regardless of where they were opened. In a post-war leisure economy built on travel and the promise of reliable comfort, this mattered enormously.

By the time Cold War trade barriers were fully in place, Smirnoff had grown in lockstep with the emerging vodka category and had come to dominate the American market almost entirely. Other brands appeared and disappeared, but by some accounts Smirnoff controlled as much as 99.5 per cent of domestic production well into the 1970s.

That dominance was not for lack of competition. In 1954, a trademark application for Vodkatini appeared in the US Patent Office Gazette, described simply as being for an alcoholic cocktail. The application does not appear to have been successful, because in the same year Smirnoff launched its own advertising campaign encouraging Americans to try a Vodkatini: Smirnoff Vodka and Vermouth mixed in your favourite proportions.

As they had under Kunett, Heublein recognized that vodka's future lay not in sipping but in mixing. Print ads instructed consumers to combine vodka with everything from fruit juices and tea to beef bouillon. Vodka was positioned as adaptable, modern and practical.

The breakthrough came when Smirnoff leaned into the one thing that set vodka apart from every other spirit on the shelf: it left no trace. No smell on the breath, no obvious evidence in the glass. The resulting slogan, 'It leaves you breathless', was a masterstroke. It told office workers they could have a drink at lunch and return to their desks. It told housewives they could pour something in their afternoon tomato juice without comment. To many Americans, Smirnoff vodka became the spirit of discretion.

Heublein placed Smirnoff in the hands of people whose intelligence or wit made the discretion angle feel sophisticated rather than furtive. Groucho Marx, Woody Allen, Eartha Kitt, Johnny Carson, Zsa Zsa Gabor. Each brought a different register of glamour, but the message was consistent: this is the drink of people who are in on the joke.

The most striking choice was Langston Hughes. In 1959, the poet and playwright, one of the central figures of the Harlem Renaissance, appeared in a Smirnoff advertisement at a time when American advertising was almost entirely segregated. Whether or not the decision was primarily commercial or reflected something more principled is difficult to say, but the effect was real. Smirnoff was quietly positioning itself as a brand for a broader America than its competitors were addressing.

The sexual register grew more explicit as the decade progressed. In 1962, Julie Newmar fronted a campaign in which she occupied most of the frame, the bottle and cocktail reduced to small details in the corner. The 'breathless' tagline had begun as a practical promise about odour. By the mid-1960s it carried suggestions of excitement and permission alongside the original assurance of discretion. Both meanings were useful, and Heublein used them both.

The numbers tell the story plainly. Vodka overtook gin as America's preferred white spirit in the late 1950s. By 1967 Smirnoff had become the best-selling distilled spirit in the United States. By the mid-1970s vodka had displaced whiskey as America's top-selling spirit category overall, a shift that would

RIGHT Smirnoff's 'It Leaves You Breathless' campaign of 1962. Discretion sold beautifully to anyone with lunchtime meetings still ahead.

have been incomprehensible to a bartender from 1945. In two decades, a drink associated with Cossacks and collective farms had become the aspirational choice of suburban America.

While the 1950s and early 1960s belonged overwhelmingly to Smirnoff, at least one American challenger briefly surfaced. Arrow Vodka, based in Detroit, positioned itself as forward-thinking and unusually technical, offering 80, 86 and 100 proof bottlings years before proof variation became fashionable. Like Smirnoff, Arrow put the vodka martini at the centre of its messaging. 'BE MODERN IN DRINKS, TOO,' ran the tagline.

Heublein, having established almost total dominance in vodka, soon turned its attention to marketing actual cocktails. By the early 1960s, the company was bottling some of the first RTD (ready to drink) products, which included two variants on a vodka martini as part of a broader range of pre-mixed Club Cocktails. One was an 11-to-1 Vodka Martini, blending eleven parts Smirnoff to one part Heublein vermouth. Another was marketed with a precision that invited more questions than it answered: a 67.5 proof Vodka Martini, bottled and poured straight from the cap. These products were promoted using authoritative figures, such as the actor and politician Wendell Corey, shown holding a martini on the rocks with the line: 'Wendell Corey votes for the Heublein Martini because most people can't make one as good.'

The intended audience was the home drinker, and making cocktails soon became a domestic performance alongside other 'masculine skills' like carving a turkey or tending a barbecue. Cocktail books proliferated, glassware adopted the same modernist geometry that was reshaping post-war architecture and interiors, and Heublein published its own party guide, using recipes to quietly reinforce brand loyalty. The home bar became a stage, and vodka was soon its most reliable prop.

Moscow Mule

The Moscow Mule was a piece of genius cocktail crafting for a spirit that had little in the way of substance. It steered vodka in the direction of familiar whiskey cocktails – with subtle spice, fragrant aromatics, sweetness and a kick – but was a drink unburdened with the connotations of the pre-Prohibition cocktails your parents drank.

50 ML/1⅔ FL OZ VODKA
15 ML/½ FL OZ FRESH LIME JUICE
120 ML/4 FL OZ GINGER BEER (GOOD QUALITY, PROPERLY SPICY)
A DASH OF ANGOSTURA BITTERS (OPTIONAL)

Fill a copper mug (or a highball glass) with ice cubes. Add the vodka and lime juice. Top with ginger beer and the bitters (if using) and give it one gentle stir. Garnish with a lime wedge and a mint sprig.

Your choice of ginger beer is important here. Brands with genuine heat, such as Fever-Tree or a craft-brewed variety, produce a fundamentally different drink to the mild commercial alternatives.

SMIRNOFF

MARTINI TIME

Of all the drinks in this book, the vodka martini is the one most likely to provoke a strong opinion from the person sitting next to you at the bar. Among serious cocktail drinkers it has a reputation problem: too simple, too cold, too devoid of the botanical complexity that makes a gin martini interesting. That argument has some merit, but it also misses the point entirely. The vodka martini is one of the most-ordered cocktails on the planet. In some bars, in some towns, and in some periods of time, it has outsold the gin equivalent by a considerable margin. Whatever the gin martini faithful may think of it, the vodka martini is a phenomenon, and a phenomenon deserves an explanation.

The story of the vodka martini's invention is, like so many stories in drinking history, one where the facts as generally accepted turn out to be only part of the picture.

A 1935 promotional pamphlet produced by Smirnoff in the early years of the brand's American operation includes a recipe that meets the working definition of a vodka martini. On paper that makes it the earliest known reference to the drink in print. In practice, it demands a degree of scepticism, because Smirnoff's pamphlets of this period were marketing exercises, stuffed with recipes designed to demonstrate vodka's versatility to an American public that largely had no idea what to do with the spirit. Vodka appeared in dozens of combinations across these pages, many of them speculative at best (Vodka Manhattan anyone?). Crucially, the pamphlet appears to have made very little impression on the bars or drinkers of the time, as it would be more

LEFT The Waldorf-Astoria in the 1930s. Ted Saucier's PR office and Manhattan's reliably connected listening post. **OPPOSITE** Ice-cold vodka, good vermouth and a patient stir. Inherently simple and yet infinitely customizable.

than a decade before we saw a vodka martini named in a cocktail book – and there were a lot of cocktail books published in the 1930s.

If we delve deeper on this subject, we encounter a richer story around vodka's introduction to vermouth and the martini glass that illustrates a shifting culture of drinking in New York during the late 1930s and early 1940s, enabled by a colourful cast of characters.

The first of these characters is Ted Saucier, who published the 1951 title *Bottoms Up* (not to be confused with the 1934 book of the same name by Jean Robert Meyer, which mentions vodka only in passing: 'a powerful Russian born from a harmless potato, certain to pep up the most listless party'). Saucier was not a bartender but a highly successful public relations man, best known as the PR director of the Waldorf-Astoria Hotel from the end of Prohibition through to the 1950s. That position made him one of the best-connected people in New York, with journalist Mel Heimer once describing him as the 'confidante of kings, queens, saxophone players and cowboy movie stars'. With recipes for around 500 drinks (making it one of the biggest cocktail book in the English language at that time) *Bottoms Up* is notable for its full-colour illustrations of semi-dressed women wrapped around, drinking from and lounging in giant cocktail glasses, which were produced by a selection of the best and brightest illustrators of the era. In that book we encounter a recipe for a 'Vodkatini' comprising ⅘ jigger vodka and ⅕ jigger dry vermouth, stirred with ice and garnished with a lemon peel.

The drink was credited to Jerome Zerbe.

Vodkatini is a portmanteau of 'vodka' and 'martini,' which suggests the 'vodka martini' had to exist first, which of course it did.

Before we get to that, it is worth establishing a working definition of what constitutes a vodka martini. There are two ways to define a cocktail: by name or by recipe. Names are unreliable, prone to reuse and mutation over time. A mixture of vodka and dry vermouth, served straight up, is a vodka martini whether someone calls it that or not. With that in mind, the recipe in *Bottoms Up* qualifies. So too does a drink that appears in David A. Embury's *The Fine Art of Mixing Drinks*.

Embury's book, first published in 1948, remains one of the most respected cocktail books ever written. Its author was a lawyer by profession, with no formal connection to the drinks trade, but his observations on spirits and cocktails were sharp and hold up remarkably well even today. On vodka, however, Embury was not very generous. In fact, the first edition does not include any vodka drinks at all, but in an addendum to his extensive chapter on the martini, Embury notes that martinis 'are also sometimes made with some other liquor substituted for gin as a base, particularly a liquor of neutral flavour such as vodka or tequila'. Lumping vodka and tequila together as interchangeable gin substitutes was not exactly an endorsement and suggests a chink in the armour of the great David Embury for conflating two very different spirits. By 1961, at which point the vodka martini had become a well-known drink, Embury was still resisting it, writing that unless you use far more vermouth than he recommended, the result would be 'nothing but raw alcohol with a faint herb flavour from the vermouth'.

Yet in the second edition of *The Fine Art of Mixing Drinks*, published in 1952, something interesting appears. Buried among the recipes is a drink made to the following specification: '3 to 4 parts vodka, 1 part French vermouth. Stir. Twist of Lemon on top.' By any reasonable measure, that is a vodka martini. Embury called it a 'Kangaroo'. Later editions also include a drink called the 'Soviet', which adds dry sherry to the vodka and vermouth combination. The cynic in me says that it reads less like a genuine recommendation than a creative workaround that allowed Embury to acknowledge vodka drinkers buying his book without formally endorsing the vodka martini itself.

The cocktail known as the Kangaroo is worth pursuing, because it predates the 1952 Embury edition by nearly a decade. In 1943, a New York bartender called Oscar Haimo published *Cocktail Digest (From Private Notes)*. Haimo had begun his career at the Ritz-Carlton in Paris and the Monte Carlo Casino before taking over the bar at the Hotel Pierre on Fifth Avenue, a 41-storey limestone-fronted building that opened in 1930 with Auguste Escoffier as guest chef in its early years. Haimo claimed to be able to 'judge the ingredients and formula of any drink by merely tasting', which is perhaps why he was made president of the International Barmen's association. On page 49 of his book, there is a recipe for a 'Kangaroo Kicker Cocktail': 60 ml vodka, 22 ml dry vermouth, shaken with ice, strained into a coupe glass, garnished with a twist of lemon. That is unmistakably a vodka martini, albeit shaken rather than stirred, making it the earliest known martini recipe that meets James Bond's specifications.

Nobody is quite sure why the drink was called a Kangaroo. One possibility is that it was named after Patrick John 'Kangaroo Kicker' O'Dea, the Australian rules football player (and later American football player), who earned his nickname for his astonishingly long, high kicks. A more likely explanation is that it followed the same naming logic as the Moscow Mule, which was invented around the same time: a vodka-based drink named after an animal that kicks, with a hint of warning about the spirit's potency.

But a recipe is only half the story. To find the first drink that carries both the right recipe and the right name, we need to go to one of the most legendary bars of all time: The Stork Club.

ABOVE Overlooking Central Park with a roof modelled after the Royal Chapel at Versailles, the Hotel Pierre opened to serious fanfare in 1930. The gala dinner was cooked by Auguste Escoffier – the king of chefs and the chef of kings.

The Stork Club was a Manhattan nightclub on West 58th Street, established in 1929 by Sherman Billingsley, a former bootlegger. For roughly 25 years it was New York's most celebrated after-dark destination, a place where old money, new fame, and serious political power collided nightly. Chauffeur-driven Bentleys and Cadillacs pulled up under its awning and the door policy was notoriously opaque. Billingsley often managed it himself, and his sole

TOP Sherman Billingsley outside his legendary Stork Club in New York City in 1946. **ABOVE** New York – the iconic birthplace of the equally iconic Vodka Martini.

criterion was money. The columnist Walter Winchell, who used table 50 as his personal office and broadcast his radio programs from the club, summarized the ethos with characteristic bluntness: 'The Stork discriminates against everybody. White, black and pink. But if your skin is green and you're rich and famous, you'll be welcome at the club.' Winchell was a sufficiently valuable social commentator that when he was called up for military service in 1939, the president himself intervened. The clientele at various points included Marlene Dietrich, Marilyn Monroe, Ernest Hemingway, the Kennedy and Roosevelt families, and Irving Berlin. Hemingway famously cashed a $100,000 check for the film rights of *For Whom the Bell Tolls* at the bar to settle his tab.

The club closed in 1965, but at the height of its powers in 1946, the writer and journalist Lucius Beebe published *The Stork Club Bar Book*. Beebe wrote a syndicated column for the New York Herald Tribune called 'This New York', which was read by millions every morning and chronicled the activities of fashionable society at venues like the Stork Club. He is credited with coining the term 'cafe society' and became so wealthy and possessed such a confident personality that he became one of the first members of high society who lived as an openly gay man. When he appeared on the front cover of *Life* in 1939, he was the first openly gay man to do so.

Beebe wrote 35 books in total, most of them about railways (he owned and lived on two luxury railway carriages as an older gentleman), but *The Stork Club Bar Book* is the one that concerns us here.

The book organizes its recipes by time of day and contains recipes for 13 vodka cocktails. Included among them, appearing in the 'Night' section, is the first printed recipe for a 'Vodka Martini' in a cocktail book (outside of the aforementioned Smirnoff pamphlet). Beebe introduces it with a note about how all mixed drinks are variations on standard

RIGHT Richard Rodgers, Walter Winchell, Marlene Dietrich and Lee Bowman at the Stork Club, around 1950. Winchell used table 50 as his personal broadcasting office.

themes, a bit like how all jokes are supposedly based on a handful of fundamental structures. He then mentions that the actress Carole Landis 'swears by a vodka martini', noting her assessment that 'if perused over any length of time it will make the customer scream next morning for a Bloody Mary'. The recipe calls for 3 oz vodka and 1 oz dry vermouth, stirred with ice and served in a cocktail glass.

Proving the old adage that 'it never rains but it pours', a second vodka martini recipe appears in the book's appendix, contributed by a bar captain named Joe Acre. He notes the drink as a favourite of crime novelist Dashiell Hammett. This version is considerably smaller: ⅔ oz vodka and ⅓ oz French vermouth, totalling one ounce of liquid before dilution, which is closer to a shot even though the recipe calls for serving it in a cocktail glass. The same proportions appear in the book's standard gin martini recipe. You might wonder if the Stork Club preferred to make its martinis very small, but I think what's more likely is that the recipe was written down by Joe Acre on a scrap of paper or back of a napkin and transcribed improperly into the book.

The Stork Club Bar Book also contains a Kangaroo Kicker recipe that is identical to Haimo's 1943 version. This is the first occasion where both the Kangaroo Kicker and the Vodka Martini appear in the same book. The key difference between them is the method: the Kicker is shaken, whereas the martini is stirred. The separation of the two drinks into distinct categories in the same publication is notable, and suggests that by 1946, New York's more sophisticated bar culture had already settled on the stirred preparation as the standard for the vodka martini.

LEFT New Year's Eve at El Morocco, 1936. Society photographer Jerome Zerbe photographed rooms like this from well inside the velvet rope. **BELOW** Zerbe became the official photographer to Admiral Nimitz during the Second World War.

This brings us back to the man credited in *Bottoms Up* as the drink's inventor: Jerome Zerbe.

Zerbe was born in Ohio to a wealthy coal family. A Yale education and an eye for a photograph led him to New York in 1934, where he became what he called 'the first and only society photographer'. We would label him as a paparazzo today, though unlike most practitioners of that trade, Zerbe was himself a member of the celebrity world he documented. He spent most of his evenings from 1933 to 1938 at El Morocco and the Rainbow Room, both of which employed him at various points as staff photographer. His subjects included Greta Garbo, Howard Hughes, Charlie Chaplin, Salvador Dalí, Jean Harlow, Dorothy Parker and the Vanderbilts.

We can assume that Zerbe spent a fair amount of time at the Stork Club too, since it was probably there that he established a close friendship with bon vivant extraordinaire Lucius Beebe, author of *The Stork Club Bar Book*.

Very close, in fact. While never publicly confirmed, by all accounts Beebe and Zerbe were in a relationship that spanned most of the late 1930s.

Now, if you will allow me a little creative freedom for a moment, I would propose the following to be the probable truth behind the invention of the vodka martini:

The growing popularity of vodka among the celebrity class in the mid-1930s would have practically guaranteed Jerome Zerbe's exposure to vodka as a society photographer. Regulars at New

York's better establishments thought nothing of asking bartenders to adapt classic cocktails to their own tastes. Switching out gin for vodka in a martini, at a time when vodka was beginning to circulate among the city's fashionable set, was precisely the kind of forward-thinking gesture that would have appealed to Zerbe. The martini was a New York institution. Vodka was exotic, still largely unknown in America, carrying a whiff of intrigue and the suggestion of something stronger. For Zerbe, a drink rooted in tradition but pointing somewhere new made a kind of personal sense.

Zerbe's relationship with Lucius Beebe is the key connective tissue in the story. Beebe referenced Zerbe in his newspaper column with enough frequency and warmth to attract comment from rival columnist Winchell, who suggested Beebe rename his column 'Jerome Never Looked Lovelier'. While neither man publicly confirmed the nature of their relationship, it was by most accounts well understood in their social circles. They spent their evenings at the same bars, photographed and wrote about the same world, and moved through New York's cocktail culture as its most attentive observers.

The Stork Club Bar Book was published six years after the relationship appears to have ended. Beebe makes no mention of Zerbe in it, which could reflect the awkwardness of that history, or simply the fact that a society photographer was not quite the kind of figure whose name was typically invoked in a glamorous cocktail book. What the book does contain, however, are two fully formed vodka martini recipes at a time when most bartenders had still never heard of the drink. Beebe's familiarity with the cocktail, the detail of his presentation of it and his confidence in citing it as the preferred drink of a Hollywood actress all suggest someone who had been living comfortably with the vodka martini for years before he wrote about it.

ABOVE The Rainbow Room at Rockefeller Center. Zerbe's other regular staff photography post, and a vodka martini's natural habitat.

Ted Saucier's attribution in *Bottoms Up* (in 1951) credits Zerbe directly. By that point, Zerbe's name was well established in New York cocktail circles, and Saucier, as the Waldorf-Astoria's PR director, was the kind of person who would have known where a drink had really come from. There is no obvious reason for him to have fabricated the attribution.

The result is something like this: The earliest printed recipe that matches a vodka martini comes from the 1935 Smirnoff pamphlet. The earliest recipe from a reputable cocktail book is Oscar Haimo's Kangaroo Kicker from 1943. The first printed recipe that carries both the correct formula and the name 'Vodka Martini' is Lucius Beebe's entry in *The Stork Club Bar Book* of 1946. The first use of the word 'Vodkatini' in print is Ted Saucier's *Bottoms Up* of 1951. The person most plausibly credited with popularizing the drink, probably sometime between 1934 and 1939 in the cocktail bars of Manhattan, is Jerome Zerbe. The world's first paparazzo, it turns out, was also one of the first people to order a vodka martini.

Vodka Martini

Two ingredients, but the decisions stack up quickly. Shake or stir? Which vodka, which vermouth, and in which proportion? Lemon twist or olive? Each choice pulls the drink in a different direction, and the range of outcomes is wider than the recipe suggests. A carelessly made vodka martini and a thoughtfully made one might as well be different drinks.

60 ML/2 FL OZ VODKA (TRY A POTATO VODKA OR A RYE, LIKE BELVEDERE)
15 ML/½ FL OZ DRY VERMOUTH

Stir the vodka and vermouth with ice for at least 60 seconds.
Getting the temperature as low as possible requires time and a little dilution.

Strain into a chilled coupe or martini glass.

Express a lemon twist over the surface and drop it in,
or add an olive or cocktail onions if that is your preference.

The ratio is a matter of taste and conviction. A 4:1 ratio is a reasonable starting point. Going drier than 6:1 is a philosophical position rather than a recipe. The vodka martini is often treated as a lesser cousin to the gin version, but the right bottle, served very cold with good vermouth and a properly expressed lemon twist, is a serious drink.

FRIEND OR FOE?

In the few short years following the Vodkatini's first appearance in *Bottoms Up*, vodka flooded American bars and reshaped the post-war cocktail landscape. Drinks that would later be treated as classics emerged almost overnight. The Black Russian, White Russian and Cape Codder all belong to this immediate post-Second World War period, laying foundations for later vodka standards such as the Espresso Martini and the Cosmopolitan.

The Black Russian, perhaps the most elegant of this early wave, was the work of Gustave Tops, a Belgian bartender working at the Hotel Metropole in Brussels. He created it in 1949 in honour of Perle Mesta, the American socialite and Democratic fundraiser whom President Truman had just appointed US Ambassador to Luxembourg. It went: two parts vodka, one part coffee liqueur, served over ice. Cold War diplomacy in the form of a cold drink.

The Black Russian – and White Russian that promptly followed – both had their roots in two chocolate-flavoured cocktails that appeared in *The Savoy Cocktail Book* (1930). The Russian Cocktail featured equal parts vodka, dry gin and crème de cacao; the Barbara Cocktail was two parts vodka, one part crème de cacao, one part fresh cream.

The White Russian found its greatest cultural moment decades after its invention when 'The Dude' from *The Big Lebowski* became its unlikely ambassador, consuming a total of nine White Russians through the course of the movie.

The Cape Codder, meanwhile, was less an invention than a product of aggressive marketing by Ocean Spray, who began promoting vodka and cranberry juice in the late 1940s as a way to shift surplus fruit. It would go on to inform the Cosmopolitan in the 1980s, which is a story we will return to later.

By the 1950s vodka occupied a curious position in America. It was the fashionable new mixing spirit, embraced by celebrities and welcomed into suburban homes. Yet it remained symbolically Russian, layered with suspicion and Cold War tension. Anti-communist sentiment intensified through the decade and in response, Smirnoff emphasized imperial Russian heritage rather than Soviet associations, positioning the brand as a relic of the old Russia rather than a product of the new one. For some consumers, Smirnoff represented a kind of victory over communism. Old Russian values, preserved, repackaged, and safely Americanized.

This contradiction may actually have been the source of vodka's power. Its Russian associations lent

LEFT Harry Craddock's, *The Savoy Cocktail Book* became one of the most enduring guides in mixology. **RIGHT** The Dude from *The Big Lebowski* abides a White Russian. He drank nine in the film, but preferred to call them 'Caucasians'.

it danger and glamour, tempered by the promise of control and refinement. Vodka was wild, but accessible. It offered flexibility and a mild sense of rebellion. These qualities aligned well with the countercultural currents of the 1960s, too. As debates around race, gender and authority intensified, younger drinkers did what younger drinkers do and rejected their parents' routines. Vodka, which carried none of the traditions of whiskey and gin, was the obvious choice.

Over in Europe, the British travel magazine *Go* ran an article around this time titled 'Vodka: Friend or Foe?', in which the author, Johnnie Cradock (the long-time partner of Fanny Cradock), attempted to dispel the lurid stereotypes of Russian-booted dancers shrieking in orgies of indulgence while… simultaneously conjuring them in vivid detail. He listed cocktails in which vodka had replaced traditional base spirits, including the White Lady and the Vodka Rickey, and offered a Vodkatini of his own: three parts vodka, one part dry vermouth, stirred with ice and strained into a cocktail glass, garnished with an olive, lemon twist or pearl onion. The tone was gently mocking, but the fact that a mainstream travel magazine felt the need to address the question at all tells you something about where vodka stood in the British imagination at mid-century. It was present and it was interesting… but it was not yet entirely respectable.

What emerges from all of this is a different story to the one vodka is usually given. Vodka did not fight its way into cocktails by proving it could rival gin or whiskey at their own game. It won by being useful and innovating a new canon of cocktails. It worked when ingredients were inconsistent, when skill levels were uneven, in the morning, on planes, at poolsides, in hotel bars and on film sets. It blended, carried, softened and disappeared when needed. That invisibility was a virtue in most circumstances. What it lacked was a personality, a set of values to borrow, a reason to choose it over the thing it was slowly replacing. For that, it needed a character. As it turned out, the character was already being written.

Ian Fleming began writing the Bond novels in 1952, not long after he finished construction of his

pages. The numbers are alarming by any modern health metric and entirely consistent with the portrait Fleming was painting: a man who operates under permanent tension, for whom controlled pleasure is part of professional discipline. Even his iconic order for a vodka martini 'shaken, not stirred' seems to hint at the personality of the man himself.

Fleming's biographer, Andrew Lycett, believed that Fleming preferred his martinis shaken rather than stirred because he thought stirring diminished the flavour. One account traces this preference to a particular encounter: after the war, while working in Berlin as a correspondent for Kemsley Newspapers, Fleming is said to have met a bartender named Hans Schröder in a bar on Fasanenplatz that became foundational to the post-war drinking culture of West Berlin through its proprietor's good connections with Allied forces. Schröder shook his martinis. Fleming drank them. The details of this origin story have the quality of a Bond novel itself, which may or may not speak to their reliability, but the shaken martini became Fleming's own habit and eventually Bond's defining one.

Jamaican estate, Goldeneye. He wrote quickly and with the confidence of a man who had spent the war years cultivating sources, running agents, and attending boozy lunches in which the choice of drink signalled who you were and who you were trying to impress. Fleming knew his spirits. He primarily drank bourbon and gin, and his personal preference ran to strong, cold and carefully made drinks. What he gave Bond was something slightly different: a sensibility about drinking that elevated it into an expression of character.

Bond himself is a considerably more prolific drinker than casual readers might assume. Across the twelve novels, he consumes a total of 317 drinks. Excluding the 36 days he spent receiving medical care or in captivity, that works out to roughly 92 units of alcohol per week, or one drink every seven

Bond drinks 19 vodka martinis (plus 16 gin martinis and five martinis where the base spirit isn't named) across the novels, as well as one Vesper Martini (see below), eight vodka tonics and two glasses of neat vodka.

The Vesper Martini, ordered in *Casino Royale* (1953), is the first significant cocktail moment across the novels. Bond specifies the recipe with exacting

ABOVE Ian Fleming: author, journalist and spy. He came up with Operation Goldeneye – a plan to undertake sabotage operations in Spain in the event of a Nazi takeover. He liked the name so much, he named his house after it.

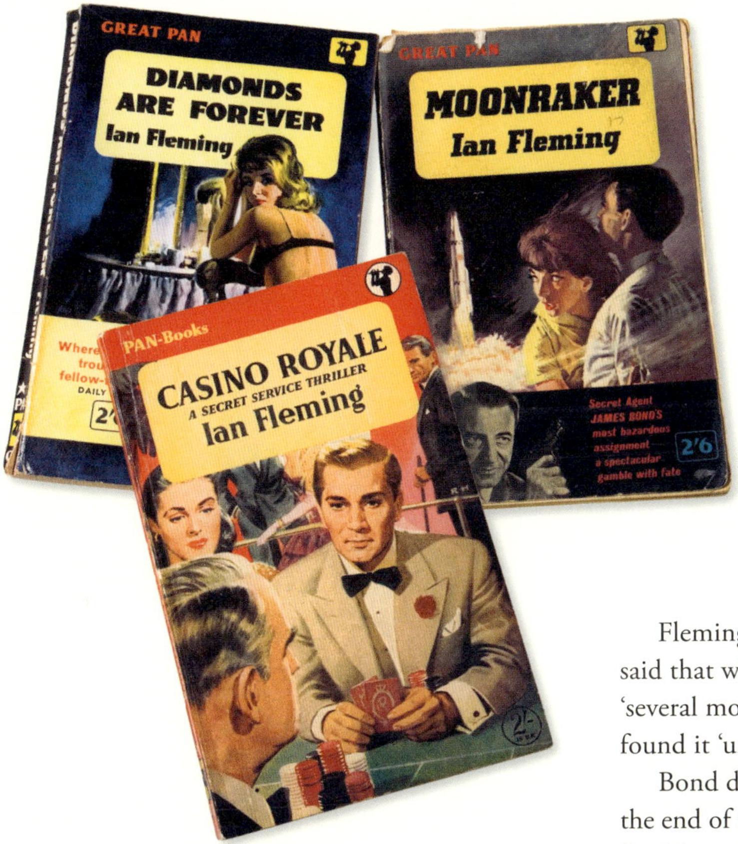

LEFT A selection of Ian Fleming's Bond novels, which in total featured 317 drinks and considerable liver damage.

detail: three measures of Gordon's gin, one of vodka, half a measure of Kina Lillet, shaken until ice-cold, served in a deep champagne goblet with a large thin slice of lemon peel. He also adds that, 'if you can get a vodka made with grain instead of potatoes, you will find it still better.'

The drink is named for Vesper Lynd, the woman Bond falls for and who then turns out to be an enemy spy. Its combination of gin and vodka places it at an interesting historical juncture. Vodka, in 1953, was still relatively unfamiliar in British drinking culture, and folding it into the martini formula alongside the established gin rather than replacing it outright was a diplomatically shrewd move. The drink was more a subtle narrative move than one of cultural observation, however. What better way to illustrate the traitorous motivations of Vesper Lynd than to sneak some vodka into a gin martini?

Fleming, in a letter to *The Guardian* in 1958, said that when he tasted a Vesper for the first time 'several months' after including it in his novel, he found it 'unpalatable'.

Bond does not order a pure vodka martini until the end of the second novel, *Live and Let Die* (1954). By *Moonraker* (1955), we see him drinking neat vodka at the fictional Blades Club with M. His boss pours him three fingers from a frozen carafe and Bond drops a pinch of black pepper into the glass before downing it in one. When M raises an eyebrow, Bond explains that it was a trick he learned in Moscow to make the poisonous fusel oil (which hadn't been filtered out on account of improper distillation) sink to the bottom of the glass.

Diamonds Are Forever (1956) contains the first appearance of the phrase 'shaken and not stirred' in print, though it reads there as an incidental detail, a waiter confirming a standing preference. The fifth novel, *From Russia with Love* (1957), deepens the association: Bond arrives in Paris, pays off his taxi, walks into the Ritz bar, and orders a double vodka martini. By *Dr. No* (1958), Bond is requesting Russian or Polish vodka specifically, and the villain's approving response, that Bond is a man who knows what he wants, functions as a neat summary of what the drink had come to represent.

By the time the films arrived, that calculation had shifted. *Dr. No* reached British cinemas in 1962, the same year Smirnoff had begun serious UK marketing, by which point the Moscow Mule had been running in American bars for over a decade. Sean Connery, embodying Bond with a quality of understated physical authority that Fleming had always intended, ordered his vodka martinis shaken not stirred and looked entirely correct doing so. In Connery's mouth, in a cinema, the phrase became a social instruction. A generation of drinkers took note.

The timing was not accidental. Vodka in the early 1960s in Britain occupied exactly the right cultural position: established enough to be sophisticated, foreign enough to be interesting, without the class associations that still clung to gin or whisky.

Fleming had created a character who lived in the space between the visible and the hidden. Vodka, the spirit that leaves no trace on the breath, was the perfect prop for him. What is worth noting is what Fleming was actually describing. The vodka martini in the Bond novels is a British drink, made with an increasingly international spirit, served according to an American cocktail tradition, against a backdrop of Cold War anxiety. That this combination became the most imitated drinks order of the twentieth century says a great deal about how culture travels through story and imagination.

The story of James Bond and, by association, Fleming, is such a potent one that mythologies around vodka martinis have even sprung up around it.

In London, the Dukes Hotel in St. James's Place is the divine home of the martini and has elevated the drink to become a spiritual experience, with all the pomp and ceremony of church. Since 1982, the house martini has been prepared tableside from a rosewood drinks trolley, in a format introduced by Salvatore Calabrese, who was Dukes' head bartender until 1994. He came up with the drink after repeated requests for a colder and drier martini from the American writer Stanton Delaplane. Calabrese went as cold and as dry as is possible by using a frozen glass, the minimum viable amount of vermouth swirled around the inside and discarded, then 120 ml/4 fl oz of near-frozen vodka or gin poured straight in. He called it the Direct Martini.

The bar gained notoriety for martinis off the back of this, and some time around the turn of the twenty-first century, a connection with the Ian Fleming was established. This appears to have happened when the former bar manager Gilberto Preti first appeared on the US TV show *Lifestyles of the Rich & Famous* in the 1990s and the host Robin Leach romanticized that he could imagine Fleming drinking martinis at Dukes. The story and the image became instantiated into legend, appearing in cocktail books (even some of mine) and news articles with increasing frequency. There is no evidence to support the fact that Fleming ever set foot in Dukes however, though the hotel, tucked around a backstreet in St. James's has always been known for its quiet discretion.

The current guardian of the bar is Alessandro Palazzi, who has held the position since 2007 and has refined the martini ritual to the point where watching him work is, as the drinks writer's standard language might put it, a spectacle. Though Fleming clearly drank his martinis wherever he could find them, Dukes has become a kind of unofficial monument to the habit… and to James Bond.

Bond made vodka martinis aspirational in a way that no advertising campaign has ever quite managed since. In some ways he was an unofficial and unpaid (at least until the birth of product placement) ambassador for the spirit, advocating for the product on page and on screen.

Interestingly, vodka had very few starring roles in late-twentieth-century cinema besides Bond, the aforementioned *Big Lebowski* and the movie *Moscow on the Hudson* (1984) where Robin Williams plays a Soviet circus musician who defects in the vodka aisle of Bloomingdale's in New York.

The reasons behind this are partly cultural and partly artistic. Vodka looks like water. A glass of whisky reads as whisky from across a room, and a martini with an olive carries decades of gin iconography. Vodka in a tumbler communicates nothing, and cinema is a medium that needs a drink to perform a role. Brown spirits had also spent most of the century building their screen presence, from the whisky-soaked Westerns and hard-boiled detective pictures of the studio era through to the boardroom dramas of the 1970s and 1980s. Vodka never accumulated that kind of visual shorthand. The Cold War added a further complication. For much of the period, the spirit carried a Soviet association that American filmmakers were reluctant to play straight, which is precisely why vodka had established itself as an anti-institutional poster child. And Smirnoff's own marketing, built on the promise that their product left no taste and no smell, told audiences there was nothing to notice. A spirit sold on its absence makes a poor movie prop.

The irony of all this is that even though vodka was rarely in front of the camera, it was doing a lot of work behind it.

Studio contracts of the 1940s and 1950s often contained clauses prohibiting alcohol on set, and the consequences of smelling of whiskey or gin were serious enough that discretion became a professional necessity. Vodka, which left almost no trace on the breath, solved the problem neatly (or on the rocks).

ABOVE Dukes Hotel, St James's. The unofficial shrine to the vodka martini, despite no firm evidence that Fleming ever drank one here.

Elizabeth Taylor was known to drink it before arriving on set, and for much of her relationship with the actor Richard Burton the pair were known to live on 'Cognac in the morning. Vodka and tonic in the afternoon. Scotch and vodka at night.' Errol Flynn carried vodka in a doctor's bag, favoured Bloody Marys in the morning, and in order to keep up with his bottle-a-day appetite was said to have injected vodka into oranges when discretion was required. Joan Crawford was another vodka lover who, in a rite of passage worthy of Peter the Great, only permitted house guests to drink neat vodka – no ice, no tonic, no soda.

Bloody Mary

The Bloody Mary had been drifting through hotel bars and airline lounges since the 1930s, a drink that offered the physical sensation of nourishment while delivering alcohol with almost no olfactory signature. Tomato juice, spice, salt and acidity masked the spirit effectively. For actors with morning calls, airline passengers (or crew) and businessmen who needed to drink without smelling of drink, vodka was the obvious choice.

Perhaps this is why it has become the de facto in-flight drink among even people who would never normally order one. The legacy of day drinking has informed our mile-high orders so that even the virgin Marys do a roaring trade from the hostess trolley where no cover up of alcohol is needed. It's certainly not the drink's opaque red hue and capacity to stain clothing during heavy bouts of turbulence that cemented its place on the in-flight beverage menu...

50 ML/1⅔ FL OZ VODKA (HORSERADISH NASTOYKA OR PERTSOVKA WORK BRILLIANTLY – SEE P30 & P72)

200 ML/7 FL OZ TOMATO JUICE

20 ML/⅔ FL OZ LEMON JUICE

5 ML/1 TSP SUGAR SYRUP

A LARGE PINCH OF SALT AND PEPPER

A DASH OR TWO OF WORCESTERSHIRE SAUCE

A DASH OR TWO OF YOUR PREFERRED HOT SAUCE

Build the ingredients into a highball glass and give it a good stir with plenty of ice. Garnish with a stick of celery and extra lemon.

Bisquit

COLD WAR COCKTAILS

'There is no Russian vodka available in the United States,' noted David Embury in the 1955 edition of *The Fine Art of Mixing Drinks*. It was a simple observation, but it carried the weight of a world divided. While American bartenders were quietly discovering what vodka could do in a cocktail glass, the spirit's homeland was sealed off behind an iron curtain, invisible to the market that would eventually make it famous.

That quintessentially vodka-like invisibility suited both sides. Between 1943 and 1959, imports of Soviet goods into the United States had fallen by around 90 per cent. In Moscow, meanwhile, no one was thinking about cocktail culture. Vodka remained what it had always been in Russia: a fiscal instrument, a social sedative and a problem the state had never quite solved.

Following Lenin's death in 1924, his successor Alexei Rykov repealed prohibition to revive a collapsed economy, introducing a heavily taxed, diluted vodka of around 30% ABV that Russians quickly and derisively nicknamed *rykovka*. Real power, however, lay with Joseph Stalin, who reasserted the vodka monopoly, ordered production maximized, and channelled the revenues into the rapid industrialization of the 1930s.

During the Second World War, vodka was formally woven into military life. Soldiers received the so-called 'Commissar's ration' of 100 grams per day. Some Russians still insist that this ration, rather than Katyusha rocket launchers, played a decisive role in turning the tide against the Nazis.

If the Kalashnikov was the hardware of the Cold War, vodka was its liquid propaganda. A soft power export packaged not in ideology but in bottles of Stolichnaya and Moskovskaya. Beginning in the mid-twentieth century, Soviet vodka began appearing on Western shelves, not just as a commodity but as a cultural emissary, an exportable image of Russian craftsmanship and resilience.

Labels evoked Red Square, onion domes and heroic workers in wheat fields. State vodka was clean, strong and ideologically sound – the proletarian's drink, refined for global consumption. Diplomats would toast with it, foreign journalists were plied with it, Olympic victories were washed down with it. Stolichnaya in particular became a symbol of Soviet modernity. It was a vodka for export, not excess, praised in the West for its clarity and quality. The irony, of course, was that while the Soviet Union

ABOVE Known by its green branding, Moskovskaya was founded in 1894 by the Russian state vodka monopoly.

used vodka to win hearts abroad, it continued to wrestle with the devastation it caused at home.

Stolichnaya belonged to a fundamentally different tradition than the private dynastic producers of the late imperial period. Where Pyotr Smirnov had built his reputation through obsessive control of quality, innovative marketing, and brand identity within a competitive market, Stolichnaya emerged from a system where competition had been abolished entirely. The brand is generally dated to 1948, during the early post-war Soviet period, when vodka production had been reorganized around central planning and uniformity. Early Stolichnaya was not originally tied to one distillery, but rather functioned as a standardized specification: a vodka made from rectified grain spirit, diluted, lightly sweetened, filtered and bottled according to state-approved norms. 'Stolichnaya' described what the vodka of the USSR was meant to be, rather than who made it – communism distilled.

ABOVE Joseph Stalin was notorious for his use of vodka as a political weapon, hosting martini-drinking sessions in which he drank very little himself. **BELOW** Soviet vodka and American cola became an unlikely diplomatic cocktail.

By the late twentieth century, Stoli spirit was largely sourced from facilities in and around Tambov, southeast of Moscow. The core expression was diluted with artesian well water, filtered through quartz sand and birch charcoal, lightly dosed with sugar, and bottled at 40% ABV.

One of the more surreal episodes in Cold War economic history came in the form of the Pepsi-Stolichnaya barter deal. In 1972, the Soviet Union, barred from holding US dollars and with limited hard currency reserves, struck an unusual arrangement: PepsiCo would market and distribute Stolichnaya vodka in the United States, and in return Pepsi would gain exclusive rights to sell its cola across the USSR. By the 1980s, the USSR had become Pepsi's largest international market and Pepsi, bizarrely, became the first American product to establish a nationwide presence in the Soviet Union.

The arrangement was a form of soft power born out of hard liquor and soft drink. Stolichnaya's presence in American bars offered a rare, palatable face to a system often caricatured as grim and grey. Its marketing leaned into exoticism: Cyrillic script, red stars, 'from behind the Iron Curtain'. For a generation of Western drinkers, Stoli was a taste of the forbidden. Meanwhile, the USSR could point to the global success of its vodka as proof that not all Soviet products were tractors and propaganda pamphlets.

Yet this vodka diplomacy came with its contradictions. While Stolichnaya gleamed on Western shelves, counterfeit vodka was ravaging Soviet consumers at home. The same state that exported elegance in a bottle often supplied its own citizens with grain alcohol diluted with water and passed off as premium. Abroad, vodka was a velvet glove. At home, it was still the same iron fist in a frosted glass. One study suggests that alcohol consumption more than doubled between 1955 and 1979, reaching 15.2 litres/4 gallons per person.

By the 1970s, dependence had reached striking levels. In 1979, the Soviet government collected 25.4 billion roubles in indirect alcohol taxes, more than from income tax that year. Contemporary sources commonly placed the alcohol share of total state revenues at around one-third, confirming a continuity with the late-imperial model, though on an even larger industrial scale.

State revenue would have been even higher if only it were possible to tax all of the illicit alcohol the nation was producing at the time. The centuries had rolled by with war and revolution, but samogon – the real drink of the people – remained endemic. One economist at Duke University in the 1970s compared official output figures with grain and sugar consumption and noted the conspicuously large quantities of grain that seemed to vanish without trace. He arrived at a staggering conclusion: illicit samogon production had effectively increased Russia's total alcohol output by a third.

Illicit production of spirits was most prevalent amongst the poorer classes. Being impoverished is one thing, but being impoverished in a system with no hope of escape is another thing entirely. Spirits offered some relief, and desperation encouraged innovation.

But the appetite for vodka was not confined to the bottom of Soviet society. The men at the top showed little more restraint. From Stalin's infamous late-night drinking sessions in the Kremlin, where guests were expected to match the General Secretary glass for glass or risk the consequences, to the open conviviality of the Brezhnev years, heavy drinking was a fixture of political life. Power and vodka, it turned out, were as inseparable at the top as they were at the bottom.

In December 1963, Khrushchev invited Finnish President Urho Kekkonen to his residence at Zavidovo, outside Moscow. Dinner was served with Stolichnaya, poured not into shot glasses but into champagne flutes. By the end of the evening, Khrushchev had to be carried from the table by his guards. Kekkonen, a formidable athlete in his younger years, watched this without comment, filled his flute one last time, and drank it off with a simple toast: 'One for the road.'

His successor was less ceremonial but no less committed. Brezhnev was fond of saying that 'life is beautiful and wonderful, if you wet your throat beforehand', and lived accordingly. His drink of choice was Żubrówka, the vodka flavoured with *Hierochloe odorata* (bison grass) whose faint vanilla and almond notes apparently suited a man who preferred his indulgences with a degree of

LEFT The Su-15TM fighter. Its hydraulic and radar coolants doubled as drinkable spirit, giving a whole new meaning to 'flight of spirits.' **BELOW** Leonid Brezhnev's drink of choice was Żubrówka, taken in his preferred 50, 100, 150 ml pyramid.

refinement. The French actress Marina Vlady, widow of the poet and singer Vladimir Vysotsky, recalled Brezhnev sharing his personal method for drinking spirits: 50 ml to open, 100 ml to continue and 150 ml to finish. A pyramid, of sorts. Whether he followed his own advice consistently is not recorded, but the Soviet mortality statistics of the Brezhnev era suggest he was not alone in the habit.

Booze saturated the Soviet military too, especially aviation where improvised vodka was made from industrial ethanol in all manner of ways. From piston aircraft of the Second World War through to Cold War jets and bombers, ethanol was used for de-icing, cooling, hydraulics, braking systems and cleaning. High-altitude flight demanded fluids that would not freeze at -50°C/-58°F or lower, and electronic systems required them to dissipate heat rapidly and reliably. Ethyl alcohol did the job. Once it arrived on base, it also solved another problem: where to get a drink.

An entire book could be written on the misadventures of Soviet pilot-come-bartenders. Each era had an aircraft type, and each aircraft type developed its own liquid folklore. On the Su-15 interceptor, junior pilots encountered *Sooltyga*, a brake coolant that was roughly 30 per cent ethanol and 70 per cent water. The aircraft carried around 7.5 litres/2 gallons. Enough to fill a 5-litre/1⅓-gallon Soviet teapot and still have some left over.

More prized was 'Shylo', the Su-15's radar coolant. The word means 'awl' or 'hole', a reference to an old naval practice where alcohol was stored in leather pouches and accessed by punching a hole. Shylo was serious drink. Around 95.5 per cent ethanol and 4.5 per cent water, with up to 20 litres/5¼ gallons carried per aircraft. With basic filtration and dilution, it passed easily as vodka.

Heavy bombers took things further. The Tu-22 earned the nickname 'booze carrier' thanks to *Shpaga*, named after the fencing sword it resembled and the dipstick used to measure coolant levels. The aircraft could carry up to an astonishing 400 litres/88 gallons of alcohol-based coolant, reportedly indistinguishable from Stolichnaya before it went into the aircraft's plumbing, but rather more tasting of metal and rubber afterwards.

The MiG-25 interceptor went further still. Its systems used a 50:50 ethanol-water mix for cooling and de-icing, nicknamed *Massandra* after the Crimean wine producer. The aircraft became known as the 'twin-tail restaurant' or the 'grocery store'. Alcohol could be traded for food, favours or parts in the shadow economy that sustained Soviet bases.

Naturally alcoholism became rife among servicemen. There was a Soviet saying that circulated quietly through air bases from the 1950s onwards: 'The only one not drinking was the autopilot.' Like most good Soviet jokes, it worked because it was close to the truth. When questioned about the sheer volume of alcohol in his aircraft, the legendary Soviet aircraft designer Artem Mikoyan reportedly shrugged it off: 'If national security required it,' he said, 'I would fill them with cognac.'

The idea of aviation fluid as drink entered popular culture in Naum Birman's *Chronicle of a Dive Bomber* (1967). In one scene, grounded pilots mix raspberry syrup with hydraulic fluid to make an improvised cocktail. The resulting concoction is tasted by the pilots, who become almost transcendent as they knock back their 'landing gear liqueur' – a term that later became a catch-all for any improvised alcohol consumed in uniform.

In Soviet cinema, vodka was rarely permitted to be glamorous. The state's ambivalence towards the drink, its simultaneous reliance on vodka tax revenue and its ideological embarrassment about a population that drank so heavily, produced a film culture in which vodka appeared constantly but was seldom celebrated. Mikhail Kalatozov's *The Cranes Are Flying* (1957), one of the great films of the Khrushchev thaw (the period in which censorship and suppresion was relaxed), uses vodka as a totem of wartime grief and moral disintegration. The bottle is passed from hand to shaking hand, not communicating pleasure but rather a desperation between men with nothing better to offer each other. In Vladimir Menshov's *Moscow Does Not Believe in Tears* (1980), which won the Oscar for Best Foreign Language Film, vodka is the numbing fuel for heartbreak across decades of Soviet life: drunk at celebrations that do not celebrate anything and passed across kitchen tables between housewives as easily as a bread and water.

Then there is *Irony of Fate*, Eldar Ryazanov's 1975 television film, which remains perhaps the most beloved piece of Soviet popular culture ever made and is still broadcast on Russian television every New Year's Eve. The premise is something akin to the 2009 movie *The Hangover*. A group of Moscow friends, following their annual New Year's Eve tradition at the bathhouse, drink so comprehensively that one of them is bundled onto a flight to Leningrad by the others as a joke. He wakes up in a city he does not recognize but which, in the relentless architectural uniformity of Soviet urban planning, contains a street with the same name as his own Moscow street, an apartment block identical to his building, and an apartment with a door that his key happens to fit. Only in a world flattened by ideological conformity and dulled by vodka, Ryazanov seems to suggest, could such confusion be possible. And yet the film is warmly comedic and the vodka-induced chaos produces love. In fact, it's probably the most optimistic thing Soviet cinema ever said about the drink.

What Soviet filmmakers could not quite say openly, the satirists slipped through in other forms. In *The Twelve Chairs* (1971), Leonid Gaidai's adaptation of the Ilf and Petrov novel, vodka finds itself as the grease of corruption. Nobody in Soviet satire is quite sober enough to be fully in control of themselves, which is the point: a population in a perpetual haze is a population that's easier to manage.

By the mid-1980s, the Soviet Union was running on borrowed time and borrowed roubles. Corruption was endemic, industry stagnant and the economy dangerously reliant on one liquid asset: vodka. With a full third of state revenue coming from alcohol taxes, vodka was soaking up an estimated 15 to 20 per cent of household budgets, and life expectancy for men was at a 50-year-low hovering at around 60 years. When Mikhail Gorbachev rose to power in 1985, promising to reform the system through *perestroika* (restructuring) and *glasnost* (openness), one of his first and boldest moves was a frontal assault on the Soviet love affair with drink.

What followed was a campaign that should have been a public health reform but played out like an attempted cultural exorcism. Gorbachev ordered the destruction of vineyards in Georgia, forced 90 per cent of the liquor shops in Moscow to close, limited opening times from 2pm to 7pm, and limited each person to two bottles only. In some districts of Moscow, vodka drinkers were known to queue for hours to secure a supply.

The effect on consumption was, at first glance, remarkable. Between 1985 and 1987, recorded alcohol sales fell by over 50 per cent, with some restaurants reporting sales plunging by 87 per cent, as customers stayed home. Key health indicators, especially mortality and workplace injuries, showed sharp improvement too. But beneath the surface, a different picture was fermenting. The crackdown hadn't quashed the taste for vodka at all – it had just driven it underground (again). Samogon surged with a vengeance, fuelling a booming black market and a flourishing second economy. The state lost control not just of consumption but also the tax revenue it provided. Gorbachev himself became extremely unpopular among hardened drinkers, leading to the following Russian joke:

'A man is waiting in line for vodka, but because of new Gorbachev laws, he's already been waiting for hours with no end in sight. He finally loses it and yells: 'I can't take this waiting anymore! I'm going straight to the Kremlin and I will kill this damn Gorbachev!' The man leaves but after an hour the people in the queue see him come back. 'So... have you done it?' whispers someone. The man replies: 'No. I got to the Kremlin, but the line to kill Gorbachev was even longer.'

Western observers, including the CIA, estimated that Gorbachev's anti-alcohol campaign cost the Soviet budget upwards of 57 billion roubles over its short lifespan, which was a financial deficit in a system that had no margin for error. By 1988, the state was staring down the barrel of a full-blown economic crisis. A nationwide survey revealed that 68 per cent of agricultural workers, 45 per cent of industrial labourers and nearly a quarter of the intellectual class were consuming homemade spirits regularly. Samogon had become a parallel institution. The campaign was quietly wound down before the decade was out, but its effect was to be fatal to the state.

The anti-alcohol campaign had exposed a fundamental contradiction at the heart of the Soviet project: a system that relied on its citizens' intoxication to fund itself could not simultaneously claim to be building a better society. And a regime that couldn't keep vodka on its shelves had, in the eyes of many citizens, forfeited the last argument for its own existence. It was one thread among many, but when the Soviet Union finally unravelled in December 1991, vodka's long entanglement with the state, as revenue source, social pacifier and political liability, came with it.

The story didn't end there though. Post-Soviet Russia inherited both the addiction and the dysfunction that flowed wherever vodka caps were cracked. Boris Yeltsin's government lifted price controls in January 1992 in attempt to rapidly transform Russia into a free market economy. Hyper-inflation ensued and official vodka prices rose sharply alongside everything else, wiping out savings and pushing millions into poverty almost overnight. The illicit market, already well-established from the samogon boom of the Gorbachev years, rushed to fill the gap. For those who could no longer afford state-produced spirits, cheap and often lethal surrogate alcohol filled the shelves. Yeltsin's administration lacked both the infrastructure and the political will to reassert control, an irony not lost on a population that watched their president's own relationship with the bottle play out on the evening news on any given evening.

But as the initial chaos of shock therapy gave way to a grim form of stability, the politics shifted. Keeping vodka affordable once again became a deliberate act of governance, as a way of managing a population with dwindling reasons for patience. By the mid-1990s, with an election looming, Yeltsin was candid enough to admit it: 'Some say that vodka is too cheap now and we should raise prices,' he told reporters, adding, 'But I haven't the courage to do so yet.' It was the oldest calculation in Russian political history.

Meanwhile, the story of Stolichnaya became one of the more dramatic legal sagas of the post-Soviet transition. The brand had been a state asset, and when the Soviet Union dissolved, the question of who actually owned it became deeply contested. The SPI Group, controlled by Russian businessman Yuri Shefler, acquired a licence to produce and sell Stoli internationally in the late 1990s following a series of privatization transactions. The Russian state, through the Federal Treasury and the state-owned spirits company FKP Soyuzplodoimport, spent years arguing in courts across Europe and North America that those transactions had been improper and that the international rights to the brand rightfully belonged to Russia. The litigation ran for the better part of two decades, grinding through Dutch, Latvian, American and British jurisdictions, with both sides scoring victories and reversals along the way. By the 2010s, the brand had effectively bifurcated: SPI Group continued marketing Stolichnaya internationally while Russia launched its own competing Stoli product for certain markets. It was a fitting equilibrium for a vodka that had always been less a single product than a projection of whoever needed it to be something.

Since 2009, SPI Group sourced its spirit from the Talvis distillery, a purpose-built modern plant that produces Alpha-grade alcohol at around 96% ABV. The spirit was not bottled at source but travelled by rail to Riga, Latvia, where finishing took place at the Latvijas Balsams facility, founded in 1900. The arrangement was a strangely apt one for a brand born from Soviet logistics. The same vodka that once represented the centralized might of Moscow was finished in the capital of a country that spent half a century under Soviet occupation. But following Russia's 2022 invasion of Ukraine, the brand was rebranded internationally as Stoli and base-spirit is now sourced from a distillery in Slovakia.

The 2000s brought a partial reassertion of state control in Russia more broadly. Rosspirtprom, a holding company, consolidated dozens of major

ABOVE During a visit to Washington D.C., Secret Service agents once found a drunk Boris Yeltsin in his underwear on Pennsylvania Avenue trying to hail a taxi to buy pizza.

LEFT A distillery worker fills bottles of Moskovskaya at the state-owned Kristall plant in Moscow, 1994.

distilleries, including the historic Kristall plant in Moscow, in an effort to restore oversight and secure the flow of capital. Excise duties were steadily raised and from 2009 minimum pricing was imposed, initially set at 89 roubles for a half-litre bottle. These measures stabilized revenue at around 300 billion roubles annually in the mid-2010s, equivalent to about 1.3 per cent of the federal budget. Recorded vodka sales declined, but excise receipts were secured, and the measures dovetailed with broader public health objectives as alcohol-related mortality began to fall.

And while the methods have modernized to include plastic jugs, pressure cookers and the occasional YouTube tutorial, the spirit of samogon remains defiantly the same: homemade, untaxed and frequently strong enough to strip paint.

Excise revenue from alcohol, once a pillar of the Soviet budget, would in time dwindle, as oil and gas took over as the economy's primary engine. Today it represents only around one per cent of state revenue, but Russia remains the biggest consumer of vodka in the world on a per capita basis at roughly half a bottle of vodka per person per month. Poland and Ukraine are not far behind.

The pattern is clear across centuries, however. Whether under tsar, general secretary or president, vodka has been treated as a revenue instrument. Its contribution has rarely fallen below material significance, and in certain periods – imperial Russia before 1914 and the USSR in the 1970s – it represented up to a third of all state income. Few commodities in history demonstrate such continuity of fiscal relevance; fewer still show the consequences so starkly when that role is disrupted – economically and socially, in the case of vodka. In Russian history, vodka has never been merely a consumer good, but a structural pillar of the entire system.

Russia's intense relationship with vodka survived two world wars, two revolutions and the dismantling of the Soviet Union in the 1990s and still remains one of the most enduring forces in the nation's psyche. It was the subject of Victor Erofeyev's 2002 Letter from Moscow feature in *The New Yorker*, entitled 'The Russian God'. Erofeyev wrote that just mentioning the word 'vodka' could cause unpredictable behaviour in Russians because 'It seems to punch a hole directly into the subconscious.' He went on to say that 'we are all held hostage by vodka', finishing the piece with: 'It menaces and it chastises, it demands sacrifices. It is both a catalyst of procreation and its scourge. It dictates who is born and who dies. In short, vodka is the Russian god.' Potent stuff.

PURE INVENTION

At the dawn of the 1980s, vodka was the bestselling spirit in the United States, shifting well over 30 million nine-litre cases a year. Bars poured it reflexively, consumers ordered it because it mixed easily and because it suited almost every occasion without drawing attention to itself. Commercial success had come through utility and inoffensiveness, but that story was nearly 50 years old now, and in spite of all of Smirnoff's success vodka remained the most anonymous bottle on the shelf.

Meanwhile, the rebellion against the steely, dry martinis of the mid-century had flipped the needle to the opposite end of the flavour dial. A new rulebook for cocktails had been written, and drinks began to inhabit bigger glasses and take on bolder colours. Everything got very sweet and sickly. The mid-1960s through to the mid-1980s (sometimes referred to as 'the Dark Ages of the cocktail') brought about three popular vodka drinks that looked starkly different to one another but that all followed the predictable formula of the era: spirit, liqueur, sweetened lengthener. The Harvey Wallbanger (1969), Blue Lagoon (1976) and Sex on the Beach (1982) all typify an era where cocktails were delivery mechanisms for alcohol dressed in fruit juice. They sold well but were not, by any rigorous standard, interesting to make or to drink.

Then suddenly, from an unexpected corner of the market, vodka found its personality.

We covered the first part of the Absolut story on page 83, when Lars Olsson Smith, the nineteenth-century Swedish distiller, made his fortune through rectification and founding the brand Absolut Rent Brännvin. A century later, with Swedish domestic spirits sales in decline and state campaigns pushing drinkers away from hard liquor, the state-owned alcohol monopoly Vin & Sprit perceived export as a commercial necessity. Its chief executive, Lars Lindmark, looked to the United States and saw the vodka trend, and in 1979 Vin & Sprit relaunched Smith's old idea for the American market. It would become one of the most strategically successful spirits launches in history.

The early responses to Absolut from American distributors were not encouraging, however. The bottle, based on an old Swedish apothecary flask discovered by Gunnar Broman and refined with colleagues at Carlsson & Broman, struck much of the trade as squat, plain and inelegant. That was precisely the point. Where Smirnoff had tended toward gilding and decoration, Absolut was stripped back, transparent and oddly confident. The name was seen as a problem too, with one early distributor famously telling Vin & Sprit that the only thing they would sell in America was 'absolute zero'.

That distributor turned out to be wrong.

The 1981 advertising campaign that changed not only vodka, but the wider field of brand marketing, was built by the New York agency TBWA. The brief

OPPOSITE Absolut reimagined vodka's place in the drinks market and reinvented brand marketing in the process...

ABSOLUT
Country of Sweden
VODKA®
This superb vodka
was distilled from grain grown
in the rich fields of southern Sweden
It has been produced at the famous
old distilleries near Åhus
in accordance with more than
400 years of Swedish tradition.
Vodka has been sold under the name
Absolut Since 1879.
80 PROOF
PRODUCED AND BOTTLED IN SWEDEN 1,0 LITER (33,8 FL. OZ.)
IMPORTED
ABSOLUT PERFECTION.
ABSOLUT VODKA. PRODUCT OF SWEDEN. 40 AND 50% ALC/VOL (80 AND 100 PROOF). 100% GRAIN NEUTRAL SPIRITS. ABSOLUT COUNTRY OF SWEDEN VODKA & LOGO, ABSOLUT, ABSOLUT BOTTLE DESIGN AND ABSOLUT CALLIGRAPHY ARE TRADEMARKS OWNED BY V&S VIN & SPRIT AB. ©1995 V&S VIN & SPRIT AB. IMPORTED BY THE HOUSE OF SEAGRAM, NEW YORK, NY.
THOSE WHO APPRECIATE QUALITY ENJOY IT RESPONSIBLY.

didn't give much to work with: a bottle with hardly any label, a liquid with no flavour, and no origin story beyond the word 'Sweden'. The solution was as elegant as it was simple – an image of the bottle, and a two-word caption in which the first word was always 'Absolut': Absolut Perfection; Absolut Heaven; Absolut Clarity. The bottle stayed the same, but the words changed, shifting to fit the mood and occasion.

The ads appeared in gay publications first, a deliberate choice by the campaign's early architects, who recognized that this community had spending power and cultural influence out of proportion to its marketing visibility. From there, the campaign spread to mainstream magazines and billboards. It was smart placement, but the real engine of the campaign's longevity was what came next.

In 1985 Andy Warhol painted the bottle, and the resulting Absolut Warhol advertisement appeared in 1986. Artist Keith Haring followed, then Francesco Clemente and Kenny Scharf, each blending their own contemporary style with the Absolut bottle. By the end of the decade, more than a hundred artists had contributed to what had become, in effect, a rolling programme of contemporary art patronage dressed as advertising. Over the 25-year lifespan of the campaign, the number of unique works would exceed 1,500. That stubby, supposedly inelegant bottle became an icon.

What Absolut did brilliantly was invent a new relationship between a spirit's brand and culture. Previous vodka marketing had leaned on heritage, imperial crests, Russian bloodlines and craft provenance.

ABOVE Andy Warhol's Absolut design in 1985, and Keith Haring's in 1986, answering the question, 'Can there be artistry in vodka?'

RIGHT Some of the Absolut flavoured range. Peppar arrived in 1986 and Citron in 1988, followed by 20 further variants of varying quality and credibility.

Absolut rejected all of that for a contemporary, unapologetically commercial approach that reimagined how vodka could show up in the market by placing itself in the worlds of art, fashion and urban culture, and doing so with wit, restraint and charm.

Absolut is made entirely in Åhus, a small town on the agricultural plain of Skåne in southern Sweden, which is unusual in an industry where base spirit routinely travels hundreds of miles before it reaches a finishing distillery. The wheat is grown on local farms, the water comes from a deep aquifer beneath the Skåne soil, and the distillation takes place within the same tightly controlled production system. The spirit is rectified to above 96% ABV through a multi-column process and bottled at 40% with no additives.

Absolut Peppar – the first modern flavoured vodka – arrived in 1986, made with green pepper extract to target the Bloody Mary market. Absolut Citron followed in 1988, and its timing would turn out to matter enormously. A lemon-forward vodka, clean and bright, it appeared at exactly the moment when a young New York bartender was looking for a base spirit to go with a pink drink he was trying to reinvent (more on that shortly).

Next came Absolut Kurrant, followed by Mandarin, Vanilia, Raspberri and more than 20 other variants including Cilantro, Acai Berry, Watermelon and something called Nights Nordic Spice.

Flavoured vodka was nothing new of course, but placing the flavour inside a commercially produced bottle that maintained its crystal-clear appearance was revolutionary. Stolichnaya and Smirnoff followed with flavoured iterations, and new cocktail trends were built off the back of vodkas that offered something tangible in the flavour department. Suddenly the base spirit of a cocktail could contribute aromatically to your drink, with a familiar taste that wasn't wedded to traditional spirit characteristics like oak and juniper.

Indeed, some brands became better known for their flavoured expressions than they did their core, unflavoured, product. Pölstar Vodka is one such example. Launched in 1996, it was made from a base of US grain spirit, which was shipped to Iceland where it was flavoured with cucumber essence and bottled as Pölstar Cucumber Vodka. Before Hendrick's Gin cornered the market on all things cucumber, Pölstar was a shining beacon of vegetal freshness in the UK that mixed very well with tonic. (Interestingly, the company that owns Hendrick's Gin – William Grant & Sons – bought Pölstar in 2002, quietly discontinued it and launched another Icelandic vodka brand, Reyka, in 2005.)

While we're on the subject of noteworthy Nordic vodka brands, another one worth a mention is Finlandia. Established in 1970 by Alko, Finland's state-owned alcoholic beverage company, it became the first Scandinavian vodka to be sold in the United States when it hit the shelves in 1971. Uniquely for the time, Finlandia grounded its marketing by focusing on its raw material and geography rather than heritage or prestige. The barley used to make Finlandia is distilled at the Koskenkorva facility in western Finland using seven columns averaging 25 m/82 ft in height, and then transported south to Rajamäki, where it is diluted with glacial water naturally filtered through sand and moraine formed by retreating Ice Age glaciers.

Finlandia's 'Frozen Ice' bottle was designed by the Finnish designer Tapio Wirkkala and conveyed the impression of an ice-cold drink from the Arctic North, with textured glass that glittered like an icicle and a label depicting two reindeer having a fight. Finlandia was an early entrant of the environmental and provenance arguments that would become standard practice in premium spirits marketing 20 years later, arriving slightly ahead of the cultural moment that could have made it a much bigger brand than it became.

Finlandia also played the flavoured vodka game, launching the first cranberry vodka in 1994 among other expressions. Its best release, by far, was Finlandia Grapefruit, which launched in 2007 and brilliantly captured the bitter zest of pink grapefruit skin.

By the early 2000s, there were literally hundreds of flavoured vodkas on the market and many bars of the era devoted huge backbar real estate to display as many of these products as possible.

Perhaps the most enduring product of this era (maybe because it wasn't technically from the era) was Żubrówka. Sitting somewhere between ancient infusion tradition and the modern flavoured vodka category, Żubrówka is made from a Polish rye vodka that is macerated with dried bison grass (*Hierochloe*

BELOW Finlandia's Wirkkala-designed bottle evoked Arctic ice before provenance was fashionable.

RIGHT This was the birthplace of Dick Bradsell's on-the-fly coffee liqueur, served cold. **LEFT** Żubrówka was one of the most popular vodka brands when I began bartending in 2001.

odorata). Its Western export push, which gained real momentum through the 1990s, carried with it a story of forests, wild bison and a flavour profile so distinctive that the coumarin compound responsible for its vanilla and almond notes was banned by US food safety regulators and required a reformulation for the American market.

'It smells of freshly mown hay and spring flowers,' wrote Somerset Maugham in *The Razor's Edge* (1944), 'of thyme and lavender, and is so soft on the palate and so comfortable, it is like listening to music by moonlight.'

The bartender-led vodka infusion movement arrived in the mid-to-late 1990s, when the generation of American and British bartenders who had grown up with the commercial flavoured vodkas began to realize they could make their own. House-infused vodkas, steeped in everything from fresh chillies and vanilla to black pepper, lemongrass, herbs, Skittles, beef jerky, sawdust and just about anything else that would fit through the neck of a bottle, became a mark of the more ambitious bar programmes of the era. The trick was to load up a bottle of vodka with whatever was close at hand, then seal it shut and let it stew on top of the espresso machine or put it through the glass washer on a hot cycle. Some of these infusions were genuinely creative and at the very least communicated a desire to innovate in the early years of modern mixology. The trend also produced a lot of undrinkable spirit.

These were the nascent years of the cocktail renaissance, as bartenders began to take a more culinary approach to cocktails, muddling fresh fruits and herbs, and squeezing fresh juices to order. In London that meant Dick Bradsell, who had begun behind the bar in the early 1980s. By the end of the decade, he was working in the bars and members' clubs of Soho that sat at the centre of British creative life: Fred's Club on Carlisle Street, The Groucho Club on Dean Street and later the Pharmacy in Notting Hill, designed by Damien Hirst. Dick had a gift for reading a room and for matching a drink to a moment and he was also technically precise in a way that was not common in British bartending at the time. His influence on a generation of UK bartenders who passed through those rooms is difficult to overstate.

In 1983, while working at the Soho Brasserie, Bradsell created what would become arguably the most culturally significant cocktail of the decade: the Espresso Martini. The story is well-documented: a young model came to the bar and asked for something that would 'wake me up and then f*** me up'. Dick later told writer Simon Difford that, 'the coffee machine was right next to the station where

I served drinks. It was a nightmare, as coffee grounds were everywhere, so coffee was very much on my mind. And it was all about vodka back then – it was all people were drinking.' Dick pulled a shot of espresso, combined it with vodka, coffee liqueur and sugar syrup, shook it hard, and strained it into rocks glass. The drink, originally dubbed Vodka Espresso, acquired several other names before finding its way into a martini glass in the 1990s and becoming the Espresso Martini.

The turn of the century was the era of the 'Neo Martini', in which any drink served in a V-shaped cocktail glass was granted the martini attribution regardless of what was in it (and most drinks were served in martini glasses). Neo Martinis were usually sugar-charged, vividly coloured and more often than not built on a vodka base: French Martini, Appletini, Porn Star Martini, Wasabi Martini, Polish Martini, Lemon Meringue Pie-tini – we won't get into the recipes for all these drinks but you get the idea. While it's easy to denigrate these drinks now, the format at the time worked for everyone because it gave bartenders creative freedom, offered consumers something that felt like a choice, and lent proceedings a degree of largely unwarranted sophistication by appending the word 'martini' to anything that fitted the glass.

One drink from this period did not quite belong to that trend, despite sharing its vessel, had been invented quietly in New York several years earlier. It then spread rapidly through the city's downtown bar scene and retreated again, before being rediscovered by the rest of the world in the late 1990s. It didn't need the martini attribution, because it already had a fantastic name of its own – Cosmopolitan.

The Odeon Restaurant was a converted 1930s automat in Tribeca, lower Manhattan, co-owned by a young Keith McNally, his then-wife Lynn Wagenknecht and his brother Brian. It opened in 1980 and quickly became one the essential rooms of New York's downtown creative world. Artists, writers, photographers and the people who moved between those worlds frequented it because it was open late, the food was reliable, and the atmosphere was precisely calibrated between accessible and cool. Warhol, Haring and Basquiat were all regulars.

It was at the Odeon, in 1988, that a young Toby Cecchini was tending bar. He had been in the job for only a year when a colleague, Melissa Huffsmith, arrived for a shift and mentioned a drink she'd encountered on a trip to San Francisco. She made it for him: rail vodka, Rose's lime juice, Rose's grenadine, shaken and poured into a V-shaped martini glass with a lemon twist. The drink, called a Cosmopolitan, tasted awful – but it looked great.

Later that night, making drinks for the waitstaff at the end of their shift, Toby came back to the Cosmopolitan and decided he could make a drink that looked the same but tasted better. The Odeon made its margaritas with fresh lime and Cointreau, which in the 1980s constituted an uncommon attention to detail for an industry swimming in sour mix, and Toby had absorbed that blueprint as his reference point for sour drinks.

Rose's grenadine went out. Fresh lime juice and Cointreau came in. Ocean Spray cranberry juice, which the bar kept for Cape Codders, replaced the grenadine as colorant. For the base, Cecchini reached for a bottle that had arrived just months earlier and that he and his colleagues had been experimenting with, mostly unsuccessfully. 'Absolut had come out with Citron several months prior,' he recalls. 'And when it came out, it was kind of hilarious because we were like 'oh my god, the flavour is inside the vodka!' It was mind-blowing to us. We were just like, that is the coolest thing ever!'

His new take on the Cosmopolitan was the perfect candidate for using the new citrus vodka. Two ounces of Absolut Citron, one ounce Cointreau, one ounce

Espresso Martini

50 ML/1⅔ FL OZ BELVEDERE VODKA
1 SHOT OF ESPRESSO
15 ML/½ FL OZ SUGAR SYRUP

Shake all of the ingredients with ice and strain into a chilled martini glass. Many recipes include coffee liqueur in the preparation of an espresso martini. This is optional, however, and I've always viewed it as largely pointless. Coffee liqueur is made from coffee, spirit, and sugar – the same ingredients as the above recipe, which begs the question, why add coffee liqueur to a drink that is already effectively a coffee liqueur?

LEFT The Odeon, in lower Manhattan. Toby Cecchini reinvented the Cosmopolitan here in 1988, then spent decades disowning it. **OPPOSITE** Absolut Citron in 1988. The lemon-forward vodka was the engine oil of the Cosmopolitan.

fresh lime juice, one ounce cranberry juice, shaken hard into a martini glass with a lemon twist. He poured it for one of the waitresses and a couple of her colleagues. They loved it. They wanted it every night. It became the staff drink for weeks, then months. Then regulars started asking for it by name, having heard about it from the staff. Then people Toby had never met started ordering it. Then he walked up the street to El Teddy's on West Broadway and saw them shaking something that looked familiar. 'There's some guy down at the Odeon making it,' they told him. 'Yeah,' he said. 'That's me.'

'Within months,' Toby recalls, it was 'everywhere in downtown New York and then within a year and a half it was like the thing that ate us alive.' By 1990 he was making 250 Cosmopolitans on a Friday or Saturday night, and the drink had become, as he would later put it, his albatross. He spent years publicly distancing himself from it, a decision that created space for other claimants. A Miami bartender named Cheryl Cook has pointed to an earlier, looser version using flavoured vodka, lime and cranberry that she called a Cosmopolitan. Others have placed variations in Georgia, San Francisco and various places in between.

Then *Sex and the City* began airing in 1998, and Carrie Bradshaw's Cosmopolitan became one of TV's most visible drinks orders. The cocktail Toby had invented for the Odeon's late-night staff, which had risen, saturated the downtown New York scene and then quietly retreated, was back. Globally this time.

By this point Dale DeGroff was serving Cosmopolitans at the Rainbow Room on the 65th floor of Rockefeller Plaza, finishing them with a theatrical twist of flamed orange zest, that got the attention of practically every bartender in the world. Dale never claimed to have invented the drink but was a huge contributor to its fame.

As the flagship drink for Absolut Citron, Absolut eventually investigated the competing stories of the drink's origin, sending a journalist to interview everyone who claimed credit. Toby's was the account that survived scrutiny, as it fitted with the documented release dates of Absolut Citron and with the testimony of the people who were at the Odeon that night.

The Cosmopolitan that most bars serve today is not the one Toby made. The proportions have drifted toward sweet, the cranberry has crept up until the drink glows red rather than blush, and the careful balance of citrus that made the original interesting is often misplaced. Toby is direct about this: 'It's exceedingly dry and even rather shrill. Bracingly dry. It needs to be super cold, super dry.'

A fact that passes many bartenders by is that the Cosmopolitan sits in the same (Daisy) family of cocktails as the Margarita, Sidecar and White Lady, and Toby's specifications place it there too – the addition of cranberry offering colour and a little dilution. That colour is a distraction in many ways, as the pink hue hides that truth that the Cosmopolitan is one of the only drinks that contains all three of the main citrus fruits: lemon (vodka), orange (liqueur) and lime (juice). It is the ultimate citrus drink, painted pink.

That attention to the details of balance and temperature that Toby communicated in the 1980s was rare among bartenders back then, but things were changing. A generation of bartenders in New York (Dale DeGroff, Sasha Petraske, Audrey Saunders, Julie Reiner), London (Dick Bradsell, Nick Strangeway, Dre Masso, Henry Bessant, Wayne Collins) and beyond were beginning to treat their work differently. Out went sour mix and in went sourcing fresh citrus. Out went sickly-sweet concoctions and in came reviving pre-Prohibition recipes. Bartenders were holding their drinks to a higher standard than had been seen for 50 years.

As the craft movement began to find its feet, an uncomfortable tension began to surface. The growing seriousness about technique and ingredient quality sat awkwardly alongside vodka's utility-first reputation, plus the fact that very few cocktail recipes from pre-prohibition America and prohibition-era Europe ever called for vodka (and those that did were more often terrible). In time, many of the best bartenders of the era begin to resist vodka's dominance, turning their attention to rum, whisky, brandy, gin, vermouth and bitters, even while still depending on vodka commercially. A spirit designed not to be tasted was a difficult fit for a revival built on celebrating flavour and provenance. Vodka demanded almost nothing from the person making the drink, and a craft movement premised on demanding everything had limited patience for that. Vodka's response to this challenge would prove multifaceted, and we will trace it across the next few chapters. But it came down to one simple aim: find a new reason to be noticed. The first move focussed not on what vodka tasted like in the glass, but about what the bottle looked like on the table. Somewhere in the background, a question was forming that the drinks industry had not previously taken seriously: could a neutral spirit be luxury? Could a category defined by the absence of character command a price that implied the opposite?

The answer was yes. But it required two things: a convincing story and a bottle that looked like it was worth the money. Both arrived before the century was out, from Poland, Holland and France, and they changed the vodka market permanently.

Cosmopolitan

The Cosmopolitan is one of cocktail history's misunderstood drinks. Toby Cecchini's 1988 original was bracingly dry, properly cold, only slightly pink and balanced across all three citrus fruits. The pink hue is a clever distraction that suggests berries and sweetness but is juxtaposed by citrus zing. Get the proportions right and you have a Margarita's sharper, more sophisticated cousin in disguise.

40 ML/1⅓ FL OZ ABSOLUT CITRON
20 ML/⅔ FL OZ COINTREAU
20 ML/⅔ FL OZ FRESH LIME JUICE
20 ML/⅔ FL OZ CRANBERRY JUICE

Shake the ingredients with ice until very cold and then strain into a chilled coupe glass. Toby's original recipe calls for a lemon twist as a garnish. Dale DeGroff made the more theatrical flamed orange twist famous while working at the Rainbow Room.

LIQUID GOLD

In the world of drinks, 'premium' is an adjective that has done so much work for so long that it has nearly worn through its meaning. It can suggest longer aged, better raw materials, higher strength or simply a harder-to-make product. There's usually something you can point to. In vodka, a spirit defined by regulation as neutral, colourless and without distinctive character that 'something' is much harder to locate. And that raises an uncomfortable question that the category has never quite managed to answer cleanly: when the liquid itself resists distinction, does premium mean anything beyond the price tag?

The audacity of the premium vodka proposition, when it arrived in force in the 1990s, was to build a category on something that technically speaking contained almost nothing that could be classed as premium. That it worked (and worked spectacularly) is one of the more instructive chapters in the history of modern marketing, and as much a part of the story of vodka as kabaks and cosmopolitans.

Premium vodka arrived fully with Absolut (as told in the last chapter) where vodka became a carrier of cultural signals. What may have looked like a cynical approach to marketing a flavourless product exposed genuinely new insights into how people use objects, including drinks, to say things about themselves. Vodka drinkers were sold not a taste or technique or even a romantic back story, but rather an idea about what being an Absolut drinker said about them.

The next step up was steeper, however, namely how you turn premium vodka into a luxury product. The challenge was taken on by a man in his late seventies, who had already made one fortune in the American spirits market by understanding that the power of suggestion is just as potent as flavour.

Sidney Frank was born in 1919 in rural Connecticut and built his first career through a combination of family connection and commercial instinct, eventually running a spirits import business. His most celebrated success until the late 1990s was Jägermeister, the German herbal digestif that had spent decades gathering dust on the bottom shelf of Central European bars. Frank looked at the bottle with its gothic script and strange deer-head label, and saw not an obscure after-dinner liqueur but a badge of rebellion waiting to be liberated. He leaned into the mystery, targeted college campuses, deployed an army of young brand ambassadors, and turned Jägermeister into a major brand.

In 1996, Frank was 76 years old and not in need of another project, but he dreamed up an idea anyway, and that idea became Grey Goose. The brief

OPPOSITE & ABOVE Sidney Frank built Grey Goose on price and packaging just when the market was ready for it.

he gave himself was blunt: create a vodka that would sell for more than anything else on the shelf – a lot more. 'Why don't I price my vodka extravagantly higher than Absolut,' he told *New York Magazine* in 2004, 'at wildly more profitable margins… and steal Absolut's market share that way?'

Grey Goose subsequently launched in 1997, retailing at $30 a bottle, almost double the price of Absolut. Frank basically sidestepped the competitive $15–17-a-bottle vodka market, and sat his product alongside single malt Scotch whiskies with 12 years of ageing behind them.

The liquid inside was made from French 'soft winter wheat' grown in the Picardie region, north of Paris, distilled in column stills by a Cognac cellar master, Francois Thibault, then shipped to Cognac and diluted with spring water from a limestone aquifer. The bottle was frosted glass with a painted grey goose in flight against a pale winter sky. Some early shipments were packaged in wooden crates like fine wines, exaggerating the sense of rarity and quality.

Grey Goose positioned itself not only as a vodka but as a French luxury product, drawing on France's centuries-long association with refined taste. At a moment when Absolut had established Sweden as a plausible source of premium vodka, and Polish brands were beginning to argue for Eastern European craft, Frank planted his flag in the country that most reliably communicated sophistication to an American consumer. He then let the price make the argument. Modern vodka is broadly speaking not a

ABOVE Belweder Palace in Warsaw, long associated with the Polish presidency, and the Belvedere bottle, distilled at Polmos Żyrardów since 1993.

product that can easily be assessed by conventional sensory means, and even spirits experts regularly fail blind tastings. Price and packagaing then becomes the primary signal of quality. If it costs more, a certain logic runs, someone somewhere must have decided it was worth more. That somebody, in the case of Grey Goose, was Sidney Frank. He decided it was worth more, and waited for the market to agree.

It agreed with impressive speed. In 2004, after just seven years, Frank sold Grey Goose to Bacardi for $2.2 billion. Few spirits brands in history have been created, grown and sold in so short a period for so much money. Frank, then 86, reportedly used some of the proceeds to throw a party for his employees. He died the following year. The hangover for the industry lasted considerably longer: every brand manager in every spirits company now had to account for why their vodka was not Grey Goose, which turned out to be an extremely productive question for the category's revenue (if not always for its honesty).

Where Grey Goose had constructed its premium credentials largely through marketing, Polish vodkas Belvedere and Chopin came with what they presented as something more grounded: specific ingredients, specific places and production decisions with genuine implications for the final spirit. Belvedere, named after Belweder Palace, which is long associated with the Polish presidency, was first distilled in 1993 at the Polmos Żyrardów facility, a distillery with roots going back to 1910. It launched in the United States in 1996, a year before Grey Goose, making a legitimate claim to have opened the super-premium category. Made from Polish rye grown on the Mazovian plains and water drawn from artesian wells near the distillery, Belvedere positioned its quality in terms that connected production to product: the character of Polish rye, the heritage of a particular distillery and a tradition reaching back centuries. Also, being a rye vodka meant that a certain peppery spice and oily texture could differentiate the product from wheat and barley vodkas.

Chopin, also Polish and named after the composer Fryderyk Chopin, went further, offering single-ingredient expressions made from potato, rye or wheat, each producing a discernibly different spirit. Potato-based vodka does have a creamier mouthfeel and character compared to grain-based spirit, sometimes exhibiting mild vanilla or marshmallow notes. Here, for once, the premium claim corresponded to something in the glass – so long as you are drinking it neat or were very restrained in the mixing.

The Dutch entry came via a different kind of pedigree entirely. Ketel One is produced at the Nolet distillery in Schiedam, a small city west of Rotterdam that was once one of the most concentrated distilling centres in the world, home to over 100 genever distilleries. The Nolet family has distilled there for 11 generations, with a founding date of 1691. The vodka, launched in 1983, takes its name from the distillery's oldest pot still, a brick-jacketed, coal fired copper vessel installed in the nineteenth century. A portion of each batch is re-distilled through this pot and others, and rested in underground tiled vats, contributing a softness and textural complexity that very subtly sets Ketel One apart from most column-distilled spirits. Here was a vodka that was attempting to trade off historic tradition, craft, and family legacy. Ketel One Vodka is now a joint partnership between the Nolets and Diageo, with the family retaining the brand rights and ownership of the distillery.

By the turn of the century, these brands and a few others occupied a new tier in the market, one that had not existed a decade earlier and would have been unimaginable to an eighteenth century Russian serf. Consumers were paying serious money for vodka and, increasingly, wearing that choice publicly.

The unique economics of the nightclub had a great deal to do with this. Bottle service – the practice of purchasing a whole bottle of spirits delivered to a reserved table with an assortment of mixers and ice – had been developing in the VIP rooms of London and New York

BELOW Schiedam was once home to over 100 genever distilleries. The Nolet family has distilled here since 1691 and Ketel One takes its name from their nineteenth-century pot still.

through the early to mid-1990s, before reaching its most bespangled industrial form in Las Vegas and Miami in the following decade. The practice had little to do with the spirit inside the bottle, and more to do with conspicuous consumption – a way of purchasing territory within a venue and broadcasting, to anyone who could see the table, exactly how much that territory had cost. The sparklers arrived with the bottle not to celebrate anything in particular but to draw maximum attention to the moment of delivery.

Vodka dominated this economy because it mixed without friction, suited any palate, and made no demands on the buyer's knowledge. A table of 12 people could agree on vodka in a way that they could not agree on rum, whisky or gin. Crucially though, the bottle had to look right, which is where the premium brands earned their table space. The emerging brands of the luxury sector were packaged like ornaments or trophies, with frosted glass, elaborate stoppers, heavy bases and silk-screened labels that read as expensive from a distance (which was the distance from which they were most often seen).

Leading vodka brands soon commanded massive budgets for promoting and packaging their product as the luxury choice. If you're making whisky, Cognac or rum, a large share of the bottle's value is tied up in sourcing and processing ingredients, labour-intensive production, and time, where years or decades of maturation lock capital away in warehouses. Vodka suffered none of these constraints. The spirit could be fermented, distilled, filtered and bottled in a matter of days, and it was cheap to make entirely because the process had been so perfectly industrialized. Like the rest of the luxury goods sector, vodka now enjoyed low production costs alongside a high price tag, and the money saved was diverted into fancy packaging and extravagant promotions.

The turn of the millennium was not a time for subtlety. The music was loud, the clothes were loud, the money was loud, and the drugs that moved through the nightclubs of London, New York and every city that wanted to think of itself as culturally adjacent to those two were not, in the main, designed to slow anything down.

Cocaine and vodka occupied the same place on the social register for most of this period. Both were odourless, both were associated with the same venues, the same faces, the same late hours. Cocaine suited vodka in the way that it suited the decade generally: it rewarded function over flavour, left no obvious trace and was reassuringly expensive. A spirit that prided itself on not announcing itself was a natural companion for a drug that prided itself on exactly the same thing. The drinks industry knew it even if it did not say so publicly.

The mid-1990s were a period of unusual cultural confidence in the UK. Bands like Oasis, Blur, Pulp and Elastica occupied tabloid front pages in ways that rock acts had not since the 1970s. The superclub circuit – Ministry of Sound in London, the Haçienda in Manchester, Cream in Liverpool – was at its peak. Vodka Red Bull had arrived from Austria, where Dietrich Mateschitz, a businessman from Graz, had launched Red Bull in 1987 after licensing the formula from a Thai energy drink called Krating Daeng and adapting it for the European palate. The product found its natural habitat almost immediately in the nightclub. In the UK, the combination became the functional drink of the club era: inexpensive, ubiquitous and formulated to keep you upright until five in the morning.

The UK even had its own satirical precursor to *Sex and the City* six years earlier, where women drank vodka heavily, dressed aggressively and conducted their emotional lives loudly. Jennifer Saunders and Joanna Lumley's *Absolutely Fabulous* made Stolichnaya into both a fashion accessory and a comedy weapon. Patsy Stone's relationship with Stoli was essentially the show's running joke about aspirational consumption gone completely feral. Generous measures of 'Stoli & Boli' did something interesting to the utilitarian Soviet vodka brand though, making it both funny and glamorous.

Perhaps the idea for combining vodka and Champagne came from Dick Bradsell who, in 1988, invented the Russian Spring Punch while working at the Zanzibar Club or possibly Fred's in Soho. The drink spread through London bars quickly through the 1990s – it's one of those cocktails that gets ordered once out of curiosity and twice because it's better than you expected.

Though she was unpaid, Joanna Lumley may have been vodka's first modern celebrity ambassador. The world had already seen Absolut partner with Warhol and Smirnoff with Woody Allen and Zsa Zsa, but what arrived next represented a deeper relationship between brand and individual. Where those earlier arrangements had essentially been licensing deals, a famous face attached to a campaign for a fee and a photograph, the new model asked celebrities to become the living embodiment of a brand, present at every launch, opening bottles, and becoming a participant in the cultural moments that the brand wanted to occupy. This model reached its most consequential precipice in 2007, when Diageo struck a partnership with Sean Combs, then known professionally as Diddy, to promote Cîroc Vodka.

Cìroc was an unusual product to begin with. It launched in 2003 as a partnership between the French producer Jean-Sébastien Robicquet and spirits giant Diageo. Robicquet's family had been in the wine business for four centuries, which was a good fit because Cîroc was to be made from grapes rather than grain: Ugni Blanc and Mauzac Blanc varieties from the Gaillac region.

The original idea for the product came from the legendary drinks innovator David Gluckman. This was the man behind Bailey's Irish Cream Liqueur, The Singleton, Tanqueray Ten and Smirnoff Black – a premium line extension of Smirnoff Vodka that was launched in the US in 1995. Smirnoff Black is made by taking regular Smirnoff and redistilling it in a copper pot still with a small amount of new-make (un-aged) whisky. The inclusion of new-make whisky was a move that sat right on the edge of vodka legality, and even to this day is not something the brand publicly talk about. It was a stroke of genius though, as the resulting spirit offers genuine character, with a subtle maltiness hints at what vodkas from the mid-nineteenth century and before might have tasted like.

The idea for Cîroc came to David in the 1990s when he was in Tbilisi, Georgia, on the search for inspiration for a new line of Smirnoff products that would each use a different cereal as its base material as a nod to agricultural diversity across Russia and the former Soviet states. 'In Georgia they don't grow much grain because it's too warm,' David told me. 'Instead they make brandy and a kind of grape vodka called *chacha*.'

Aware of the old mantra that you should 'never mix grape and grain', David's idea was a vodka made from grapes that might suit a night of wine drinking.

Like Smirnoff Black and Ketel One, Cìroc was made from a rectified spirit that was redistilled in copper pot stills. This, along with the use of grapes as a raw material, gave Cìroc a faintly different character to most vodka – lighter, with a trace of fruit (citrus more than grapes) that regulation required to be minimized but could not eliminate entirely.

Sales of Cìroc were slow at first. Diageo decided that they needed someone to change that and found the model for doing so in Sean Combs. The Cìroc arrangement was structured not as a conventional endorsement, which had been the norm up until this point, but as a genuine business partnership.

Russian Spring Punch

The origin story of the Russian Spring Punch goes that a couple of friends were throwing a party they couldn't quite afford, and Dick Bradsell's solution was to stock the bar with glasses pre-loaded with vodka, lemon juice, sugar and cassis, then have guests bring their own Champagne. Better bottles got a better drink. Bradsell later described the drink as 'basically a spiked Kir Royal over ice,' and the name followed the same logic: Russian because it's vodka, spring because it's fresh, and punch because it follows the blueprint for a punch (strong, sweet, sour, lengthener, aromatic or spice). By Dick's account, it was lethal, with people falling down the stairs and dancing around in wild abandon, much like an episode of *Absolutely Fabulous*.

50 ML /1⅔ FL OZ STOLICHNAYA VODKA
20 ML/⅔ FL OZ FRESH LEMON JUICE
15 ML/½ FL OZ CRÈME DE CASSIS
5 ML/1 TSP SUGAR SYRUP
CHAMPAGNE OR DRY SPARKLING WINE, TO TOP UP

Build in a Collins glass over ice. Add the vodka, lemon juice, cassis and sugar syrup. Give a stir and then top up slowly with Champagne. Finish with another gentle stir and garnish.

Combs would take half the brand's profits in exchange for driving its commercial growth, giving him a stake in the outcome rather than a flat fee for his image. Cìroc subsequently became embedded in hip-hop culture with a thoroughness that no advertising campaign could have manufactured: music videos, live performances, lyrics, social media. In 2009, Combs even performed a live blind tasting on *The Ellen DeGeneres Show*, appearing to pick out Cìroc among a vodka set that included Ketel One and Absolut, 'I can tell it's mine because it's the smoothest,' he declared proudly.

Combs helped build a cultural context for Cìroc and introduced a world in which Cìroc was the drink of a particular kind of success. By 2012, the brand was selling in excess of two million cases a year.

What Combs and Diageo had demonstrated, and what the industry studied with close attention, was that the right celebrity with genuine commercial involvement could generate growth that would require many multiples of a standard marketing budget to achieve by conventional means. The lesson rippled outward and, in the decade that followed, barely a major spirits brand existed without a celebrity attachment, and barely a major celebrity existed without a spirits brand attached to them.

The Cìroc relationship between Diageo and Combs came to a messy end in June 2023, though it couldn't have happened sooner from Diageo's perspective as, in late 2023, Sean Combs faced civil allegations, including allegations of rape and sex trafficking. Federal criminal charges were announced in September 2024. Diageo claimed that Combs made 'nearly a billion dollars over the course of [the] 15-year relationship'.

The celebrity vodka sector produced both genuine commercial successes and a quantity of novelty items selling the name and the bottle shape rather than anything you might reasonably want to drink. Crystal Head, launched in 2008 by the actor Dan Aykroyd and the painter John Alexander, occupied a position somewhere between the two. The spirit inside was a respectable Canadian vodka, made from Newfoundland water and filtered

LEFT & BELOW Cîroc launched in 2003 as a collaboration between a French wine maker, a global spirits giant and a hip-hop artist.

through Herkimer diamonds, a form of extremely clear quartz crystal. The bottle was a glass skull. It was striking, in a gothic sort of way, and the sort of bottle you felt bad about throwing away when it was empty. The brand sold well, and Aykroyd proved to be a genuine enthusiast rather than a passive face on a label, and his conviction, however unusual its premise, gave the brand an energy that distinguished it from most celebrity novelty products.

Trump Vodka sits firmly in the latter category. Launched in 2005, remarkably, it was probably the first celebrity-backed vodka brand of the modern era, though in this instance the celebrity in question – Donald Trump, a teetotaller – has gone on record saying he has never tasted the product. With the accompanying tagline 'success distilled' the spirit was originally produced by Drinks Americas in the Netherlands from a base of wheat. The tall gold bottle flopped in the US, but enjoyed some success in Russia, before the brand was quietly discontinued in 2011.

Or so we thought.

While Trump Vodka vanished from American shelves, it quietly found a second life in Israel, where it was sold as a kosher-certified product made from potatoes. With Trump's political rise after 2015, Israeli demand increased, especially after his recognition of Jerusalem as Israel's capital in 2017. A vodka that couldn't survive in its home market had become both a geopolitical souvenir and passover luxury.

Then, in 2016, a Jerusalem Post investigation found that many Trump Vodka bottles on Israeli shelves were not actually kosher at all, and the manufacturer had bottled vodka made from unspecified leavened (grain) ingredients. Police subsequently raided a warehouse in Haifa and uncovered bottles carrying counterfeit kosher certification labels.

Then, in another plot twist befitting of the name on the bottle, in 2025 Eric Trump announced the brand's US relaunch, with pre-orders opening on Black Friday under the tagline 'The Great American Spirit'. The new version is made from corn, bottled in Miami and certified gluten-free. The golden tower bottle is gone. So is the original tagline.

By the mid-2000s, the premium vodka boom had produced an awkward problem for the category it had created. The shelves of any serious bar now held a considerable selection of bottles, each asserting exceptional provenance, artisanal production and superior quality. Terms like 'luxury', 'ultra-premium', 'craft' and 'handcrafted' had been applied so broadly that they had shed almost all meaning. Filtration through activated charcoal, quartz sand, silver-impregnated carbon and materials approaching the mystical had all been deployed as marketing narratives. Bottles had been embossed, frosted, hand-blown and encrusted. Distillation counts climbed, water sources were glorified and grains acquired single-estate and organic status.

The problem was that vodka had been defined precisely by its resistance to the kind of sensory differentiation these claims implied. In theory, you could produce a technically excellent vodka with carefully selected grain, longer fermentation, skilled distillation and restrained filtration, because making those moves would produce a more interesting and complex spirit. But the regulatory framework governing vodka in most markets was designed to minimize, not celebrate, the evidence of those choices in the finished product. The luxury tier had made enormous amounts of money and brought many new consumers to the category, but it had done so partly on a promise that the spirit could be something that it couldn't. All of which begs the question: what is vodka?

WHAT IS VODKA?

The ice bucket arrives at the table. It's flanked by two sparklers fizzing white light across the white leather booth. The music pumps on the dance floor as the waitress pours from the frosted magnum of vodka. The liquid is clear, cold and faintly viscous. It's topped off with a colourful mixer, and the first sip goes down without resistance. The bottle cost this Ibiza club €50. They have sold it to you for €1000. The difference between these two numbers is the business model, and vodka, because it is cheap to produce and commands a price that bears no relationship to its production cost, is the most profitable spirit this nightclub can sell. The economy of this venue – the lighting rig, the door staff, the DJ, the podium dancers – is underwritten by the difference between what that liquid costs to make and what you are willing to pay for it in this setting.

But if we rewind far enough back, the scene changes completely.

All vodka begins its life in a field.

Before the milling, cooking, fermentation, distillation, filtering and dilution with water, long before the liquid is put in an expensive bottle and sent to Miami, Ibiza, Las Vegas or Dubai, someone had to decide what this vodka will be made from.

Wheat is the most common base material among global vodka brands. It produces a spirit that tends toward softness and a faintly sweet, clean profile, which is why the majority of large commercial vodkas use it. Absolut, Grey Goose, Ketel One, and practically all Russian vodkas (Stolichnaya, Russian Standard, Imperia, Beluga, Moskovskaya) are made from wheat. Wheat is cheap, widely available and relatively easy to process.

Rye is the traditional grain of Polish vodka, and it produces a spirit with more body, a peppery spice and a faintly oily texture. If you have ever tasted Wyborowa, Belvedere or Chopin's rye expression alongside a wheat vodka, the difference is instantly apparent, even after extensive rectification. Rye is harder to work with than wheat because the grain is rich in beta-glucans and arabinoxylans – non-starch polysaccharides that form a thick, sticky gel when mixed with hot water. The resulting mash is considerably more viscous than a wheat mash, which clogs pumps, slows heat transfer, and makes the whole system more prone to foaming during fermentation. Rye also yields less fermentable sugar per kilogram than wheat, so you need more grain per litre of alcohol. But it carries flavour in a way that wheat does not, which is why Polish producers have historically been willing to absorb those costs.

Corn is the grain of choice for much of the American vodka industry including American-made Smirnoff (wheat is used elsewhere) as well as what is now the country's largest-selling brand, Tito's Handmade Vodka. At least two other entrants from Texas – Dripping Springs and Deep Eddy – also use corn as a base, but it is much less common outside of the US and Canada. Corn spirit tends to be rounder and slightly vegetal, sometimes with a suggestion of sweetcorn on the nose. It is usually the cheapest

grain, abundant in the US, and the equipment knowhow for processing it into neutral spirit at industrial scale is already there, originally built to supply the bourbon and ethanol industries.

Barley appears in some Scandinavian products as well as a few smaller, craft brands who make vodka alongside whisky. Finlandia, for example, uses six-row barley grown in Finland, distilled at the Koskenkorva facility in the western part of the country. Finland's leading domestic vodka brand, Koskenkorva, also use barley as a base. Reyka is a barley-based vodka, its base spirit originating from the Girvan whisky distillery in Scotland. Barley vodkas sometimes have a slightly nutty, biscuity quality, with a hint of toasted grain or mild cocoa, and a drier finish than wheat.

ABOVE A country road through a Russian wheat field is a stark contrast to the places where Russian vodka is consumed today. **BELOW** Potatoes yield a noticeably creamier vodka, but cost two to three times more than wheat, which deters most producers.

You typically need 700–850 g/1 lb 10–1 lb 12 oz of barley, corn, wheat or rye (costing between £0.11 and £0.14 based on 2026 commodity prices) to make a 70 cl bottle of vodka. Switch to potato, however, and the material cost jumps two or three fold. You need around 2.7 kg/6 lbs of potatoes to make a bottle of vodka, the mash and subsequent waste are harder to handle and the fermentation is slower. Put all this together and potato vodkas can cost five times as much to make as grain spirits. But

potatoes produce a vodka with a distinctly creamy mouthfeel, sometimes accompanied by mild vanilla or marshmallow notes. Potato vodkas are often detectable in a blind tasting and it is the reason brands like Chopin, Karlsson's Gold, Ogilvy, Boyd & Blair, Vestal and Chase have built their brand identities around the ingredient.

Chase was founded by William Chase (who made his first fortune with Tyrrells potato crisps before selling 75 per cent of the business for around £40 million) in 2008. He took delivery of a copper column still and began distilling vodka from King Edward, Maris Piper and Lady Claire potatoes grown on his own farm. The potatoes were harvested in late summer, stored in dark cold rooms, peeled, mashed at 95°C/203°F, fermented, and distilled through a 22-m/72-ft copper column. The whole process, from soil to bottle, took place within the same postcode. It was a remarkably ambitious project for an English distillery in 2008. However, Chase was sold to Diageo in 2021, the distillery closed not long after, and production was moved to Diageo's massive Cameronbridge distillery in Scotland. As of 2026, 'potato' seems to have been quietly removed from their marketing materials.

Beyond the traditional cereals and potatoes, a growing number of vodkas are made from materials that would have puzzled a nineteenth-century Polish or Russian distiller.

Grapes provide the base for Cîroc as well as other brands found in notable wine-producing regions: The Guillotine brand is distilled in a 100-year-old distillery in Aÿ-Champagne, France, using Pinot Noir, Pinot Meunier and Chardonnay grapes; Idol is made from Pinot Noir and Chardonnay grapes in the Burgundy wine region. Over in Australia, Cooranbong and Bombora brands both use grapes from the Barossa Valley. In California, Hanson of Sonoma use organic Sonoma grapes, and in Alameda, Hangar One combine wheat and grapes for production of their vodka. Founded by Jorg Rupf and Lance Winters of St. George Spirits in 2002, the grape component of Hangar One typically accounts for 10–20 per cent of the blend, and it gives the liquid a faintly floral texture. Rupf sold the brand to Proximo Spirits in 2010.

Grapes are by far the most expensive material used to make vodka. You need around 4 kg/9 lbs of grapes for every bottle, which can cost from anywhere from £2.00 to £4.00 ($2.70–$5.40) – up to 25 times the price of a grain alternative. Grape vodkas can offer a mildly citric or floral quality, so when you put it all together the 'ultra-premium' positioning isn't entirely marketing fiction.

At the other end of the cost scale there is sugar beet molasses (the byproduct from refining sugar beets into sugar) the latter of which is widely used in industrial European neutral spirit production and for white label brands, where the cost per bottle there can be as little as £0.08, and ready-to drink products (RTDs). Sugar beet molasses comes at a cost to flavour however, where even with aggressive distillation and filtration, a burnt, vegetal note can sometimes be detected.

The sugar beet itself is also used by some producers, such as BĒT, in Minnesota, who produce a vodka from what is effectively table sugar refined from sugar beets. Then, in the UK's Lake District, Grasmere Sugarbeet Vodka is made from 'turnip wine', where the beets are mashed and fermented in-house, producing a spirit with subtle fruity notes.

Liquid whey is another of the more exotic ingredients used to make vodka. The byproduct left after milk has been separated into curds for cheesemaking, whey has almost no commercial value at the farm gate, and is typically sold for animal feed for pennies per litre. You need about 20 litres/5¼ gallons of whey to make a 70 cl bottle of vodka, but that still keeps the typical cost below £0.50 a bottle. What makes it expensive to produce is everything that comes after. Lactose doesn't ferment with standard distiller's yeast, so specialist strains are required, and the resulting milk beer is weak enough to demand significant energy and labour to bring it up to distillation strength. Black Cow, the West Dorset dairy farm that put the whey vodka category on the map, and a handful of other producers have

ABOVE Pinot Noir grapes used by Cîroc and others; sugar beet, the cheapest base material; sorghum, popular with so-called 'gluten-free' craft distillers; and whey separated from curds, the byproduct powering Black Cow Vodka.

followed the same logic: Broken Shed in New Zealand's Southern Alps, Copper Crow in Wisconsin – the first Native American-owned distillery in the United States – and Hartshorn in Tasmania, which makes its vodka from sheep's whey in batches of 80 bottles at a time. Since whey from cheesemaking is frequently a waste product, there is a reasonably strong sustainability argument to be found among the whey vodka category.

Rice, which trades at roughly the same price as other cereals, is used by a small number of producers in Asia and increasingly by craft distillers elsewhere, yielding a very clean, light spirit. Sorghum appears in some African production and has attracted attention from American craft distillers keen to market their vodka as gluten-free. It's worth noting however that gluten, the protein present in wheat, barley, rye and spelt, does not pass through the rectification process that all vodka must undergo. It is simply not there in the finished distillate of any unflavoured vodka, regardless of base material.

While large molecules like gluten don't pass through the still, smaller aromatic molecules do leave a trace in the finished spirit, which can signal what the product was made from. The legal and commercial tension at the heart of modern vodka is that regulation has historically asked the production process to erase those traces, while marketing has increasingly asked the consumer to notice them.

Whatever the raw material, the first task in production is always the same: convert starch into sugar and sugar into alcohol. If you're working with grain, the starch must be released from the kernel by milling, then broken down into fermentable sugars. This is done by adding hot water and enzymes, either from malt (the traditional method) or from commercially produced enzyme preparations (almost universally in modern practice). The result is a warm, sweet liquid called a wort in English, *brzeczka* in Polish and *suslo* in Russian.

Potatoes follow a similar path, though the starch requires more aggressive treatment. The tubers are typically mashed with water at temperatures above 90°C/194°F for 30 minutes or longer. Enzyme addition is essential, and the resulting mash (*zacier* in Polish; *braga* in Russian) is thicker and more difficult to pump and manage than a grain mash.

Yeast is then added, and fermentation begins. Most large-scale vodka producers use continuous fermentation, where fresh wort/mash is fed into one end of a series of fermenters and fermented beer is drawn off the other. Fermented beer/wash typically sits somewhere between 8 and 12% ABV, depending on the raw material and the yeast strain. Some producers, notably those making premium or craft claims, ferment for longer and at lower temperatures, which can produce more of the delicate, fruity flavour compounds that may or may not carry some character into the finished spirit.

Absolut Elyx, the single-estate luxury expression from Åhus, uses a proprietary yeast and ferments for roughly 48 hours to around 10% ABV, in batches kept separate from the standard Absolut production. Stoli Elit claims a 72-hour fermentation with fresh yeast. These are subtle differences, but in a category where the raw materials and the distillation process are designed to converge toward neutrality, they represent a rare moment where a producer can introduce genuine variation beyond the base material.

The column still remains the foundational technology of vodka production. A modern vodka distillery typically runs a series of connected columns, each performing a different function. The first, sometimes called the beer column or wash column,

uses steam to strip the alcohol from the fermented liquid. The second, the rectification column, pushes the spirit to very high purity by selecting only the fraction of the spirit vapour with a specific boiling point and removing nearly all of the water. Additional columns may follow to remove specific unwanted compounds: a hydro-selection column uses water to capture fusel oils (isoamyl alcohol, amyl alcohol and isobutyl alcohol), which have hot, solvent-like characteristics; while a methanol column separates out methanol and other light fractions from the spirit. Methanol is almost indistinguishable from ethanol in smell and taste, but highly toxic, so a methanol column is more about safety and meeting regulations

ABOVE In a modern vodka distillery, fermented beer or wine feeds into a series of connected columns (and sometimes a pot), each with a specific job: stripping alcohol from wash, rectifying to high purity, capturing fusel oils and removing methanol. The near-neutral spirit is then diluted, filtered and bottled.

(the EU permits 0.0375 g methanol per litre of 37.5% spirit) than taste.

The spirit that emerges from a well-run multi-column system typically sits between 95 and 96.5% ABV. At this strength, very little of the original raw material's character survives.

It is worth pausing on the phrase 'six times distilled' or 'ten times distilled' that appears on many vodka labels. In a modern column still, the spirit vapour rises through a series of perforated plates, condensing and re-evaporating at each level. Each plate performs what is effectively a single distillation. A column with 40 plates therefore achieves 40 small distillations in a single pass. When a brand claims its vodka is 'distilled six times' it may mean the spirit has passed through six separate columns, but in reality all vodkas are distilled many more times than that in order to achieve the necessary strength and purity.

Speaking of column stills… not all 'vodka distilleries' have one. A significant number of vodka brands, including some of the most successful in the world, do not distil their own base spirit. Instead, they purchase grain neutral spirit (GNS) from large industrial distilleries and then optionally redistil, filter, dilute and bottle it at their own facility. The major GNS suppliers in the United States include Archer Daniels Midland (ADM), Midwest Grain Products (MGP) and Grain Processing Corporation (GPC), companies whose names are unknown to most vodka consumers but whose output fills a remarkable share of the bottles on the shelf.

Tito's Handmade Vodka, which has grown from a single pot-still in Austin, Texas, to become the best-selling vodka in America, is the most prominent example of this model. Bert Butler 'Tito' Beveridge II obtained the first legal distilling permit in Texas since Prohibition in 1995, and built his early reputation on a small-scale operation, from making flavoured spirits at home and giving them to friends, then gradually teaching himself to distil using improvised copper stills built from pipe fittings and outdoor fryers. The growth that followed was extraordinary. By 2016, the brand was selling approximately 3.8 million nine-litre cases in the United States, representing a seven per cent market share.

But growth at that scale requires a supply chain that no single pot still can support. The corn-based neutral spirit that forms the bulk of every bottle of Tito's is produced at one or more of those industrial distilleries and trucked to Austin, where it is redistilled through one of ten copper pot stills, cut with water and filtered through activated charcoal. Practically every word of the tagline 'Handmade Vodka Crafted in an Old Fashioned Pot Still by America's Original Microdistillery' has been contested over the years, and it became the subject of a 2014 class-action lawsuit alleging that the description was misleading. Tito's settled the case, adjusted some of its language, and kept growing. Smirnoff is still a bigger brand globally, but Tito's has largely confined to the US – until 2026 that is, as they plan for a European launch.

Reyka offers a different variation on the same sourced spirit model. The brand, owned by William Grant & Sons, starts with neutral grain spirit distilled at the company's Girvan facility in Ayrshire, Scotland, producing base spirit that is also used to make Hendrick's Gin. The spirit is shipped to Iceland, where it is cut with water from the Grábrók spring and redistilled through a 3,000-litre/790 gallon copper Carter Head still. During distillation, the vapour passes through a basket of lava rock, intended to purify the spirit in a manner analogous to charcoal filtration. The distillery in Borgarnes, a coastal town of fewer than 2,000 people, runs on geothermal energy and has zero emissions. It is a neat story, and a smart looking brand, but the alcohol in the bottle was made from Scottish grain by a Scottish distillery.

LEFT Reyka vodka and the Icelandic town of Borgarnes. The base spirit is distilled at William Grant's Girvan facility in Scotland, then redistilled in Iceland.

Ketel One (see p169) is another high-profile brand that buys in their wheat-based neutral spirit and then processes it in-house to produce their vodka. This is not a scandal, but rather how much of the vodka industry has come to work – and indeed, did work – in Russia, prior to the twentieth century.

The question remains though, does redistillation in a pot still actually do anything to the spirit? By the time a vodka has been column-distilled to the legally required minimum strength, it is already close to pure ethanol. The case for then running it through a copper pot still rests on two claims. The first, that copper strips out residual sulfurous compounds by reacting with them to form copper sulfide. This is true, and it's why copper is used in the production of most whiskies, brandies and many rums. However, the effect is rendered redundant at the level of purity produced by a well-run column distillation, where all of the sulfurous compounds have already been stripped out. The second claim is that copper actively generates fruity and floral esters through catalytic reactions. This has some support in the research literature, but applies far more meaningfully to spirits distilled at much lower strengths (like whisky, brandy and rum) where there are enough congeners present for the copper to interact with. For a near-neutral spirit, the effect is marginal at best. Some producers genuinely believe the redistillation adds a subtle roundness or textural quality to the finished vodka, and it may do, but attributing that with any certainty to the copper rather than the base material, the water or method of filtration is difficult. Like so much of the modern vodka category, the pot still is more a story than it is a flavour modifier.

Even if a copper pot still can engender some character into a product, the next part of the production story after distillation is filtration, where the goal is once again to strip character from the product. We already learned about the history of filtration in vodka, from Lowitz's charcoal experiments in eighteenth-century St Petersburg through to Ostrejko's activated carbon patents and the modern industrial process. In modern production, charcoal filtration remains almost universal, though the specifics vary enormously.

Most large producers dilute their spirit to 40–50 per cent and pass the spirit through columns packed with activated carbon made from coconut shell, birch or other hardwoods. The alcoholic strength of the liquid is important, because the trace quantities of organic compounds being removed (esters, ketones, higher alcohols) have a stronger affinity for water than for ethanol. Diluting the spirit first pushes those compounds into the water component, where activated carbon can adsorb them more efficiently. Contact time, flow rate, pressure and the age and grade of the carbon all affect the result. Stoli Elit makes a further adjustment, employing a proprietary 'freeze filtration' process in which the spirit is chilled to -18°C/-0.4°F before passing through carbon. At that temperature, certain impurities become less soluble and are more easily captured. Whether this produces a measurably superior product is debatable, but it does produce a measurably more expensive one.

Some producers go the opposite direction, minimizing or eliminating filtration entirely. Vestal is Polish potato vodka launched in 2010 by Willy Borrell. It was made at the Gospodarstwo Podole Wielkie distillery near Gdańsk and, uniquely for a vodka brand, bottled unfiltered expressions in annual vintages, arguing that the character of the potato and the specifics of each year's harvest are better preserved without carbon stripping them away. It was a position that runs directly counter to the mainstream assumption that filtration equals quality, and one that connects more closely to how whisky, wine and many other drinks approach the question of character and quality. And it's thanks to this restrained approach to production that Vestal have bottled some of the most characterful vodkas on the market today, on occasion exhibiting subtle tropical aromas, aromatic spice, baked potato, florals and more. Vestal Vodka has sadly wound up production as of 2023, but vintage bottles can still be found online and they are worth tracking down.

Water, the other essential ingredient in vodka, receives less attention than it deserves considering it constitutes the majority of the liquid in the bottle. Most producers use reverse-osmosis treated municipal water or well water that has been demineralized and softened. A few make specific claims about their water source: Absolut draws from a deep aquifer beneath the Skåne soil; Reyka uses Icelandic spring water; Chase formerly used a borehole beneath the farm's orchard. These claims are rarely spurious, but the extent to which water source affects the taste of the finished product, once both spirit and water have been processed to high levels of purity, is a subject on which producers are considerably more excited about than the available evidence warrants.

If you have read this far, you might reasonably assume that a bottle of vodka contains two things: ethanol distilled from an agricultural raw material, and water. However, this simply isn't true for most vodkas.

It has long been common practice to add small amounts of other substances to vodka before bottling. The most prevalent are sugar, glycerol and citric acid. These are not flavourings in any conventional sense but rather processing aids and texture modifiers, added in quantities small enough to remain below most people's conscious perception but large enough to alter the feel of the spirit in the mouth and improve our conscious appreciation of it. That sensation of 'smoothness' that appears so reliably on tasting notes and marketing copy? It may come from careful distillation and filtration. It may also come from a few grams of glycerol.

Glycerol, also known as glycerine (food additive E422), is colourless, odourless and about 60 per cent as sweet as table sugar. Its primary function in vodka is to increase viscosity, giving the spirit a rounder, silkier mouthfeel without substantially altering its flavour. Sugar performs a complementary role, mellowing the peppery bite of ethanol and adding a subtle sense of body. In many modern Russian vodkas, a trace of honey is still the preferred softener, which is a nice nod to the past. In Western production, refined sugar is more common. Citric acid, meanwhile, adjusts the pH and can mask certain harsh notes in a spirit.

The legal position varies by market, and the gap between what is permitted and what is disclosed is wide. In the USA, a 1956 revenue ruling established that sugar up to 0.2 per cent and 'trace amounts' of citric acid were acceptable in vodka without being considered flavouring agents. The meaning of 'trace amounts' remained vague for nearly four decades until, in 1995, the Bureau of Alcohol, Tobacco and Firearms (ATF) investigated and found that citric acid levels in commercial vodka had climbed significantly since the 1980s, from a historical range of roughly 49 to 150 parts per million (ppm) to considerably higher concentrations. A 300 ppm limit was briefly imposed, but the eventual ruling (ATF Ruling 97-1) settled on permitting up to 1,000 ppm, roughly one gram per litre. The Bureau's position was that, 'consumers have been purchasing vodka which contains citric acid in varying ranges of up to approximately 1,000 ppm for more than a decade without any complaints,' and because nobody had complained about an undisclosed ingredient in a product marketed on the basis of purity, the ingredient must be acceptable. In other words, the absence of complaint was treated as evidence of consent, in a market where consumers had no way of knowing the ingredient was there in the first place.

Sugar is permissible up to two grams per litre, and glycerol is also allowed up to a limit of 2.5 per cent, which is very high indeed and unlikely to be a limit that any producer is close to. Crucially though, none of these additives need to be declared on the label. If vodka were subject to the same ingredient disclosure rules as food, many bottles would read something like: 'Ingredients: rectified potable water, ethanol of agricultural origin, sugar, glycerine, citric acid.'

The EU has a sweeter tooth. Regulation 2019/787 permits sweetening of up to 10 grams per litre (expressed as invert sugar) 'to round off the final taste'. That is a remarkably permissive threshold for a spirit nominally defined by the absence of flavour, and it means that a vodka bottled in the EU can contain a teaspoon and a half of sugar per 70 cl bottle without any obligation to declare it.

Poland, characteristically, takes a harder line. Polish legislation stipulates that vodka produced in Poland may not contain any additives except water. No sugar, no glycerol, no citric acid. This prohibition applies to all Polish vodka, and it is one of the clearest differentiators underpinning the Polska Wódka Protected Geographical Indication (PGI). When Polish producers argue that their vodka is a different product from the mass-market Western competition, the absence of additives is part of that argument, even if most consumers don't realize there is something in their vodka in the first place.

The additive question is an important one, because it sits at the intersection of two of vodka's defining tensions: The first is between the official definition of vodka as a neutral spirit and the commercial reality that neutrality is difficult to achieve consistently, which incentivizes the use of small additions to smooth over inconsistencies. The second is between the marketing language of purity, which is central to how most vodka brands present themselves, and the production reality that many of those brands contain ingredients the label does not mention. The tequila industry is currently being forced to confront this same tension through a wave of class-action lawsuits and independent laboratory testing. Vodka, so far, has avoided that reckoning, largely because the permitted additive levels are lower and the consumer expectation of what vodka tastes like is different. But the principle is the same: if a product is marketed on the basis of what it does not contain, the consumer has a reasonable interest in knowing what it actually does.

CRAFTING LAWS & THE LAWS OF CRAFT

Global vodka production is dominated by two regulatory frameworks, established by the EU and the US.

The EU definition states that vodka must be produced from ethyl alcohol of agricultural origin, obtained by fermentation and distillation. It must be distilled to at least 96% ABV and the minimum alcoholic strength for bottling is 37.5% ABV. Sweetening is permitted to round off the final taste, up to a maximum of 10 grams of sweetening products per litre. Flavouring is also permitted within the scope of traditional practices specific to particular member states. The critical element, and the one that provoked the biggest regulatory fight in the category's recent history, concerns raw materials. Recital 18 of the EU regulation states that 'adequate information should be provided on the raw material used where vodka is made from raw materials of agricultural origin other than cereals or potatoes or both'. In other words, if your vodka is made from grapes, sugar beet or anything other than grain or potatoes, you must say so on the label.

The American definition is slightly different. The Trade and Tax Bureau (TTB) historically defined vodka as a type of neutral spirit, distilled at or above 190 proof (95% ABV) from any material, then 'so treated after distillation with charcoal or other materials, as to be without distinctive character, aroma, taste, or color'. So no requirement to disclose the base ingredient, but a requirement to eliminate any trace of it from the finished product.

However, in April 2020, the TTB issued a rule that changed this. The 'without distinctive character, aroma, taste, or color' clause was removed entirely. The Bureau acknowledged that the old definition no longer reflected consumer expectations, given the variety of base ingredients, production methods and flavour profiles now found in the vodka market. It was a quiet bureaucratic moment with significant implications, because it officially conceded what producers had been demonstrating for years: that vodka made from different materials, by different methods, does taste it different, and that this

RIGHT In Poland, vodka is woven into national identity and routinely served chilled with food.

difference might in fact be a feature rather than a bug. Whether or not the American market has yet caught up with the regulatory change is another question entirely. Most consumers still reach for vodka precisely because it does not taste of much. But the legal door is now open for American producers to make vodka with genuine character and sell it as such, without fear of having their product reclassified.

Between 2006 and 2008, just before the craft gin boom dented vodka's ego, vodka was the subject of one of the most contentious legislative battles in the history of European spirits regulation. The argument centred around whether or not only vodkas made from cereals and potatoes should be allowed to call themselves vodka.

The 'vodka belt' countries, led by Poland, Finland, Sweden, Estonia, Latvia and Lithuania, said yes. For these nations, vodka was a cultural product with deep historical roots in specific raw materials. They argued that allowing grape-based or sugar beet-based spirits to be bottled as vodka was misleading to consumers and damaging to the traditional producers who had built the category.

On the other side of the argument stood the UK, France and a number of southern European countries, whose producers used grapes, sugar beet molasses and other non-traditional materials to make spirits they had been selling as vodka for years. The UK in particular had a substantial vodka industry built on a variety of base materials, and saw the proposed restriction as protectionism dressed up as tradition.

The European Parliament debated the issue, lobby groups on both sides mobilized, and the resulting compromise, reached in 2008 and later carried forward into Regulation 2019/787, effectively split the difference: vodka could be made from any agricultural raw material, but if the base was anything other than cereals or potatoes the label had to declare it. A vodka made from grapes must say 'made from grapes'. A vodka made from sugar beet must say so too. Only grain and potato vodkas were exempt from disclosure.

The compromise satisfied nobody completely, which is usually a sign that it was roughly fair. Polish and Finnish producers felt it did not go far enough because consumers were unlikely to read or understand a small-print ingredient declaration on the back of a bottle. British and French producers felt it was unnecessary and burdensome. But the principle it established was significant: that vodka's identity is, at least in part, tied to what it is made from, even though the production process is designed to erase the evidence. Even in the twenty-first century, vodka remains an unusually contested spirit: officially neutral, but still loaded with ideas of place, tradition and agriculture that refuse to be distilled away.

The Polish response to the vodka wars was to stake their own claim on raw materials and production standards. In 2008, Poland secured a Protected Geographical Indication (PGI) for Polska Wódka, registered under the EU's geographical indications framework. The PGI establishes a set of binding requirements: the spirit must be made from Polish-grown cereals (rye, wheat, oat, barley or triticale) or Polish-grown potatoes, and it must be distilled and bottled in Poland. You can't import spirit from elsewhere and finish it in Poland, and it must be additive free.

OPPOSITE LEFT The Olustvere manor distillery in Estonia dates back to the nineteenth century. **BELOW LEFT** Rye is the traditional grain of Polish vodka, giving peppery spice and oily texture. **LEFT** Heads of barley – used by Finlandia, Koskenkorva and Reyka for nutty, biscuity character. **BELOW** Oats drying in the traditional way in northern Sweden. Oats are permitted under both Swedish and Polish vodka GIs as base material to make vodka.

In spite of its vodka-making heritage and the quality of its products, Poland was surprisingly late to the GI game. When Sweden and Finland joined the European Union on 1 January 1995, both countries brought their vodka GIs with them. The designations had been in place since 1989, secured under the EU's foundational spirits regulation before either country had a seat at the table.

Swedish Vodka must be produced from grain cultivated in Sweden (wheat, rye, barley or oats) or Swedish potatoes, with distillation and rectification both occurring on Swedish soil. Dilution and bottling may happen elsewhere. Finnish Vodka follows the same guidelines, though nearly all of the vodka made there is from Finnish barley. All raw materials must be of Finnish origin, and the water used for dilution must be groundwater or spring water clean enough to require no further chemical treatment.

The Baltic states came next, their GIs formalizing in 2008. Estonia, Lithuania and Latvia were each included in the first wave of protected designations alongside Poland, Finland and Sweden, though the specifications they brought to the table differ slightly.

Estonia's GI is the most technically precise of the three. Raw materials are restricted to rye, wheat or potato, all grown in Estonia, and the grain must be coarsely dry-milled to wholegrain consistency, with at least a quarter of the resulting flour consisting of particles larger than 1mm. That milling requirement is unusual among vodka GIs and reflects a deliberate

ABOVE The Chopin bottle. Single-ingredient expressions from potato, rye or wheat, each tasting discernibly different.

effort to preserve grain character in the spirit. The specification notes that winter rye, the country's dominant crop, produces a more robust and spicy result, wheat gives fruitiness and softness, and potato contributes sweetness and body.

Lithuania's GI, registered under the name *Originali Lietuviška Degtinė* (Original Lithuanian Vodka), allows only for grain in its raw material, which must be Lithuanian-grown rye, wheat or triticale, and the spirit must be filtered through quartz, sand and birch charcoal. The nation's top producer – also called Originali Lietuviška Degtinė – uses gold and silver as a filter medium too.

Latvia's GI sits on the register but is the least defined in practice. The country is better known internationally as a production and bottling location for Stolichnaya than as a distinct vodka style in its own right, which perhaps explains why its specification has generated less attention than its neighbours.

All of the above GIs prohibit the use of colourings but the Polish GI is the only GI that forbids additives altogether.

While a GI is designed as a means of trade protection, it also adds a layer of legitimacy to the relationship between spirit and place. Scotch whisky, Cognac, tequila and a range of other spirits carry geographical indications that tie their identity to a place and a set of production standards. Vodka GIs demonstrate that even vodka – the spirit most associated with anonymity and neutrality – can be a product of specific agricultural tradition, shaped by specific grains grown in specific soil, and that this specificity has commercial and cultural value worth defending.

Polish brands like Belvedere, Chopin, and Żubrówka (all of which have established global distribution), can now carry the Polska Wódka mark, but whether or not consumers in London, New York or Tokyo will recognize or care about it is another matter. The distilleries themselves present a particular challenge. Unlike a Scotch whisky distillery set in a Highland glen or a Cognac house surrounded by rolling fields of vines, a Polish vodka factory does not naturally lend itself to the romantic visitor experience that has helped other spirits' categories build emotional connections with consumers. The provenance argument is strongest when you can see the place. For vodka, most brands would prefer you didn't.

Interestingly, Russia does not have an EU-recognized PGI for vodka. After the collapse of the Soviet Union, ownership of some brands, such as Stolichnaya, became entangled in disputes between private groups and the Russian state. Its ownership has been contested for decades between the Russian state enterprise FKP Soyuzplodimport and SPI Group, the private company founded by Yuri Shefler. Production itself has been split across jurisdictions, with spirit distilled in Russia and finished in Latvia, and parallel versions produced inside Russia.

ABOVE Belvedere have recently transitioned all of their production to organic certified Polish rye.
LEFT A 2008 Stolichnaya 'Choose Authenticity' ad. The campaign defended Russian provenance just as the EU vodka wars redefined the category.

In that environment, agreeing on a unified definition of 'Russian vodka' for international protection is tricky. Who would control the specification? The Russian Federation, a state company, or private rights holders? And how would a brand produced partly outside Russia sit within a framework based on tightly defined geography?

Russia's relationship with vodka remains complex on many fronts.

As we saw in the chapter Peter & Polugar (see p46), Russia's ancestral grain spirit was a

LEFT Boyd & Blair pot-distils from local potatoes and bottle every batch on site. Vestal embraced terroir and vintage, in a similar manner to wine-making.

pot-distilled, grain-forward drink made from rye or wheat at around 38.5% ABV. It tasted of bread crust and carried the fingerprint of its raw material. Polugar and the khlebnoe vino that came before it was what Russian vodka was, for centuries, before the state monopoly of 1895 redefined legal vodka as the product of industrial rectification and outlawed traditional pot distillation.

That ban has never been lifted. Boris Rodionov, the historian who did more than anyone to recover the production methods and flavour profile of polugar, was forced to set up his distillery in Poland. Even today, a craft distiller in Moscow who wanted to produce grain spirit the way it was made before the column still arrived would be breaking the law. So the country that gave vodka to the world will not permit anyone to make its own oldest version.

If you wanted a single image to capture the tension between vodka's history and its regulatory present in Russia, that would be it.

Polugar fits all of the generally accepted criteria of a craft product: independent, small scale and prioritizing quality of quantity – with the added bonus of historical recipes and authentic production methods. The question of whether or not a vodka can be 'craft' is another thing, and has been nagging at the category for the better part of two decades. The honest answer is that it depends entirely on which part of the production process you are looking at.

Several of the producers profiled in the previous chapter genuinely control every stage from raw material to sealed bottle. Boyd & Blair pot-distils from locally sourced potatoes and hand-fills every bottle. Vestal bottled unfiltered, vintage-dated potato vodkas that tasted different from one year to the next. Absolut Elyx segregates its single-estate wheat and redistils through a near-century-old copper pot. These are real points of difference, and when tasted alongside mass-market vodka, the effect is usually apparent. If craft means legitimate control over ingredients and process at an increased cost to the producer, these brands qualify.

But they are a minority. A large number of brands that use the word 'craft' on their labels are redistilling purchased neutral grain spirit, which means the most consequential production decisions – the choice of raw material, the mashing, the fermentation and the primary distillation – were made by someone else entirely. The previous chapter discussed what redistillation in copper actually does to a near-neutral spirit, and the conclusion was honest if a little deflating: the effect is real but marginal, and difficult to separate from the influence of water, filtration and the base spirit itself. Calling that process 'handmade' or 'small batch' puts more weight on the language than it can honestly support.

The deeper problem is around the regulatory framework which, at least in Europe, demands distillation to a minimum of 96% ABV. The cultural expectation, built over a century of marketing, is a

RIGHT Absolut Elyx is one of a handful of super-premium iterations that have emerged from established brands, leveraging artisanal production methods for added value.

spirit that is clean, neutral and inoffensive. The craft producer is therefore trying to introduce character into a product that the system has been engineered to strip character out of. In single malt whisky, regulation protects flavour by specifying pot distillation only. In vodka it's the reverse, because character is technically a defect.

The 2020 TTB revision in the US, by removing the 'without distinctive character' requirement, opened at least a theoretical door. It meant that an American producer can now make a flavourful, grain-forward vodka and sell it under its own name without regulatory challenge. Whether many will walk through that door remains to be seen. The market still rewards neutrality, and consumers still reach for vodka precisely because it stays out of the way. If flavour-forward vodkas are going to succeed, I would expect it to happen in cocktail bars and in martinis – the places where flavour is progressive, price is less sensitive and drinkers are open to experimentation.

The cynic's answer to 'can vodka be craft?' is that the word on the label is usually a marketing play rather than anything pertaining to production, and that in a category where most consumers cannot reliably distinguish one product from another in a blind tasting, the argument is more about storytelling than flavour. The optimist's answer is that a small number of producers are doing things that genuinely matter, sourcing specific ingredients from specific places, distilling with care and transparency, and making spirits that reward the attention of anyone willing to pay it.

Both answers are true at the same time, which is perhaps the most honest thing you can say about a spirit that has spent its entire modern history trying to fit in everywhere.

FINDING VODKA

For the best part of 50 years, vodka was the biggest-selling spirit in the United States, and by extension the biggest-selling spirit in the world's most valuable drinks market. It peaked in 2021 at over 80 million nine-litre cases, a number so large it is difficult to hold in your head. If you tried to serve all of those bottles from one bar, the shelf would stretch the entire circumference of the earth. Three times.

Vodka was a category that seemed immune to fashion, taste and economic changes.

But then it started to fall. By 2024, US vodka volume had dropped to around 74 million cases, a decline of roughly 8% in three years. Revenue fell too, with the category pulling in approximately $7 billion (£5.5bn) in 2025, down 3% on the previous year. For the fourth consecutive year, vodka was shrinking. Tito's, the volume leader in the US, recorded its first ever decline in 2024, down 1.5%. Smirnoff dropped 6%. Svedka dropped 6.2%. Absolut fell 4%. Of the top five brands by volume, only New Amsterdam held steady.

The obvious question is: what took vodka's share? The answer comes in two parts. The first is tequila, which grew its US revenue by nearly 300% between 2003 and 2023, reaching $6.5 billion (£5.2 bn) and over 30 million cases – that's less than half the volume of vodka but it beats vodka on total revenue. Tequila is a premium product and its appeal was built on exactly the things vodka had spent a century ignoring or avoiding: clearly defined raw material, cultural identity, artisanal production stories and above all, taste.

American whiskey took share too, driven by the same cocktail culture that was turning its back on vodka. Bourbon and rye offered what the new generation of bartenders wanted: depth, complexity, barrel character, a production story that connected the drink to a specific place, a specific grain bill and a specific cooper's decision about char level. Vodka, the spirit designed not to be noticed, found itself in a market that was increasingly rewarding the opposite.

The moderation and no/low-alcohol movement adds a further layer of pressure, particularly among younger drinkers. Surveys consistently show Gen Z consuming less alcohol than previous generations, with over a third of American adults in that cohort identifying as teetotal. Vodka, as the default 'mindless' spirit, the one people reach for without thinking, is particularly vulnerable to a cultural shift that asks people to think more carefully about whether they want to drink at all.

The decline of bottle service culture, which we discussed previously, removed one of vodka's most profitable distribution channels. The VIP table, sparklers and the frosted bottle in the ice bucket spectacle still exists in pockets of Las Vegas, Miami and Dubai, but it is a smaller and less culturally dominant force than it was in the mid-2000s. The craft cocktail bars, speakeasies and restaurants with serious drinks programmes were not kind to vodka.

The craft cocktail movement, whose early stirrings were noted with the arrival of the Cosmopolitan and Espresso Martini, built its identity on flavour, technique and historical reference. Bartenders reached back to pre-Prohibition recipes and rediscovered spirits that had been eclipsed by vodka's long dominance: rye whiskey, gin, aged rum, Italian Amaro, vermouth. A spirit designed not to be tasted was a difficult fit for a revival premised on tasting everything.

The rejection was not total, however. The Vodka Martini, after years of being dismissed by cocktail purists as a characterless version of the real thing, has made a quiet comeback in the 2020s, partly because a new generation of drinkers encountered it without the baggage of the debates that preceded them, and partly because a very cold, very clean Martini made with good vodka and decent vermouth is, by any honest assessment, a fine drink.

The Espresso Martini, meanwhile, has grown again in popularity. Dick Bradsell's creation (see p161) had a second life as a global bar staple, powered by the coffee culture boom and social media's appetite for photogenic drinks. By the early 2020s, it was among the most-ordered cocktails in many markets.

FAR LEFT Tito's, where claims of craft wrestle with remarkable sales volume. **LEFT** Tequila grew nearly 300% in the US between 2003 and 2023. **ABOVE RIGHT** The Espresso Martini, reborn for a new generation in the 2020s.

LEFT The vodka soda. Invisible in cocktail books but omnipresent in bars.

Then there is the vodka soda, the drink that nobody writes about and everybody orders. A vodka and soda requires practically no skill to make (just enough ice please!), no premium ingredients and no explanation. It is vodka's truest expression: alcohol delivered with maximum efficiency and minimum friction.

Finally, and perhaps most importantly, there is the ready-to-drink (RTD) cocktail, a category that barely existed in 2018 and by 2025 was nearing $4 billion (£3 bn) in US sales. Spirits-based RTDs alone nearly quadrupled their volume in five years, leaping from 23.5 million cases to over 85 million. Vodka accounts for around 45% of the spirit-based RTD market so if you crunch the maths you find that, in 2025, American consumers drank over 10 million nine-litre cases of vodka sequestered into cans and bottle. This has a meaningful implication for how one might interpret vodka's apparent decline. A significant and growing portion of vodka consumption has effectively migrated into RTDs, where it's counted differently. Consumers haven't necessarily stopped drinking vodka, they've just stopped buying a bottle and started buying a can of something that contains it.

The picture is murkier still if we look to the so-called malt-based RTD category, which commands 80% of the overall RTD market. Brands such as White Claw are classified as malt-based for regulatory reasons, which means the base must be brewed like a beer. That beer is then filtered of all its colour and malt flavour, before being re-flavoured, carbonated and canned. While the malt beer isn't distilled, the goal is the same as grain-neutral-spirit distillation – to produce a characterless alcohol that can be dressed up with other flavours. This isn't technically vodka, but rather a legally required workaround to make an accessible vodka-like beverage.

The direction of travel for natural-tasting alcohol then, is clearly not in decline but rather migration – from the out of the bottle category and into a format that the traditional spirits industry did not see coming, and whose explosive growth is now cited as one of the primary reasons bottled vodka is struggling. This is vodka succeeding on its own terms, in a container it does not get credit for.

OPPOSITE White Claw is malt-based, but the principle is the same: characterless alcohol dressed up with flavour. **RIGHT** Ready-to-drink cocktails have grown from 23.5 to over 85 million cases in five years. Many of them are based on vodka.

The problem for vodka brands is that the evolution does not carry their names.

Over in Russia, the population has witnessed the most significant shift in drinking behaviour in the nation's history, and vodka has been at the centre of that change. In the early 2000s, per capita alcohol consumption was among the highest in the world, with vodka dominating both culturally and economically. Since then, overall alcohol consumption has fallen sharply in Russia. Estimates from the World Health Organization suggest a drop of roughly 40% between 2003 and the late 2010s, with the steepest decline coming from strong spirits. Vodka's share of total alcohol consumption has steadily contracted, from 81.4% of total alcohol sales in 1995 to only 36.4% in 2018. It was replaced, in part, by beer in the 2000s and, more recently, by wine and lower-strength drinks in urban centres. What was once the default drink across almost every social setting has become more occasional, more generational, and increasingly regional.

Some traditions are hard to unlearn though. Harking back to its fifteenth-century roots, vodka is still used medicinally in parts of Eastern Europe and Russia, especially for sore throats or rubbed on dry or sore skin. During the Chernobyl nuclear disaster of 1986, Ukrainians gargled vodka to minimize the effects of radiation poisoning. Vodka has also maintained a reputation as a household detergent, anti-bacterial treatment and all-round household essential for some people.

In spite of its myriad uses in and around the home, the global vodka market has lost somewhere in the region of 150–200 million nine-litre cases since its 2010 peak. Russia remains the largest vodka producer in the world, accounting for over 30% of global production, but over 90% of that is consumed domestically according to global drinks data and insight provider IWSR. The US has essentially held steady and is now the more significant swing market, while Brazil, the UK and parts of Asia represent a modest growth story.

Twenty-first century Russia still found space to introduce some new brands to the world. Russian Standard was founded in 1998 by Roustam Tariko, a Tatar-born entrepreneur who had made his early

LEFT Russian Standard was founded in 1998 by Roustam Tariko in post-Soviet Russia.

money importing Ferrero Rocher chocolates and distributing Martini & Rossi in post-Soviet Russia. Tariko looked at the Russian vodka market and saw that it was dominated at the top end by imported Western brands. Absolut, Smirnoff and Finlandia were selling premium vodka to Russian consumers in a country that had been making vodka for five centuries. He set out to build the first genuinely Russian premium brand.

Russian Standard claimed to follow the 'principles for vodka established in 1894 by famed Russian scientist Dmitri Mendeleev', and the bottle carried his signature. As we established previously, the connection between Mendeleev and the 40% vodka standard is considerably more complicated than the brand implies. Mendeleev's doctoral thesis concerned alcohol-water solutions at concentrations above 70%, and the relevant regulatory benchmarks were set by von Reutern's 1866 decree and later instantiated into law under Alexander III's monopoly of 1894, long after Mendeleev's thesis and well before the brand existed. What Tariko had done, with considerable commercial skill, was to take a genuinely important figure in the history of Russian science and retrofit him as the founding father of a vodka brand.

Production takes place at a purpose-built facility near St Petersburg, using winter wheat from the Russian steppes and glacial water from Lake Ladoga. The spirit is filtered through charcoal and quartz crystal. Within two years of launch, Russian Standard had overtaken every imported premium vodka on the Russian market. The portfolio expanded: Platinum was introduced in 2001, the ultra-premium Imperia in 2004 and Gold in 2008. By 2018, the brand held a 30% share of the Russian premium segment and was selling over 3.5 million cases domestically, with distribution in more than 80 export markets.

Beluga Vodka was launched in 2002 and produced at the Mariinsk Distillery in Siberia. The brand leans heavily on ideas of remoteness, purity and refinement, all wrapped up in highly polished packaging and a quasi-caviar sensibility that fits its sturgeon-derived name. Unlike many large vodka brands that market neutrality as a virtue, Beluga tries

to suggest craft and texture, drawing on a base of malted wheat spirit from the Itkul factory (roughly 675 km/420 miles to the south) and then softening the final product with a series of additions and treatments, including sugar, honey, oat, milk thistle extract and vanillin. The result is a vodka that is smoother, slightly more characterful and more obviously 'designed' than many of its rivals, which makes it useful as a case study in how modern premium vodka often relies less on raw material transparency than on the careful manufacture of luxury itself.

These brands, among others, represent attempts to reclaim Russian vodka as something worth paying attention to, after decades in which the category's most successful brands were Swedish, French, Dutch and American. Whether these brand can sustain that positioning in a market that has, since 2022, become deeply uncomfortable with the word 'Russian' on a vodka label is a question the next decade will answer. Stolichnaya quietly rebranded to 'Stoli Vodka' for international markets in 2022, dropping the Russian name just weeks after the invasion of Ukraine. Russian Standard, with the country of origin embedded in its very name, had no such option. Beluga was purchased by the Noblewood Group in 2022 and now markets itself as a Russian-heritage brand, with spirit produced in Latvia and bottled in Montenegro.

The connection to beluga caviar is an interesting one, and food represents a realm in which vodka can generate real, authentic credibly. In the west, vodka is a bar drink that you order in a cocktail, or with a mixer, or occasionally as a shot; you do not, as a rule,

ABOVE Russian Standard draws its glacial water from Lake Ladoga, just north of St Petersburg.

THIS PAGE Beluga vodka and the zakuski tradition. The potent flavours of -pickled herring, cured meats, salted cucumbers and caviar on blini, are tempered by the sweet burn of chilled vodka on the tongue.

sit down to dinner and ask for a bottle of vodka alongside your main course. This practice in the west would seem odd to a Russian, a Pole, a Finn, or anyone from the vodka belt, where the spirit has always been a table drink, served with food as a matter of course.

The Russian *zakuski* tradition, which stretches back centuries, is built on the interplay between small, intensely flavoured dishes – pickled herring, cured meats, smoked fish, salted cucumbers, caviar on blini, hard-boiled eggs with roe – and shots of chilled vodka. The food is rich, salty, oily and designed to provoke thirst, which is satiated by a cold swallow of spirit that resets the palate before the next bite. *The Buffalo Times* reported in 1932 that Russians drink vodka only with food, declaring: 'Give a Russian a drink of vodka and you have to give him a slice of bread, too.'

In Poland, the equivalent tradition is *zakąski*, and in Scandinavia it connects to the *smörgåsbord*. The principle in all cases is the same: vodka is not a flavour to be savoured alongside food in the way wine is. It is a punctuation mark – a palate cleanser that sharpens the senses for what comes next.

Leonid Shutov, the Russian-born owner of Bob Bob Ricard in London's Soho, has built this principle into the fabric of his restaurants. Russian Standard is the standard pour there, served at -18°C/-0.4°F in tiny cut-crystal glasses, and the menu opens with a section of zakuski designed to be paired with it. The restaurant shifts over 50,000

RIGHT SKYY, launched in San Francisco in 1992. One of the first American-made premium vodkas, it's now owned by Campari.

shots of vodka a year and Leonid's position is straightforward: 'Unlike wine, when you drink vodka with food, the flavours don't merge into something new. Instead, the vodka helps to amplify the flavours in the dish.' He describes a fine Russian vodka as so heavily distilled and purified that the connection to its wheat base is 'just a delicate hint of breadiness. It's like smelling spring water, it's so ephemeral.'

The case for vodka at the table is essentially a case about temperature and texture. A spirit served at -18°C/-0.4°F has an almost oily viscosity that coats the mouth briefly before evaporating. The alcohol cuts through fat, and the cold resets the palate between courses of rich or oily food. It is the same logic that underpins the Japanese practice of pairing *shochu* or sake with small dishes, or the Scandinavian tradition of schnapps with pickled fish. The spirit is not there to compete with the food but to create space for the next mouthful.

Whether this tradition can translate into Western restaurant culture at scale is doubtful. Wine is too deeply embedded in the economics and rituals of dining for vodka to displace it. But as a minority practice, a way of beginning a meal or accompanying a specific course, chilled vodka with food deserves more attention than it currently receives. The ingredients are not expensive and the effect is immediate. It is simply unfamiliar, which in a restaurant industry that prizes novelty, may eventually work in its favour.

Several brands that have not featured prominently elsewhere in this book deserve mention for their scale, their approach to production or what they represent about the contemporary vodka market.

SKYY was launched in San Francisco in 1992 by Maurice Kanbar, an inventor and entrepreneur. It was one of the first American-made premium vodkas and its cobalt-blue bottle made it immediately recognizable on the backbar. SKYY arrived before the super-premium wave and was positioned as a credible domestic alternative to the European imports at a time when 'serious vodka' still meant Absolut or Stolichnaya. It is now owned by Campari Group and remains a solid mid-tier brand.

Svedka, a Swedish vodka launched in 1998 and now owned by Constellation Brands, occupies an interesting space in the category. It is one of the highest-volume vodkas in America (around 3.5 million cases in 2024), sold at a price point well below Absolut and Grey Goose, and marketed with an irreverence that sets it apart from the premium category's provenance claims. Its growth story is essentially the value play: decent Swedish vodka at a price that makes the premium competition look overpriced. In a market where premiumization is beginning to stall and value brands are growing again, Svedka's position looks increasingly shrewd.

New Amsterdam, produced by E. & J. Gallo and launched in 2011, followed a similar playbook to Svedka and reached approximately 5.3 million cases in 2024, making it the third-largest vodka brand in America. It is the brand that nobody in the drinks industry really talks about and that an enormous number of consumers buy. Its success in the retail channel is built on price, availability and the fact that for many vodka drinkers, the liquid in the bottle matters less than the numbers on the receipt.

NOW YOU SEE ME...

The novelist and bon vivant Kingsley Amis once described vodka as 'a drink for people who don't really like drinking'. It's a dismissive line, but contains more truth than Amis perhaps intended. Long before its clean odour and clarity of colour made vodka the discreet choice for mixing, Russian peasants were swilling back khlebnoe vino and polugar out of need rather than preference. Their appetite for the spirit that would eventually become vodka crossed a tipping point of fiscal relevance to the state, pitching addiction against revenue in a conflict that governments consistently resolved in favour of the latter. The near-neutral vodka that lines liquor store shelves today is, therefore, a product of centuries of technical refinement orchestrated by states dependent on populations that return to the bar, drink without restraint, and do so with minimum cost to the state.

For some, function over flavour remains the whole point of vodka. But the story of vodka is considerably stranger and richer than that.

It is a spirit of agricultural origin that traces a path back to early European distillation, through great fields of rye and wheat, joined by potatoes when they arrived from the New World. In Russia it was taxed, banned, monopolized, banned again and taxed more heavily still. It crossed the Atlantic quietly in the luggage of migrants and then more loudly in the mind of one Russian émigré named Kunett. It soon found its way onto American menus via the cocktail culture of the early part of the twentieth century, and then spent the second half colonizing every corner of the Western bar. The Espresso Martini, the Cosmopolitan, the Vodka Soda, the White Russian: these are not drinks that have much in common with the polugar of a nineteenth-century Russian tavern, yet they all trace a line back to the same column still and the same centuries-long philosophy of something clean, strong and easy to drink.

The cocktail renaissance of the 2000s was initially reluctant to acknowledge vodka as a serious ingredient, and in some respects the scepticism was fair. In the first book in this series, published in 2013, I wrote that 'vodka had been shunned from cocktail lists, declared insipid, characterless and without honour...'

But the bar world came around, not by persuasion so much as by demand. 'Vodka pays the bills' is a common hospitality industry saying. Drinkers kept ordering vodka drinks, kept asking for Sex on the Beach, kept mixing vodka with orange juice, coke, soda, lemonade and basically anything else that they liked the taste of and thus didn't want that taste to be compromised by a flavoursome spirit.

In parallel, vodka migrated into an entirely new format without anyone really noticing. The ready-to-drink boom that reshaped global drinks sales from the early 2020s is powered largely by vodka, even when it doesn't say so on the can. The vodka category hasn't so much contracted as the headlines might make you think as much as it has shape-shifted, leaking out of a glass bottle and into an aluminium can.

Adaptability remains vodka's greatest strength as demand for a spirits that don't announce themselves continues to grow. While whisky, rum and gin surf waves of fashion, vodka moves like a Soviet submarine beneath them: undetectable, unwavering and very much still out there.

Meanwhile, the premium and craft producers who have spent the past three decades arguing that vodka can carry the weight of terroir, raw material and production philosophy have slowly, and against considerable commercial headwinds, started to make that case land. Not everywhere, not always honestly or convincingly, but enough to suggest that the question this book has tried to take seriously – whether a spirit defined by its neutrality can still tell a meaningful story – has an answer that is at least sometimes 'yes'.

Perhaps Amis was on to something. Vodka is a drink for people who don't really like drinking, and the historical record supports that statement in ways he probably never considered. But it is also a drink that has built an empire, shaped agriculture, funded revolutions, inspired artistry behind the bar, fuelled a lot of fun in front of it and generated some of the most creative marketing the drinks industry has ever produced. For a liquid designed to taste of nothing, vodka sure has a great deal to say.

Six hundred years in, it is still saying it.

INDEX

PICTURE CREDITS

Key: a = above; b = below; l = left; c = centre; r = right.

2 Addie Chinn; 4 centre Addie Chinn; 4 bl nordroden/Adobe Stock; 4 br Addie Chinn; 5 al Mr. Music/AdobeStock; 5 b Addie Chinn; 7 Addie Chinn; 8–9 Fahd Reja/Adobe Stock; 10 Archivist/Adobe Stock; 11 ar Historic Collection/Alamy; 11 b Photo 12/Alamy; 12 Historic Collection/Alamy; 13 Erica Guilane-Nachez/Adobe Stock; 14 PhotoStock-Israel/Alamy; 15 BTEU/RKMLGE/Alamy; 16 acrogame/Adobe Stock; 17 fifg/Adobe Stock; 18 Science History Images/Alamy; 19 Ivy Close Images/Alamy; 21 Grazyna Nowicka/Adobe Stock; 22 Audrius Merfeldas/Adobe Stock; 23 a Boumenjapet; 23 b Irina/Adobe Stock; 24l Bjorn B/Adobe Stock; 24r Kirill/Adobe Stock; 25l Iryna/Adobe Stock; 25r photography/Adobe Stock; 27 rgraz/Adobe Stock; 28 Album/Alamy; 29a Album/Alamy; 29b dikson/Adobe Stock; 31 Addie Chinn; 33 Addie Chinn; 34 Archivist/Adobe Stock; 35 bbsferrari/Adobe Stock; 37 The Picture Art Collection/Alamy; 39 Addie Chinn; 40 b201735/Adobe Stock; 41 Album/Alamy; 42 Artem/Adobe Stock; 43a Mannaggia/Adobe Stock; 43b acrogame/Adobe Stock; 45 Addie Chinn; 46 Artem/Adobe Stock; 47 fifg/Adobe Stock; 48 Elena Odareeva/Adobe Stock; 49a wowinside/Adobe Stock; 49b Dead_inside/Adobe Stock; 50l Anatoliy Sadovskiy/Adobe Stock; 51al 13smile/Adobe Stock; 51ar jefwod/Adobe Stock; 51 (bottles) www.polugar.com; 51 (logo) www.polugar.com; 52 PRISMA ARCHIVO/Alamy; 53 Erica Guilane-Nachez/Adobe Stock; 54 Erica Guilane-Nachez/Adobe Stock; 55 Georgios Kollidas/Adobe Stock; 56al marmoset/Adobe Stock; 56ar makasana photo/Adobe Stock; 56b trianatio/Adobe Stock; 57 Alexander Gutkin/Adobe Stock; 59 Addie Chinn; 60 Georgios Kollidas/Adobe Stock; 61a Fotokon/Adobe Stock; 61b far700/Adobe Stock; 62 Dmitro/Adobe Stock; 63al Patryk Kosmider/Adobe Stock; 63b Tommy Lee Walker/Adobe Stock; 64 History and Art Collection/Alamy; 65 piemags/Alamy; 67 markrobe/Adobe Stock; 67ar Callum Jonston/Wirestock; 67br Aleksabdr Matveev; 69 Hum Images/Alamy; 70 Emilija/Adobe Stock; 71 Lance Bellers/Adobe Stock; 73 Addie Chinn; 74 Mistervlad/Adobe Stock; 75a Hum Images/Alamy; 75b Penta Springs Limited/Alamy; 76 Juulijia/Adobe Stock; 77 Archive Collection/Alamy; 77 inset a vectorgoods/Adobe Stock; 77 inset b Dotters/Adobe Stocks; 77br Artem/Adobe Stock; 78a Sergii/Adobe Stock; 78b Historic Images/Alamy; 79 Album/Alamy; 80 piemags/Alamy; 81 The Picture Art Collection/Alamy; 82 Ryhor Bruyeu/Alamy; 83 piemags/Alamy; 85 piemags/library/Alamy; 87 Addie Chinn; 88 New Africa/Adobe Stock; 89a Dietmar/Adobe Stock; 89b CoreRock/Adobe Stock; 92 ARCHIVIO GBB/Alamy; 93 nortivision/Adobe Stock; 94 Sergey Kohl/Adobe Stock; 95 Heritage Image Partnership Ltd/Alamy; 97a Juulijis/Adobe Stock; 97b CupOfSpring/Adobe Stock; 98 CPA Media Pte Ltd/Alamy; 99 romanevgenev/Adobe Stock; 100 Underwood Archives, Inc/Alamy; 101 Shawshots/Alamy; 102 Archivist/Adobe Stock; 103 Archivist/Adobe Stock; 104 Mannaggia/Adobe Stock; 105 Larry/Adobe Stock; 106 Archive PL/Alamy; 107 acrogame/Adobe Stock; 108 Morphart/Adobe Stock; 109 Joe Vella/Alamy; 110 Larry Gibson/Adobe Stock; 111 Mannaggia/Adobe Stock; 112 Album/Alamy; 113 Addie Chinn; 114 Profile Books Ltd; 115l Editions Demangel Paris; 115c William Heinemann Ltd; 115r S. Bornemann; 116 Addie Chinn; 117 Cerib/Adobe Stock; 119 Addie Chinn; 120 SJArt/Alamy; 123 Addie Chinn; 125 adsR/Alamy; 127 Addie Chinn; 128 Chronicle/Alamy; 129 Addie Chinn; 131 Chronicle/Alamy; 132a SuperStock/Alamy; 132b Andrew Deer/Adobe Stock; 133 PictureLux/The Hollywood Archive/Alamy; 134a Sueddeutsche Zeitung Photo/Alamy; 134b Archive Farms Inc/Alamy; James/Adobe Stock; 137 all Addie Chinn; 138 Art Directors & TRIP/Alamy; 139 LANDMARK MEDIA/Alamy; 140 Everett Collection Inc/Alamy; 141 Chris Howes/Wild Places Photography/Alamy; 143 chrisdorney/Adobe Stock; 145 Addie Chinn; 146 Mdv Edwards/Adobe Stock; 147 Anton Ivanov Photo/Adobe Stock; 147bl JRJfin/Adobe Stock; 147br Kuganskiy/Adobe Stock; 149l sikaraha/Adobe Stock; 149r Terence Waeland/Alamy; 152 Suddeutsche Zeitung Photo/Alamy; 153 Richard Ellis/Alamy; 155 Retro AdArchives/Alamy; 156l Retro AdArchives/Alamy; 156r adsR/Alamy; 157 Nattawit/Adobe Stock; 158a monticellllo/Adobe Stock; 158bl Ruslan/Adobe Stock; 158br pil76/Adobe Stock; 159 Barry Lewis/Alamy; 161 Addie Chinn; 162 jonbilous/Adobe Stock; 163 Alejandro/Adobe Stock; 165 Addie Chinn; 166 victoriap_107/Adobe Stock; 167 Retro AdArchives/Alamy; 168l Q77photo/Adobe Stock; 168r mychadre77/Adobe Stock; 169 David Taljat/Alamy; 169 inset www.ketelone.com; 173 Addie Chinn; 174l Inshots/Adobe Stock; 174r Q77photo/Adobe Stock; 177a jahmaica/Adobe Stock; 177b Robert/Adobe Stock; 178l kraichgaufoto/Adobe Stock; 178r Bits and Splits/Adobe Stock; 179l bubbers/Adobe Stock; 179r New Africa/Adobe Stock; 180 www.blackcow.co.uk; 181al Сергей Голуб/Adobe Stock; 181ar Lance Bellers/Adobe Stock; 181bl nordroden/Adobe Stock; 181br nordroden/Adobe Stock; 183l Andriy Stefanyshyn/Adobe Stock; 183r Ascannio/Adobe Stock; 186a Andrey Kusmin/Adobe Stock; 186b justasc/Adobe Stock; 187 AS Photo Family/Adobe Stock; 188a Mykola Iegorov/Adobe Stock; 188b Magnus/Adobe Stock; 189a Ingrid/Adobe Stock; 189b jojoo64/Adobe Stock; 190l Q77photo/Adobe Stock; 190r victoriap_107/Adobe Stock; 191a Q77photo/Adobe Stock; 191b adsR/Alamy; 192l www.boydandblair.com; 192r @vestalvodka Instagram; 193 Walter Cicchetti/Adobe Stock; 194l Rosemarie Mosteller/Adobe Stock; 194r Addie Chinn; 195 Addie Chinn; 196l Brent Hofacker/Adobe Stock; 196r (both) Archlane/Adobe Stock; 197 Pixels Hunter/Adobe Stock; 198l victoriap_107/Adobe Stock; 199 Александр Оборотов/Adobe Stock; 200al Artem Shadrin/Adobe Stock; 200ar SellStock/Adobe Stock; 200b Anna Khomulo/Adobe Stock; 201 www.skyyvodka.com; 203 sonyachny/AdobeStock.

ACKNOWLEDGEMENTS

While most of the books in this series have required extensive periods of travel and on-the-ground research (drinking), *Vodka Chronicles* has been a far lonelier experience, though one that was rewarding in other ways. If you have finished the book, I expect you can appreciate that no small amount of historical research was conducted in its making. In a world where AI can have a reasonable stab at doing this for you, it turns out a human is still better. The human in this case was Marin Jones, who pored over research papers and historical texts for months in order to tease out the most interesting and honest strands, handing them over to me for knitting together.

As usual, the brilliant studio photography was done by the man who has photographed all of my books, Addie Chinn, with guest stylist Hannah Reynolds graciously accommodating all of our silly (read: creative) requests. Nathan Joyce has once again honoured me by project managing and editing the book into something we can all be proud of. Thanks also to Megan Smith for design, Yvonne Doolan for promotion, and all of the rest of the team at RPS. Finally, I'd like to thank Julia Charles and Leslie Harrington for their enthusiasm and continued belief in these books over the years. Julia commissioned the first *Curious Bartender* book in 2012. This one, published in 2026, is dedicated to Julia and Leslie.

Senior Designer Megan Smith
Series Design Geoff Borin
Editor Nathan Joyce
Senior Editor Abi Waters
Editorial Director
Julia Charles
Head of Production
Patricia Harrington
Creative Director
Leslie Harrington

Drinks Photography
Addie Chinn
Prop Stylist
Hannah Reynolds

Map Design Emily Breen
Indexer Ruth Ellis

First published in 2026 by
Ryland Peters & Small
20–21 Jockey's Fields,
London WC1R 4BW
www.rylandpeters.com
email: euregulations@rylandpeters.com

10 9 8 7 6 5 4 3 2 1

(Full picture credits see page 207)

Printed in China.

ISBN: 978-1-78879-766-5

A CIP record for this book is available from the British Library. US Library of Congress cataloging-in-Publication Data has been applied for.

The authorised representative in the EEA is Authorised Rep Compliance Ltd., Ground Floor, 71 Lower Baggot Street, Dublin, D02 P593, Ireland
www.arccompliance.com